Listening to Olivia

Other titles in

THE NORTHEASTERN SERIES ON GENDER, CRIME, AND LAW
edited by Claire Renzetti, St. Joseph's University

Jody Raphael

Listening to Olivia

VIOLENCE,

POVERTY, AND

PROSTITUTION

Northeastern University Press

BOSTON

Northeastern University Press

LIBRARY OF CONGRESS CATALOGING-IN-PUBLICATION DATA

Raphael, Jo Ann, 1944–
    Listening to Olivia : violence, poverty, and prostitution / by Jo Ann Raphael.
       p. cm. — (The Northeastern series on gender, crime, and law)
Includes bibliographical references and index.
    ISBN 1-55553-596-8 (pbk. : alk. paper) — ISBN 1-55553-597-6 (cloth : alk. paper)
   1. Olivia. 2. Prostitutes—Illinois—Chicago—Biography. 3. Prostitution—Illinois—Chicago. I. Title. II. Series.
  HQ146.C4R26 2004
  306.74′2′092—dc22   2003019321

Designed by Janis Owens, Books By Design, Inc.

Composed in Joanna by Coghill Composition Company, Richmond, Virginia. Printed and bound by Edwards Brothers, Inc., in Ann Arbor, Michigan. The paper is EB Natural, an acid-free sheet.

MANUFACTURED IN THE UNITED STATES OF AMERICA
08 07 06 05 04   5 4 3 2 1

For Sheila I. Wellstone (1943–2002) in loving memory
and for Sarah E. Rowley and Claire Renzetti

Every human being is of sublime value, because his experience, which must be in some measure unique, gives him a
unique view of reality, and the sum of such views should
go far to giving us the complete picture of reality, which
the human race must attain if it is ever to comprehend its
destiny.

— REBECCA WEST, *Black Lamb and Grey Falcon*

Contents

Listening to Olivia

Prologue

There is a draught that we must drink or not be fully
human. . . . I knew that one must know the truth. I knew
quite well that when one is adult one must raise to one's
lips the wine of the truth, heedless that it is not sweet milk
but draws the mouth with its strength, and celebrate com-
munion with reality, or else walk forever queer and small
like a dwarf.

— REBECCA WEST, *The Return of the Soldier*

The wispy twenty-seven-year-old African-American woman had
walked into the social services agency at the close of the afternoon on
a typically cold and windy early April day in Chicago. Dressed in black
jeans, a blacksweat shirt, and white sneakers, her hair in a ponytail,
Katrinka (not her real name), plied the streets on the near West Side,
trading sex for money. A heroin addict for six years, Katrinka appeared
to have something close to pneumonia. On top of that, she revealed
she was pregnant and afraid that the child protective services would
take her baby if she sought help. Katrinka said she had gone back
to church. "It's not working. I'm still on the streets," she sobbed in
desperation.

She devoured the food the case manager offered like someone who
had not eaten in days. Then Katrinka nodded off and had to be awakened. As the organization was soon to close for the day, the worker
gave her a referral to a city agency that would transport her to shelter

and drug treatment. But Katrinka would have to walk the ten or so blocks herself to get there. I seriously doubted that she would. It seemed likely that Katrinka was immediately going to return to the streets to get money for her next heroin fix.

Although as a researcher I wanted to better understand how Katrinka had come to such a pass, and why she could not leave prostitution when she desired to do so, the question that struck with greater force was this: Who were these men who would find it desirable to pay for sex with a pregnant, drug-addicted young female in such broken health?

I knew that a young woman like Katrinka—in the throes of addiction and ill health—would not be in a good position to answer this question. About four months later, a forty-five-year-old prostitution survivor named Olivia[1] walked into my life. Soon I understood that Olivia had been Katrinka and had lived her life, down to the sweatshirt and that ponytail. And Olivia had a lot of answers.

In her sophomore year of high school, Olivia left her alcohol-soaked and violent home in Chicago for a residential Job Corps program. Once there she took up with older girls who introduced her to the streets. When she left the Job Corps after ten months with her GED and a nurse's aide certificate, Olivia found a job as a barmaid on the South Side with one of her new friends from Job Corps. A month later, Olivia heard about Rush Street in downtown Chicago, an area north of the Chicago River noted in the 1970s for its numerous bars and strip-clubs. A new friend from the bar found the club first, and Olivia soon followed her to the strip joint. Olivia was sixteen years of age.

> I was very naive. I had been to dancing school. I thought I was this great dancer, and I thought, all my lessons are paying off. For about a month. It doesn't take long to see what is going on in the club.

But the attention, the glamour, and the money for the sixteen-year-old from a South Side housing project kept her at the club. Olivia began to use more and more alcohol to enable her to get up there and take off her clothing, and later, to engage in prostitution in the club's back rooms.

You learn to put up with a few things, and every time you do
an act, it better prepares you to do a little bit more next time.
You kind of desensitize yourself to what is really happening, and
you are using more and more alcohol. I soon knew what the
guys were looking for, and it didn't take long to figure out the
scene. How did I do it? I was always in an altered state of mind
before I got there. I came in drunk. I'd be half blasted before I
arrived.

That Rush Street stripclub led to a nineteen-year involvement in prostitution—a progression from dancing in strip clubs to an ever-spiraling
heroin habit that left Olivia homeless, trading sex for money on the
street, and dependent on a violent partner who procured the drugs for
them both with the money she made from turning eighteen to twenty
tricks a night.

Yet Olivia managed to break away from prostitution and drug addiction. Today, fourteen years sober and fourteen years out of prostitution, she is director of addiction services at a community counseling
center in the western suburbs of Chicago, and president of Exodus, a
new organization dedicated to supporting women in Chicago after
they exit the sex trade. [Note: This work will use the terms "prostitution" and "sex trade" interchangeably.]

During our first conversation when Olivia gave me the broad outline of her story, she cried only when she described her rescue on a
bleak, rainy October day in 1990. Actually, we shed tears together.
Almost immediately I realized that this was a rarely heard tale. Yes,
researchers have interviewed women on the streets to capture some of
their experiences, but we almost never hear from women who have
left prostitution after so many years.

Olivia chose to share her story because of her concern for all the
poor women still left behind. She wants to lead an exodus of such
women from poverty, violence, and drug addiction.

I am one of the few women who have survived this life style. I
am telling my story to give hope, so that other people understand
the dynamics of prostitution and do not judge so much. I have
a responsibility to others to offer my story.

6   By telling her story Olivia hopes to motivate people to view women in prostitution as fully human and to help them. Almost immediately, she saw that I had no particular expertise or point of view about prostitution and for this reason could serve as a useful messenger: "You were in the arena with the people who need to know."

Between January 2001 and January 2003 Olivia and I met for taped interviews. Her decision to speak so frankly was made at great cost. Dwelling in depth on her days in stripclubs and on the street caused her to vividly relive experiences she had put behind her, a process that often retraumatized her. Knowing her own limits, Olivia would signal her need to terminate our interview. In the beginning, realizing the effects of this project on Olivia, I was always relieved and gratified to find her smiling on the doorstep for our next interview.

Olivia stayed the course. And despite the pain she often endured, she remained brutally honest about herself and her experiences. Never were there any excuses or sugar coating. Early on I realized that it would be important for me to convey a sense of Olivia's uncompromising approach to speaking the truth, which has been such an important element in her recovery and her current approach to life.

Now that our collaboration is completed, Olivia has told me that she viewed with interest my struggle to comprehend her experiences and to put myself, as best as I was able, in her place: "I saw how you really wanted to understand our perspective, and that made me trust you." To see the self-confident social service administrator who is Olivia today as the frail, ninety-pound street addict of the past remains an effort. Olivia said she found my difficulty empowering because it continually reminded her of how far she had come. And the approach, centered as it was on fully discovering Olivia, proved to be successful. Olivia said she never felt that I was judging her or treating her like a victim.

Readers may find some of the material in this work rough going, but fidelity to the truth requires that there be no sanitization. Because Olivia is not able to remember a great deal of the violence and abuse she suffered from customers, everything is, in fact, not here. To try to bring back more details would deeply retraumatize her and prevent her from successfully continuing to navigate her new life. Olivia has also chosen to protect the privacy of her husband, her sister, and three children. For this reason, this work will not provide details of their lives and struggles, except in the most general way.

Although parts of the story are grim, the reader should understand that this is a tale with a happy ending. Fundamentally, it is a story of hope. Olivia's perseverance, grit, and determination to succeed will move you, as will all the kindnesses of strangers who offered her a helping hand along the way. Ultimately, it is a story that reaffirms for us the intrinsic worth of all human beings and spells out what our obligations to them should be.

Once you read her story, you will more fully understand that Olivia's choice to describe her experiences and to use her own name in the process is a matter of profound courage. The decision not to use a pseudonym was hers: "Now to use the name Olivia is a total acceptance of who I am." Olivia, who has her own strong notions of right and wrong and what she expects from herself and others, will look back and judge her own decisions and actions over the years. Now she realizes that when in prostitution she had buried and silenced her inner voices and values.

For some feminists, prostitution is the ultimate expression of sexual freedom, representing as it does women's choices to use their bodies and their sexuality in ways contrary to patriarchy's prescriptions. For still others, prostitution is the ultimate expression of patriarchy, a process in which women become only their bodies for the use and enjoyment of men. One group wants to legalize prostitution, the other to abolish it; one advocates for women's rights to trade sex for money, while the other argues that prostitution itself is a human rights violation.

This work makes two contributions to the current polarized debate about prostitution. First, it enables us to hear the voices of low-income women of color in prostitution. Although women of color participate in prostitution in larger numbers than would be warranted by their percentage in the general population, their stories and viewpoints have been largely absent from the literature. Living in drastically impoverished and marginalized circumstances, they remain largely invisible to us. Instead, the experiences of White feminist women in the sex trade find their way to publication. Their motivations for entering prostitution are not the same, the length of time they spend in prostitution is generally shorter, and, as a result, their experiences can be radically different.

Olivia does not claim to represent all the women and girls in prostitution, but from her work with thousands of women in the sex trade and her experiences over nineteen years, she is certain that her story is typical for far too many low-income women and girls of color: "There is a mass of women who are invisible that I must be the voice for."

Second, the prostitution debate has been conducted in the abstract, without reference to new research data or an up-to-date understanding of the organization and structure of the now global sex trade industry. In the last ten years, a significant amount of research data has surfaced concerning women in indoor prostitution venues such as stripping and escort services who probably make up the bulk of the women in prostitution in North America. Unfortunately, many of these articles are contained in inaccessible and obscure professional journals. Grounded in new research data and in the realities of today's multi-billion-dollar sex industry,[2] this work provides new perspectives to inform decisions about the acceptability of the industry on the landscape.

Olivia's story is my second work in a planned trilogy describing how and why so many poor girls and women in the United States become enmeshed in violence, and the many ways in which that violence keeps them trapped in poverty. All too often, explanations of women's poverty look to imperfections in the women themselves or to social structures of inequality that keep the poor from economic opportunity. Yet disadvantages stemming from gendered circumstances—from the upbringing of the girls to the agency of men in their lives—work to constrain these low-income girls in gender-stereotypical roles that imprison them in poverty and violence.

In *Saving Bernice: Battered Women, Welfare, and Poverty*,[3] the first book of the trilogy, I demonstrate how the men in the lives of many women on welfare, threatened by their attempts at economic self-sufficiency, sabotage them with violence and threats, and how lack of support, education, and financial resources make it difficult for these women to escape. I argue that women on welfare are magnets for low-income abusers, who encourage welfare dependency as a means of control, and that for battered women, the institution of welfare, which begins as a helping hand, over the long term becomes a mechanism that traps them in poverty.

At sixteen years of age, Bernice Hampton fled her violent, alcoholic, and dysfunctional home for a romantic relationship that promised the healthy nuclear family she so desired, but that so tragically failed to deliver and thus made her into a poor and battered woman. Olivia's story illustrates another response to the same problem. Repelled by what she saw of love and marriage in a childhood home dominated by domestic violence and alcoholism, Olivia took a different path than Bernice's. Eschewing romantic relationships, at sixteen she turned to stripclub dancing, which she thought promised her glamour, attention, big money, personal power, and independence from men. In the end, she found herself trapped as much as Bernice in violence and much worse in drug addiction. I will demonstrate how the sex trade industry as an institution, like welfare, plays a strong role in trapping needy women and girls in poverty, and how no antipoverty strategy for women can be effective unless it squarely confronts the recruitment strategies of the industry.

To look at Olivia today is to see a strikingly beautiful and intelligent woman with verve and a sparkle in her eye. Readers will soon learn how her vivacity, sense of humor, love of adventure, and profound courage helped her cope with her chosen lifestyle and to succeed in what became a dangerous escape. Nonetheless, Olivia almost lost the struggle and probably would be dead today if it had not been for the many individuals she met along the way who helped her persevere, including special mentors Edwina Gateley and Richard Booze. How unbearably sad it is to think of all the other women like Olivia out there, unable to make the same journey because we have not chosen to reach out to them. It is for them that Olivia shares her story.

CHAPTER ONE

Groomed

It is as if a number of people were set down in a desert,
and some had compasses and some had not; and those who
had compasses treated those who had not as their inferiors,
scolding and mocking them with no regard for the injustice
of the conditions, and at the same time guiding them, often
kindly, to safety. I still believe childhood to be a horrible
state of disequilibrium, and I think we four girls were not
foolish in feeling a vast relief because we had reached the
edge of the desert.

— REBECCA WEST, *This Real Night*

The alcoholism in Olivia's household was rampant. Her father, an African-American who paved streets for the city of Chicago for twenty-two years until his diabetes took over, was never without a drink, and Olivia's mother, who was of Polish ancestry, kept up. There were weekend poker parties at home and at other people's houses. And family trips to sit in bars. Olivia grew up in bars with her parents. But a lot of the drinking was done at home.

Olivia knows now that her parents were alcoholics. Her father always had a pint or more in his lunch pail. First thing in the morning, he would shake, needing a drink for his "wake up."

*My father was a very controlling man. I know the drinking had
a lot to do with it, because we didn't see a lot of fighting when*

they weren't drunk. I can't remember when they weren't drinking and when they weren't sick.

The fighting was continual: "He didn't spank us girls, but he beat the
living daylights out of my mother." It didn't happen every day, but at
least four or five times a month.

> Punching, slapping, kicking, throwing her against the wall,
> dragging her by her hair. We kids would huddle together during
> these two-hour episodes. We lay in bed hearing it and we would
> go to sleep hearing it. We didn't know what to do as kids. We
> talked about calling the police, but we thought that would make
> it worse. It was pretty horrible.

The next morning Olivia's mother's face would be a mess.

> He would be sorry the next morning. He would tell us, your
> mother knows she shouldn't have said that to me, but you girls
> know how much I love you and her. And my mother would buy
> that. She and her women friends would be sitting at the table
> all with black eyes, laughing and joking about it, how much in
> love they were.

Because the violence was for the purpose of control, the beatings could
be over anything. For the children, the brutal battering created a lot of
fear and, under the fear, anger.

> We were scared a lot. That our mother was going to die, or it
> would turn on us, that we were next. I remember a couple of
> times both my sisters and I screaming, "Don't hit her any
> more, stop, please stop." It always fell on deaf ears. We were
> told, "If you don't shut up, you're next." It never happened,
> but we didn't know if it would or not.

At the age of eight or nine, Olivia started to drink as a method of
numbing herself, disassociating herself from the violence.

> When I tasted booze, I liked it. For many reasons. I wouldn't
> be as fearful at night when my parents started fighting. The

> drink desensitized me to what was really going on. I would see
> a glass and sip the drink. It would calm me and make me pass
> out, or it didn't devastate me as much. It was very easy to go
> out there and take what I wanted, which was the bourbon. After
> I drank, I found that sense of satisfaction, that warm glow and
> sense that I could deal with this. I was always a real nervous
> child, very nervous.

Olivia knew that the violence would occur whenever her father came home from drinking and gambling, whether he had won or lost. Even as a small girl, she began to prepare for it by numbing herself with alcohol in advance. That enabled Olivia to simply pass out and not hear the beatings at all.

The violence against Olivia's mother resulted in emotional abuse for the children. Olivia's mother gave her father his insulin shots. Regularly, following a brutal beating that resulted in a black eye, her mother would tell the three girls, "Don't worry about it, when I give him his shot tomorrow, I'm going to give him water."

> My baby sister would cry all the time, thinking our mother was
> going to kill our father. She never did, she never would. It was
> revengeful thinking. It didn't bother me for some reason, but I
> remember telling my sister, "Don't worry, she said that last
> week. It isn't going to happen." It was pretty nuts, pretty nuts
> at home.

Olivia's father's parents had been killed in a flood, and he had been placed in a series of foster homes.

> We'll probably never know what happened in some of these
> foster homes. He had one foster father whom he hit over the
> head with a washboard. He did a lot of time in juvenile homes
> and as an adult he did some time in prison for attempted mur-
> der. Men act out trauma differently than women.

Olivia says her mother was twenty-five when she met Olivia's father. She was also emotionally needy. One of Olivia's mother's sisters had developed chronic arthritis at a young age and was unable to walk. The whole household revolved around the needs of this sister, whom family members carried everywhere. Undoubtedly, thinks Olivia, her mother became vulnerable and needy owing to the lack of attention and care from her parents and other siblings.

Between Olivia's two parents there was a twelve-year difference in age. Nothing could make her mother's family reconcile themselves to their daughter's marriage to a Black man. The age difference between them and the isolation from her family probably made Olivia's mother very dependent upon her husband, increasing his power over her. Olivia is certain that these dissimilarities between them made Olivia's father an exciting partner for her mother who was young and impressionable.

Olivia thinks that the lack of relatives contributed to the family dysfunction.

> My father was an orphan, and my mother's family almost completely removed themselves from her life when she married.
> Being biracial was also a large factor. When my girlfriends would get mad at me, they would say, oh, she thinks she's cute because her mother's White. As a biracial child, I didn't know where I fit into society. It is part of the identity problem and part of the self-esteem problem.

Physically, Olivia's parents were there in the home, but they were absent emotionally, busy with their drinking and their parties and recovering from their hangovers. Always they took the three little girls with them to the parties. "I realize now that they did love us, and they did the best they could with what they knew," Olivia says. "I don't think that they understood that wasn't appropriate, I really don't."

At the parties, the men played poker and drank, and the women talked and drank. While the adults imbibed their alcohol, the girls were put in another room where they entertained themselves before falling asleep. This was the era of the Supremes. The girls would tease their hair up, put on matching outfits, and practice their song and dance routines in that side room.

> It started that way. We would begin performing there, for these drunks. Our parents would show us off. The more voluptuously

> I danced, the more I shook my rear end, the more my father's
> friends would say, "Oh, she's going to be a star one day." All
> kinds of little comments. I remember that it really fed my self-
> esteem. The more they hollered and gave money, the nastier I
> would dance. We must have started at seven, eight, or nine years
> of age—a couple of bucks, singles, fives. I never related how
> that played a part until I got sober later. When I look at it
> now, I see that I've been prostituted all my life.

Whether child sexual abuse occurred at these parties remains an open question, but there are some signs that it did. Olivia has had flashbacks.

> I saw a hand. I was a real little girl lying on the bed. I saw a
> very young child's private parts, and a man standing over her.
> I could never get to the face. I have often wondered if it was my
> father, or one of his friends. I don't doubt that something hap-
> pened. Everybody's drunk, the kids are in the room asleep, the
> door was never all the way closed. My sister thinks that she
> may have been, too, and we both can't be wrong. It was proba-
> bly so early on that subconsciously we just buried it.

The more Olivia's parents drank, the more her father controlled and beat her mother, and the more often Olivia slipped drinks. She was always happy to volunteer to clean up after parties, when she could down the drink remains as she cleared the room.

Undoubtedly, Olivia's mother's situation affected her abilities to be a good parent for her children. Because she was numbing herself with alcohol, how much could she give? She also had to deal with the physical and mental abuse from Olivia's father, and her own displaced anger had an effect on her parenting. Olivia makes clear, however, that her mother was a good caretaker: food was always on the stove, the clothing for the school week was always washed and ironed, and lunches were always ready for school. "I recently attended my eighth-grade class reunion," Olivia says, "and one of the things that I told my sister that really threw me was that everybody there still remembered that we girls always had the best lunches."

School and reading were Olivia's refuges. Books became an escape, a salvation. Because danger was the norm at home, school became the safe environment, and Olivia spent a lot of time there with after-school activities. She believes that she worked so hard academically so that her parents would never have to be called to the school.

> I never knew what would happen if they summoned my parents
> up to school. I didn't know if they would be drunk, or what.
> You overachieve so that there is no reason to be called. Since I
> was ashamed of what happened at home, I wanted to make the
> outside look good, so people didn't think that it was so screwed
> up at home.

The three girls all had different reactions to the family dysfunction. Older sister Alta, who also geared herself to school achievement, was the worrier. Olivia says her parents held Alta accountable for anything that happened, dispensing physical punishment if her two sisters suffered any harm. For this reason, Alta was always watching and supervising. Animosity grew between Olivia and Alta that was later to have tragic consequences, because although Olivia did not want to listen to anybody, she especially did not want to listen to her bossy older sister. Tanya, the youngest, was the rebellious one. She reacted differently to the family situation by playing the clown, getting into fights, and not getting good grades.

Alta, interviewed many years later, remembers the young Olivia as precocious.

> She always was a people person, she attracted people to her.
> Everyone looked at her, she always had a kind of star quality. She got a lot of attention, and by her being as small as she was, she did not get a lot of discipline. Things that my younger sister and I couldn't get away with, Olivia sometimes did. That, and being the center of attention in terms of growing up, made her feel that was where she should always be, and so she did things to make sure she was the center of attention.[1]

When Olivia was nine or ten, her father's diabetes became worse and he was unable to work. This caused a traumatic change in the economics of the household. Money, now in short supply, became increasingly important to the girls.

Olivia had an Uncle Billy who lived in a senior citizens' building directly across from Olivia's family on Chicago's South Side. Uncle Billy was much older than Olivia's parents.

> *We would be sent over there to go to the store for them. I remember him beginning to grab my hand and putting it on his genitals, and telling me not to tell. When I got ready to leave, he would give me five, then eventually it became twenty dollars. I was twelve years old when it started. When I found out it was happening also with my younger sister, she and I would get in cahoots to go over there and get this money. It bothered me; I remember feeling disgusted, especially after the first four to five months when it came to the part of unzipping him and taking his genitals out, and him pressing against me. I never saw him release, but he derived some pleasure out of it, because he continued to do it. He made the mistake one time of approaching my older sister who went and told. That was the end of it. I remember my younger sister being angry with her because she had blown our money.*

And then there was "Uncle" Jimmy, who lived in an upstairs apartment. He would take Olivia's mother shopping Thursday nights. Whichever child had done well that week would get to go shopping with mother and "Uncle" Jimmy. He would buy all the groceries for the week.

> *I'll never forget it. I'm sure my mother saw him at different times. Thursday must have been his payday. When my father was physically abusing my mother, I would hear little innuendos relating to "Uncle" Jimmy, about her seeing him. She liked "Uncle" Jimmy more than him, she had better get the money from him, things like that. There definitely was prostitution, and the controlling and the violence very likely had to do with it. At times she was doing it against her will, I am sure.*

Alta remembers her mother saying that their father eventually became angry about her mother's visits to "Uncle" Jimmy. With the father's ironclad control over the household, it would appear unlikely that their mother could have taken up with this man without her husband's approval. But when it really became necessary for the family's survival, after he was too ill to work, Alta believes that their father began to resent the necessity of her mother's involvement with "Uncle" Jimmy.[2]

Later, when Olivia had been in the clubs for a while, it suddenly dawned on her what had been going on in her home when she was growing up. The language seemed the same, and previously inexplicable things began to make better sense. The children had always heard that their mother had been a "26 girl," a woman who rolled the dice in bars. That was how she had met Olivia's father. Olivia knows now that in those days the "26 girls" were often women in prostitution. As they were growing up, the girls sometimes heard that before they were born, their father had had eight other women besides their mother living with him in a one-room apartment. The story was that Olivia's father ceased being involved with these other women after the marriage.

Olivia thinks now that these women were active in the sex trade under the control of her father. Several of them, she knows now, were living in the house when the three children were young. "I think he had my mother out for awhile," she explains. "They were together five or six years before even getting married, and that was their lifestyle. She wound up deciding to marry him."

After Olivia had been involved in prostitution in stripclubs, she talked with her mother about it. Olivia's mother admitted she had had a few guys or tricks whom she kept for a long time.

> She didn't see it as prostitution. It was a way to make ends meet. Was it coerced? It was a part of their lifestyle. Whether she was involved in it prior to my Dad, I'm not sure, but it was a part of the lifestyle that they both knew. At times she was doing it against her will. I think about all her drinking, all the fights they had over it.

The involvement in the sex trade, Olivia thinks, was a by-product of her father's life on the street. With no family support, perhaps he created his own sense of power and control by coercing others and reaping financial rewards from it.

How did Olivia feel when she later discovered the existence of prostitution in her home?

> At the time I found out, it seemed like we had something in
> common. It was so sick. We'd be drinking and talking, and she
> would be telling me about a certain guy she had, the streets
> weren't as bad as now, and there weren't the hard-core drugs
> involved, just alcohol, so the scene was different. We had a
> connection, a kind of a sick connection.
>
> In recovery it really started bothering me. He abused her,
> but the anger over her prostitution came all the more. His ac-
> tions helped to normalize prostitution. It didn't surprise me that
> was the lifestyle that I turned to. The whole progression of it.
> As I began my own healing process, the anger came up, and I
> just didn't see that as a kid. When I put two and two together,
> I got very angry. It was lucky he was dead by then.

Olivia's oldest sister, Alta, didn't turn to alcohol or drugs. Olivia thinks Alta remained in her "good girl" role, being a hero and keeping everything okay all her life. "She grew up in a role in which you didn't do anything to the extreme. She wasn't going to rock the boat, whereas I acted out my issues."

Alta agrees: "I stayed busy taking care of everybody else. I didn't allow myself. I wouldn't be able to watch over them."[3]

Olivia's younger sister Tanya died of a drug overdose just before her twenty-first birthday. She too was involved in prostitution.

⤷

Research conclusively demonstrates that many women and girls in prostitution come from households like Olivia's where drugs and alcohol, domestic violence, and incest are prevalent.[4] The Center for Impact Research survey of 222 women in various prostitution venues in Chicago, sampled in 2001, found that overall 83 percent of respondents had some substance abuse occurring in their households while growing up, and 86 percent had used one or more substances themselves as teens.[5] Eight additional prostitution research samples have measured childhood household alcohol and drug use, finding from 58 to 81 percent of parents drinking excessively and 40 to 65 percent using illegal substances.[6] Inciardi and colleagues found that prostitution was associated with significantly earlier drug use in their sample of 100 seriously delinquent Miami youth aged twelve to seventeen. Like Olivia, the girls in the sex trade (87 percent reported a mean number of 200 acts of prostitution within the last twelve months) used marijuana and alcohol at mean ages of eight and ten, and by age twelve were trying cocaine and heroin.[7] In another study, adolescents who were not in prostitution were more likely to use marijuana compared to girls in the sex trade who used drugs such as cocaine, acid, and amphetamines.[8] Kuhns and colleagues also found that the mean ages for first alcohol intoxication, initiation of daily drinking, and experimentation with drugs other than alcohol were lower for girls involved in prostitution than for other female arrestees.[9]

Having a deceased mother is a remarkably common theme. In two separate West Coast samples, 33 percent had a deceased mother,[10] and in Chicago 40 percent experienced someone's death while they were growing up, and of these 25 percent were the biological mother.[11] Separation, divorce, and the death of a father were also common occurrences.[12] In one recent study in Victoria, B.C., researchers found that 57.2 percent of their sample of 201 individuals in prostitution had at some point been in foster care, group homes, or other state-funded institutions. Eleven percent had lived on their own before they were fourteen years of age.[13]

Large percentages of women also had parents who were incarcerated while they, the women, were growing up. In a San Francisco sample, 19 percent of the women's fathers, 32 percent of their stepfathers, and 11 percent of their mothers had been convicted of crime—overall, 41 percent of the subjects' close family members had faced criminal penalties.[14] Thirty-six percent of the Los Angeles County jail sample had either a mother, father, or both parents in jail during childhood.[15]

Although household domestic violence, perpetrated against the mother of a woman in the sex trade, can be a key factor in causing a young girl to leave her home for the streets, researchers neglect it. Rates of domestic violence in prostitution samples are over twice the reported national prevalence. Fifty-one percent of women interviewed in San Francisco saw their father hit their mother violently, and of these, 75 percent reported that the violence was a regular occurrence (once a month or more often), with 19 percent of the cases occurring several times a week.[16] In a recent research project in the Cook County (Chicago) jail, 62 percent of the women in prostitution stated they had witnessed violence in the home, as compared with 52 percent of the entire sample, and 51 percent had experienced physical abuse themselves, as compared with 38 percent of the entire sample.[17] Almost 62 percent of the women answering the question in the Center for Impact Research Chicago sample had viewed domestic violence in their childhood home, and 40 percent reported serious levels of violence, including beatings, rapes, and threats with a weapon. Over half identified their mother as the victim of this violence, and 44 percent reported that their mothers were victims of the more serious violence. Ninety-one percent indicated that the perpetrator was the father, stepfather, or mother's partner.[18] Half the women reporting domestic violence stated that they themselves had also been objects of physical abuse while growing up, a figure that more than ten other research studies corroborate.[19]

Most researchers have tended to view these elements of family dysfunction as important because they result in the teen girls running away from home, an occurrence thought to directly lead to prostitution.[20] Domestic violence in the home, however, may play a key part in teen girls' perceptions about power and control that can also affect prostitution entry. As a teen observes her mother as a victim of domestic violence, she makes certain assumptions about relationships, love, and sex. The girls see their mothers controlled, beaten, and crushed. Without a doubt, many low-income teen girls, as Olivia herself now understands, eschew monogamous relationships—or any conventional dating arrangements—as too controlling.

For Claudine O'Leary, who was involved in prostitution as a teen, and who now helps young women exit the sex trade, it was all about having a sense of control that her mother, twenty years in a violent and abusive marriage, lacked. When Claudine's father deserted the family, her mother worked a graveyard shift to support herself and the two children. Claudine's prostitution activities took her to clubs and parties.

> We never had a car. Suddenly we're down in Palos Heights
> [a far southern suburb of Chicago]. You feel like you are

> going places and doing things. I didn't feel like I was being
> controlled. It was exciting. . . . My mom worked in plastic
> dipping in a factory. I didn't want to end up like that.[21]

Nothing could persuade Claudine to date one guy at a time. She saw her mother, and she saw other girls being controlled by their boyfriends: "I saw young girls having to report on the phone, guys picking them up, never being allowed to go anywhere. It seemed so stupid. I didn't want to be a part of it."[22]

Thus some needy girls become enmeshed in violent relationships, while others, in their efforts to avoid domestic violence, are attracted to prostitution, which appears to offer more power in sexual relationships. By rejecting marriage-like arrangements, they attempt to increase their own independence and efficacy. But the decisions made for these laudable goals result in an ultimate diminution of power for some girls.

Most prostitution research has simply missed exploring the intergenerational patterns of prostitution. D. Kelly Weisberg's early pioneering study of adolescents in the sex trade cites Newman and Caplan's study of juveniles involved in prostitution, reporting that one-third of the girls had mothers who were also active in the sex trade.[23] Four percent of the Pines and Silbert sample had a close relative arrested for prostitution, and 4 percent stated that a family member sent them out to earn money for the household through sex trade activities.[24] Weisberg commented in 1985:

> The influence of the prostitute mother does not appear to
> have been given the attention it deserves, and it is an area
> that merits further research. Especially interesting would be
> an examination of situations in which mothers actually
> "turn out" their daughters, since some evidence of this
> phenomenon exists.[25]

The father's or male partner's role in the mother's prostitution involvement also deserves research. A Chicago study found that almost one-third of the 206 women who answered the question stated that in their youth there was someone in the household who regularly exchanged sex for money (two or more times a week for at least a month). Of these, almost 42 percent indicated that biological mothers were involved; 40 percent had sisters who were active, 6 percent had brothers, and 13 percent aunts.[26]

About a third of these respondents indicated they had relatives outside the household while growing up who regularly exchanged sex for money. Aunts and cousins constituted the majority of these relatives participating in prostitution. Almost 20 percent stated that when they were growing up someone in the household was involved in an adult entertainment business. Twelve percent of these stated they had mothers in the business, 20 percent cousins, and 17 percent had aunts. A quarter of the women answered that there was someone in the household who received money from the prostitution activities of another person, and almost 14 percent stated that there was someone in the household who forced someone to make money through prostitution by using threats, violence, or control.[27]

Claudine O'Leary explains how household prostitution activities influence the actions of teen girls:

> They may have seen their mothers trade sex for the rent money, they have seen women getting by. This is what all women do. If you have no other examples in your life, or very few examples in your life, of women who don't do that, you might think to yourself, this is what women do.[28]

Sadly, coercion by other family members also plays a part in prostitution entry. One nineteen-year-old in the Chicago sample, who was interviewed in the streets after a spell in a stripclub, said that family members had threatened her with expulsion at thirteen if she did not cooperate in prostitution endeavors. Her family kicked her out of the house at fifteen or sixteen, "when I refused to make it with some old geezer my mom or her folks wanted me to be with." The girl's mother was involved in prostitution, and one of her mother's live-in partners had raped her at twelve years of age.[29] Another girl, age eighteen, had a mother who kept three men living with them for as long as she could remember. One was a drug dealer who turned her and her sisters out into prostitution between the ages of twelve and fifteen. He drank, shot cocaine and heroin, used pain pills, and gave the girls the drug ecstasy.[30]

Large percentages of women and girls in the sex trade have also been victims of childhood sexual assault. In twenty recent prostitution studies, the lowest percentage of women sexually abused as children is a third, with a high of 84 percent; using a conservative national figure of 17 percent, the prevalence in prostitution samples is thus three to five times that of the general population.[31] Farley and Barkan found an average of three different perpetrators in San Francisco.[32] Norton-Hawk discovered that the episodes usually occurred between the ages of six and nine,[33] and Dalla established that the sexual abuse in her sample in a midsize Midwestern city lasted an average of almost five years.[34] Nixon and her colleagues determined that 64 percent of their sample of forty-five women from three Canadian prairie provinces who began prostitution before the age of eighteen had been involved in the child welfare system as a result of this kind of abuse.[35]

Greater levels of childhood physical and sexual abuse increase the likelihood of involvement in prostitution. Fifty-three percent of the women in prostitution in a 2001 Cook County (Chicago) Jail sample reported being sexually abused as children, as compared to 38 percent of the entire sample of jailed women.[36] In a sample of more than 1,000 women in the Cook County Jail between 1991 and 1993, detainees who had experienced childhood sexual abuse had substantially higher rates of ever being involved in prostitution (44 percent, compared with 28.5 percent for detainees with no history of abuse), and of routine prostitution (almost 35 percent, compared with 21 percent for nonabused detainees). Childhood sexual assault nearly doubled the odds of entry into prostitution during the lifetime of the respondent.[37] Research with a nationally representative sample of 528 shelter youths and a multicity sample of street youths in 1992 found that both street and shelter youths were twice as likely to report engaging in survival sex (defined as trading sex for survival items such as housing or food, instead of money) if they also had suffered physical abuse from family members.[38]

Although the large prevalence of childhood sexual assault among women in the sex trade indicates some kind of relationship, the fact that most incest victims do not proceed into prostitution raises questions about the exact nature of the connection, which will be explored more fully in the next chapter. As the following story illustrates, however, the ways in which childhood sexual assault can predispose girls for the sex trade are not difficult to understand.

Diana Russell recounts the story of Lara Newman, whose sixty-year-old grandfather sexually abused her at four-and-a-half years of age. The abuse continued for eight years during the thrice-yearly visits her family made to her grandparents' home. Lara adored her grandfather, who would reward her with sweets, ice cream, or money. When she was older she learned to demand more expensive items, such as a tape recorder.[39]

Lara has never been involved in prostitution on a regular basis, but she considers herself a person groomed to be a "whore." Russell identifies important aspects of this training. Lara's grandfather encouraged her to be sexually provocative and an available object of desire. He also trained her to be compensated for her sexual services, to expect rewards for her sexual submission.[40]

At the same time, Lara finds that sex now makes her feel powerful because she can make men ejaculate. Because of her sexual power over her grandfather, Lara changed from feeling like a victim to believing that she was in control: "I get such a thrill from being in charge and being in power and making a man totally want sex."[41] Despite being happily married, Lara now constantly seduces men, encourages their obsessive adoration of her, demands payment for sex, and then hurts and rejects them, all as a means of feeling powerful.[42] Lara believes that she only feels in control in the context of a use/abuse situation, when she is able to turn herself from being a victim into a position of power. She admits, however, that "This complete juxtaposition of being in power and being a victim doesn't make sense."[43]

Lara's story describes two separate prostitution-related phenomena, of which the first is grooming. Incest teaches the child that love, attention, and financial rewards follow from sex. Prostitution survivor Norma Hotaling relates how at age five she learned to get candy money in the playground from men who paid her to view pornography with them.[44] David Finkelhor, an expert on sexual abuse, confirms that incest shapes a child's sexuality in developmentally inappropriate and interpersonally dysfunctional ways, producing what he calls traumatic sexualization. Offenders reward sexually abused children for sexual behavior that is inappropriate to their level of development. Because of these rewards, sexually abused children learn to use sexual behavior, appropriate or inappropriate, as a strategy for manipulating others to get their needs met.[45]

Second is the issue of power and control. Although a woman's sense of control has disappeared through sexual assault, she can reclaim power by using the sexual allure she can exert over men. Remaining in the sexual arena to grab the power back, women in prostitution, the majority of whom are incest victims, end up developing personal power only in relationship to men and sex, or within sexually defined gender roles.

Incest, alcohol and drug abuse, and domestic violence in the home have reduced many girls, like Olivia, to a state of powerlessness, a situation worsened by the effects of persistent disassociation, a kind of tuning out to avoid feeling pain. Then along comes adolescence, and a newfound realization that they are attractive to others. Is it any wonder that so many low-income teens harness this single asset and use it to their advantage? As researcher Leon Pettiway observes, the structure and functioning of their families and their childhood environments make it impossible for these girls to imagine or desire anything materially different. He calls their decisions "structured choices," because circumstances have limited the agency of these girls at critical turning points in their lives.[46]

One treatise on adolescent girls sums up the attraction of prostitution for low-income teen girls who have been rendered powerless by incest and domestic violence:

> Prostitutes operate within the arena of sexual behavior, in which teen girls are given the most confusing message of all. They are supposed to deny sexual feelings and yet be attractive to men. Because of their youth and freshness, teen prostitutes are the most sought after, thereby commanding higher prices. Thus the teen prostitute holds a strange kind of power over others. This experience of being valued by others (the johns and pimps) may serve to repair a self-esteem damaged by the normal adolescent struggles and history of family dysfunction.[47]

⌘

Historian Ruth Rosen has reviewed eight available survey reports on prostitution conducted by urban researchers during the Progressive Era

(1900–1920). That so little has changed since the early twentieth century about the complex, interconnected causes for entry into prostitution in the United States is startling.

Like Olivia's, many of the surveyed women's families were not originally destitute but sank into poverty owing to conditions that interfered with the breadwinner's ability to support the family, such as parental desertion, death, or illness.[48] One study of 378 women in New York's sex trade between 1907 and 1915 found that 25 percent had no parents and 60 percent had a parent absent from the home because of separation, divorce, or death, with a much lower percentage of such losses among working women who were not in prostitution.[49] This disruption of economic stability may have created immediate needs for funds that only prostitution could meet. The illusion that prostitution may provide a certain upward economic mobility is one shared by women in prostitution then and now, as the sex trade continues to attract poor girls because of its seemingly glamorous lifestyle. One young woman in prostitution told a researcher in the early twentieth century, "I thought I'd get style like the other girls do. . . . I saw them dress swell and make nice money."[50]

Women in the Progressive Era began in prostitution between the ages of seventeen and twenty-one years.[51] Many of these young women's families also had a history of alcoholism and incest, which Rosen believes may be synonymous with parental neglect or emotional deprivation.[52] For example, a 1911 publication reports that thirty-two out of seventy-two girls brought before the juvenile court in Chicago were incest victims.[53] Researcher Maude Miner found that many of the girls brought before night court for prostitution in New York had been on the street since they were children, dodging their drunk and abusive parents.[54]

Based on her review of this early research, Rosen believes that the lack of good family relations or support may well have been an important factor in the women's decisions to become involved in prostitution.

> Furthermore, to practice prostitution, women had to risk
> familial rejection. Thus it is probably not coincidental that
> women from broken homes or the daughters of immigrant
> families more frequently turned to prostitution than did the

foreign-born women or daughters of closely knit families. Without close family ties, such women may have lacked the familial restraints and controls that kept other women from entering prostitution. If no one seemingly cared, or if family bonds were sufficiently torn by constant generational conflict, a daughter may have felt free to choose an illegitimate means of achieving upward mobility.[55]

Because of the persistence of prostitution into the twenty-first century, Rosen concludes that "It should be understood that the basic class structure and gender system that supported the existence of prostitution during the Progressive Era have not changed substantively."[56] She concurs with other analysts who find that the "sexual revolution," the frank use of sexuality in advertising, and the growth of the pornography industry at the end of the twentieth century may serve to increase, rather than decrease, the historical lure of prostitution for low-income girls.[57] Despite many positive changes in American life at the turn of the twenty-first century for women and girls, the prostitution industry has continued to entice the same kinds of low-income girls for the same complex of reasons it did at the turn of the twentieth century—a profoundly depressing conclusion.

CHAPTER TWO

Reeled In

> But this made us still more determined not to marry. She
> had committed herself to this marriage without knowing
> what it was going to cost her. If we who had seen her pay
> the price condemned ourselves to such misery, even for the
> same reward, there would be something suicidal about it.
> . . . Indeed, marriage was to us a descent into a crypt where,
> by the tremendous light of smoking torches, there was cele-
> brated a glorious rite of a sacrificial nature. But we meant
> to stay in the sunlight, and we knew no end which we
> could serve by offering ourselves up as a sacrifice.
>
> — REBECCA WEST, *This Real Night*

As Olivia became a teenager, her father's health deteriorated even further. His kidney failure, owing to his diabetes, required dialysis. "The
next thing I remember," Olivia relates, "we were on public aid and
moved into the housing project. This is just at the age when kids want
to start dressing differently and start doing things. The lack of money
was the key."

Olivia desperately wanted to leave home because of the violence
and the drinking. The year before, her older sister Alta had enrolled in
Job Corps, a residential youth education program. Years later Alta told
Olivia that she had learned about Job Corps from a teacher in whom
she confided. "She did find someone whom early on she had told
about the dynamics at home," Olivia says. "In our home atmosphere

you were taught that you didn't trust, you didn't talk, and you didn't tell. Emotionally I wasn't as mature as she was to seek help."

Alta explains that in her junior year, because of problems at home, she simply stopped going to school: "I didn't go to class for an entire year. That was my way of acting out because of bad things at home. I was wanting attention. It happened that I didn't get it. Nobody said anything when I failed all my courses."[1]

So Alta returned to school, but when she confided in a male teacher who announced he was available to help the students, her grades substantially improved. As Job Corps was only available for dropouts, Alta actually had to leave high school again in order to enroll.

Unfortunately, Olivia was still in high school and a good student. But she desperately needed a quick way out of her house. Since she was also too young for Job Corps, Olivia had to lie about her age to get in.

> I just wanted to go to this place that I found where you could live there and only have to come home on the weekends, and then you could choose to come home. I told Job Corps I would quit school if they didn't let me come. My sister was out of the house. My envy was that great, and I know that it was a survival instinct, because I was much closer to my younger sister, and I didn't even think twice about leaving her. That survival instinct to get out of that dysfunctional house blew my opportunity for further schooling or even thinking about college.

Job Corps, however, fundamentally failed Olivia. While there she gravitated to a partying crowd of older girls. When they were able to get a pass, they would all go out to bars and to dinner, drinking "cocktails with the umbrellas," dating older men, and leading what they thought was the glamorous life. These fast girls were attractive to Olivia. They taught her about using makeup and all the other things that she couldn't learn from her emotionally absent mother or from her older sister, who had been too busy "in her hero role of just trying to keep things okay at home." In Job Corps Olivia really learned to hang out in bars.

Armed with her GED and a nurse's aide certificate, the sixteen-year-old looked in the newspaper for a job after she had completed the Job Corps program.

> I remember how many jobs there were. Why the bar job stood
> out to me is beyond me. Maybe there was just a connection that
> I could be around the booze that I had begun to really love by
> then. Bars were pretty much all I had ever known. I was at-
> tracted, I think, to the fast life and the fast money.

For another thing, Olivia knew she didn't want to get married and be abused as her mother was. That was her view of love and marriage, and it wasn't for her. "What I saw of marriage was not what I wanted in my life, so I wasn't looking for a Prince Charming."

> I wanted to leave home again, so a friend of the bar owner's got
> me a room for a week in a hotel. After the first week was over,
> the rent for the next week was due. I remember calling him to
> come over. I hadn't been to bed with him yet, but now he was
> expecting it. I remember lying on the bed and saying, "I don't
> want to do this," him bending my fingers back, and slapping
> me around. He had sex with me against my will. So that was
> my first experience and I was sixteen.

Olivia soon found out the facts of life: after all that, the rent still wasn't paid, so back home she went. A month later she located a coemployee at the bar who had disappeared. She told Olivia she was at a downtown Chicago Rush Street stripclub, where she made "a hell of a lot more money than we were making at the bar." When Olivia joined her there, she found out her friend was right. Without being involved in prostitution—just by stripping and pushing drinks—Olivia earned $900 to $1,000 a night, an enormous amount of money for a poor teenager.

Today, Olivia often thinks about why she sought such a job. Why not work as a nurse's aide? After all, she had the training and the certificate. Olivia wonders if being sexually abused made her feel stripped of power, and whether the activity she chose gave her a sense of regaining that control.

> Power over men, period. I could decide after I danced who I
> could go to, or who I would sit with. Prostitution gave me self-
> esteem and this false sense of power over men. And that is why

> I still tend to think that something may have happened early on
> that I felt totally stripped of power. Because why else would I
> seek that kind of job? Those aren't the jobs that attract most
> adolescents. . . .

The clubs had a real attraction to the sixteen-year old.

> I don't know exactly what I was looking for, but whatever it
> was, it was some sense of self and where you fit in this world.
> It certainly filled some kind of need. As humans we go back to
> whatever is comforting at some level. The clubs filled something
> that was empty at one time.
>   I gave no thought to what I was doing. I don't even think
> I thought of it as prostitution. I was enjoying the glamorous
> lifestyle, being self-sufficient.

Looking back, Olivia sees that Job Corps was just a time-out.

> I was there ten months, but ten months doesn't erase what you
> have known and seen all your life. I think it was a reprieve, and
> thank God for it, I don't know if I would have gotten a high
> school diploma had I not been there. But I ran from that back
> into the same lifestyle. Cognitively, I wasn't developed enough
> to make good choices, and the heavy drinking during Job Corps
> definitely delayed my development. All the GED did, though,
> was lead me to Rush Street quicker.

Later, in the course of her recovery, Olivia learned that she was not
responsible for everything that happened to her: "I didn't have the
structure or guidance I needed at home, with alcoholism as rampant as
it was in my house. I realize now that I was reared in a house that was
centered around prostitution activities. That wasn't what I should have
been exposed to."

On the other hand, Olivia is more than willing to take some responsibility for the choices she made later on, when she stayed in
prostitution at the point that she recognized that something was very
wrong.

> I get very angry at me, because I see the woman who really was
> inside of me, and I volunteered myself in a lot of ways. I was

really attracted to that lifestyle, and I stayed in it because of
that. It became a violent life. I stayed high enough not to let
the fear paralyze me into not doing it. At the time I did the best
I could with what I knew.

ॐ

Research studies with women and girls in prostitution in North America find that, like Olivia, large percentages begin as teens, a fact that should ultimately shift the entire debate about prostitution.[2] Fifteen percent of the women in the sex trade surveyed in the Cook County (Chicago) Jail in 2001, for example, began in prostitution before the age of thirteen years, and 21 percent began between the ages of fourteen to seventeen years.[3] In another recent study in Chicago, about 3 percent of the women reported they first exchanged sex for money before they were eleven years of age, and of these, several were used by parents or guardians to make money. Almost 33 percent first exchanged sex for money between the ages of twelve and fifteen, 26 percent between the ages of sixteen and seventeen, and 26 percent between the ages of eighteen and twenty-one.[4] Sixty-two percent of the women in the sample thus first became active in prostitution before their eighteenth birthday, and 87 percent before the age of twenty-one. A number of other recent research studies, some of which, like Chicago's, involve women in both indoor and outdoor prostitution, corroborate these figures, with mean ages of sixteen and seventeen years.[5]

Women who begin in prostitution as young teens—"younger starters"—share many common characteristics with ominous implications. In the Chicago study, for example, they were more likely to have used drugs while growing up. Only a quarter of those who began between twelve and fifteen achieved a high school education. Younger starters undertook more prostitution activities than older starters and were significantly more likely to have had someone else in their household exchanging sex for money. Having a mother in the sex trade also affected age of entry: 54 percent of those with a mother involved began prostitution activities between twelve and fifteen years of age. Seventy-two percent of those who began between twelve and fifteen ran away from home, as compared with 23 percent whose first experience occurred between the ages of twenty-two to twenty-five. The younger a respondent had started in prostitution, the more health problems she reported later in life, and being HIV-positive (22 percent in the sample stated they were) was also associated with early entry into prostitution: 44 percent of those women with HIV had started in prostitution by age fifteen, and 60 percent of the women with HIV had begun sex trade activities before eighteen.[6]

Another study found a relationship between younger starters and household drug use. Subjects whose parents were addicted to drugs and who were physically abused as children were significantly more likely to have traded sex for money before the age of fifteen.[7] In a Minneapolis sample, those who had begun as juveniles were involved in more total months of prostitution and higher average sexual exposures per month.[8]

Younger starters were more apt to begin prostitution activities on the street, according to another research study. In interviews with twenty-four women and girls, half of whom were involved in the streets and half in legal brothels, massage parlors, or escort agencies in Australia, researchers found that those on the street began earlier in prostitution (mean age of seventeen) than those in brothels (mean age of almost twenty-five). The researchers concluded that the younger women were more passive with their clients and less able to exert control over the encounters, which made them more vulnerable to abuse.[9] In a sample of 240 women in prostitution in three United Kingdom cities surveyed in 1999, those outdoors were also younger and had been involved in prostitution at an earlier age.[10] Researchers questioning women on the streets in Glasgow found that those injecting drugs all had started in the sex trade at younger ages than those who did not.[11]

Research, however, with stripper samples in North America, establishing that the majority begin in their late teens, does not bear out this United Kingdom finding that indoor workers begin in prostitution in their mid-twenties. Thirty exotic dancers in southern Ontario surveyed in 1998 all began their careers in their late teens or early twenties.[12] Holsopple's 1996 survey of eighteen women (ages eighteen to thirty-four) in Minneapolis area stripclubs found that the age of entry into stripping ranged from fifteen to twenty-three, with a mean age of eighteen years and ten months,[13] while the women in Wesley's sample of exotic dancers began at an average age of nineteen.[14] The vast majority of the women in a recent survey of twenty experienced strippers stated that they had participated as children in dance, modeling, or theater activities that put them in the spotlight and focused on their bodies. Like Olivia, many of the women had dreamed as children of dancing in ballet companies or in music videos.[15]

Although there is a large concern in the media about the trafficking of children into prostitution, interest in adults involved in prostitution is not as great. Yet research shows that the majority of women in prostitution began as teens and have not been able to exit, a fact that has escaped the media and the general public and has been ignored in the prostitution debate. As one provider has stated, "We are talking about the same women here. It's not like these young women are so overwhelmed with great opportunities when they turn eighteen that they just get out of prostitution."[16]

Officers in the prostitution unit of the Chicago Police Department remarked in late 2000 that women on the streets of Chicago were getting younger and younger, and sicker and sicker. One described a girl back on the street after surgery a mere seven days earlier, another nine months pregnant, and one who had delivered a baby the week before. Another officer mentioned a young girl he had recently picked up who suffered from tuberculosis, HIV, and hepatitis, was coughing, and had visible open lesions.[17]

In a newspaper interview, San Francisco cab driver Jeff Anderson stated that the girls in prostitution in that city were also getting younger and younger: "In the last six months, I've seen girls on South Van Ness—some of them look like they're babies." Although he sees plenty of fourteen- and fifteen-year-olds, he estimated that the majority started trading sex for money around seventeen. He said that they last about four years. "The girls start looking hardened after that," he explained. "Then they disappear, fall off the face of the earth. Years later you find they're dead or in jail." Anderson took the reporter through the streets, where "shadowy men in jogging suits lean against buildings—pimps minding the store," and "past armies of tarted up teeny boppers with bottle-blond hair."[18]

Because many women in prostitution leave home early, like Olivia, running away from home is thought to be one of the intervening variables predicting prostitution involvement. Some experts believe that 70 percent of street youth engage in prostitution to meet daily needs.[19] Research certainly confirms a correlation; the overwhelming majority of women in prostitution samples ran away from their childhood homes, with figures ranging from 96 percent in San Francisco,[20] 75 percent in Vancouver[21] and in a Canadian national sample,[22] 72 percent in a northeastern U.S. city,[23] 61 percent in Los Angeles,[24] 56 percent in Chicago,[25] and 40 percent in a Midwestern city.[26] And most of the women said they left home for good at extremely early ages. In a sample in a northeastern U.S. city, for example, 15 percent had left permanently between the ages of ten and thirteen, and 49 percent by the age of sixteen.[27] In Victoria, B.C., the average age the women began living without a legal guardian was sixteen years; 11 percent were living on their own before the age of fourteen.[28]

Not surprisingly, one survey of jail detainees in Chicago has found that the women with a history of having run away entered prostitution at a younger age than those who did not, and those who reported ever having run away from home were significantly more likely than nonrunaways to have ever been in the sex trade (almost 45 percent, compared with almost 30 percent) and to have engaged in routine prostitution (almost 36 percent, compared with almost 22 percent). Those who reported sexual abuse first ran away at a slightly younger mean age than nonabused women (12.6 years, compared with 13.2 years for nonabused women). The researchers found that running away affected entry into prostitution only in the early adolescent years, increasing the likelihood of prostitution entry by more than forty times. "In short, the analysis provided strong support for the hypothesis that sexual abuse and having run away influence entry into prostitution, although these risk factors were found to have distinctly different impacts over the life course."[29]

Three other research teams exploring the relationship between child abuse, running away, and prostitution have corroborated the Chicago findings. Between 1985 and 1986 Seng interviewed seventy sexually abused and thirty-five prostitution-involved children (mean age of fourteen) in Chicago. He found that the prostitution-involved children had more extensive runaway histories than did the abused group: more had run away at least once (77 percent, compared with 44 percent), and 34 percent had run away eleven or more times, compared with 8.6 percent of abused children. From these data he concluded that "the link between sexual abuse and adolescent prostitution is not direct, but requires runaway behavior as an intervening variable."[30]

Simons and Whitbeck came to a similar conclusion. Their work in Des Moines in 1991 found that early sexual abuse indirectly increased the chance of prostitution by elevating the risk of running away, substance abuse, and other forms of "delinquent behavior."[31] The work of Nadon and colleagues also confirms the importance of running away. Comparing the characteristics of forty-five female adolescents in the sex trade with thirty-seven adolescents not in prostitution (recruited from some of the same locations), they determined that a significantly greater proportion of the girls in prostitution in the sample were classified as runaways (87 percent as compared with 61 percent of the non-prostitution-involved respondents). Having found, however, nearly identical household factors—parental alcoholism, domestic violence, and childhood sexual and physical abuse—among girls in both groups, they caution against drawing conclusions about prostitution entry without researching further appropriate comparison groups:

> In the present study, adolescent prostitutes ran away from home significantly more often than nonprostitute adolescents. Given that the groups did not differ with respect to home experiences, nor in adolescent personality variables, this suggests that background factors may be necessary but insufficient conditions to justify prostitution activity.[32]

One prostitution survivor believes that the potent combination of childhood sexual assault and running away leads a girl to the sex trade:

> Incest is boot camp. Incest is where you send the girl to learn how to do it. So you don't, obviously, have to send her anywhere, she's already there and she's got nowhere else to go. She's trained. And the training is specific and it is important: not to have any real boundaries to her own body; to know that she's valued only for sex; to learn about men what the offender, the sex offender, is teaching her. But even that is not enough, because then she runs away and she is out on the streets and homeless. For most

women, some version of all these kinds of destitution needs to occur.[33]

Clearly, then, running away from home is an intervening variable that predicts the likelihood of involvement in prostitution. Does running away take the girl into an environment of poverty, homelessness, and the street, in which the sex trade already plays a strong part, or does running away symbolize for the girls a breakdown of family bonds, attachments, and commitments that propel them toward unconventional activities such as prostitution?

Maggie O'Neill, who has interviewed many girls in prostitution in the United Kingdom, puts a slightly different spin on it. She reminds us that most low-income girls are without economic power but do not turn to prostitution. She believes that involvement in the sex trade results when emotional neediness combines with poverty. The girls, she writes, have a "poorly experienced and underdeveloped sense of personal power."[34]

Unlike O'Neill, most prostitution researchers have not considered how the sex trade industry itself works to entice emotionally and economically needy young girls like Olivia. If the research from the earlier Progressive Era is accurate, girls are entering prostitution at even earlier ages now than they did one hundred years ago. As we follow Olivia's experiences in stripping and other segments of the industry, we would do well to bear in mind the role that the business played in her entrapment in prostitution. Considerable evidence supports the proposition that the prostitution industry in the United States today is built to create and satisfy a demand for teen girls. What happens when we focus more on this demand and less on the individual motivations of the girls for participation in the sex trade? Doesn't supply inevitably follow demand?

Prostitution survivor Norma Hotaling, who works with prostitution customers arrested in San Francisco, maintains that pimps actively recruit teen girls, bringing them to San Francisco from other cities:

> Vulnerable and naive thirteen and fourteen year old blond, blue eyed, white girls (supply) are brutally and cunningly recruited from our schools, streets, and shopping malls of the mid-west and Canada and delivered to major cities

through the U.S. to fill the demand side of prostitution: comprised mostly of educated, middle and upper class men.[35]

Hotaling also asserts that male customers begin prostitution with adult women and then move to using children. These adults engage in prostitution with complex needs and emotions, she says, and they attempt to satisfy them with youth.

> They use many justifications for their actions such as "they are poor and I am feeding them," "They kept coming back, therefore, they must like it. . . ." The world of prostitution, whether legal or illegal, provides an area where laws and rules which constrain sex with minors can be evaded. . . . Prostitution potentially provides instant access, often to a selection of children.[36]

Evidence of the demand for youth is all around us. Directories of escort services emphasize their girls as "hot, young, and tight." The sites indicate the girls are nineteen years of age, but, regardless of their age, their pictures make them appear younger.[37] Inspector Ron Reynolds of the San Francisco Police Department's sexual assault unit has also indicated that pimps make their girls look younger than their age to attract customers.[38] Women dressed as schoolgirls (tartan skirts, demure white blouses, clutching schoolbooks) are common in Internet and print advertisements for escort services.[39] Researcher Norton-Hawk's recent interview with the owner/manager of an escort service uncovered the fact that some customers ask women to wear a private girls' school uniform, including ankle socks, pleated skirt, and saddle shoes.[40]

Certainly these ads play to some men's fantasies about young girls. A nationwide hunt for users of child Internet pornography recently arrested 1,300 monthly subscribers, among them prominent politicians and professionals in the United Kingdom, with a total of 7,200 Britons reported to be under suspicion. Although viewing child pornography does not indicate that the individuals are actually buying sex from minors, it does demonstrate that men do indulge in sexual fantasies involving children; some of the files the men reviewed were named "Child Rape" and "I am Fourteen," and others contained sexually explicit photographs of children as young as five years of age. One child pornography expert said it was unlikely that people would view such Web sites out of curiosity: "There's only one reason they access it, which is that it allows them to generate sexual fantasy around children and use it for masturbation."[41]

Trafficking of girls and women from other countries into the United States, where they are then held in conditions of slavery to work in the prostitution industry, has attracted considerable media interest. The U.S. Department of Justice believes that 45,000 to 50,000 women and children are trafficked annually to the United States, mostly by small crime rings and loosely connected criminal networks. Once in the States, women's passports are confiscated, their movements restricted, and their escape prevented through violence and threats of violence. Traffickers may also make threats of physical abuse against family members back home. The women and girls may be moved around from city to city to avoid detection and to further isolate them.[42]

With a steady stream of reports of recruitment and trafficking of teen girls born in the United States, it also becomes clear that varying degrees of trafficking or "reeling-in" strategies are employed to recruit U.S. teen girls, closely mirroring the tactics used in international trafficking. Indeed, in retrospect, to believe that the male behavior seen in international trafficking and exploitation does not occur within U.S. borders is naive in the extreme. Now and then a news story surfaces illustrating that the exploitation of girls in the United States can be identical to that in developing countries.

In 2002 young girls in refugee camps in Sierra Leone, Guinea, and Liberia claimed that UN peacekeepers had required them to pose naked for pictures in exchange for much-needed food. The children said there were also many girls who traded sex for money or gifts. Most of the girls were between thirteen and eighteen, but others were between four and twelve. They identified at least sixty-seven individuals involved in this sexual coercion.[43]

A similar exploitation of powerless girls has been documented in an Alabama juvenile detention facility. Within moments of arriving, a sixteen-year-old girl, incarcerated for violating probation owing to truancy and running away from home, heard the other girls talk about performing oral sex on male lockup workers. At least three dozen girls corroborated her story about the male guards' inappropriate comments, suggestions, and demands for sexual relations. The girls uniformly reported that having sexual relations with staff members was an easy way for them to obtain preferential treatment and rewards such as Cokes.[44]

The sex trade industry employs many diverse strategies to hook teen girls. Advertisements are particularly important. Olivia's friend lured her to the stripclub, but at the same time she had also seen advertisements for exotic dancers and escort services. In giveaway publications available in downtown coffee shops, the ads guarantee $2,000–$4,000 a week, living quarters, and transportation expenses. They emphasize the ability to earn top dollars while making your own hours, with no experience necessary.[45]

Olivia says that the advertisements for the industry played a crucial role in her decision to strip dance.

> It is very attractive, how to make quick money, with little resources or background that would really qualify you to walk into a corporate job at the same price range. They are recruiting you. That is what they are there for, not only for customers, but to catch someone's eye, come in and try this.
>
> They want to show you on television, just the woman up there smiling, closing her eyes, and looking like she is in heaven. If you read some of the advertisements to get girls or women to come in and begin dancing, it is so attractive. It isn't glamorous when someone reaches up and pinches your nipple, or someone pours a drink on you, or someone gooses you. They don't talk about the incidents when the guys grab you and the bouncers have to intervene. They don't show you the club owners beating someone's butt, or forcing you to use the back room with one of their co-partners, or turning the police on for free, they don't show that piece of it. So the part everybody sees and the people they talk to are the people who are new to the field who are really into the bright lights and the beauty of it. They paint this picture: this is the glamorous life.

The advertisements play into young girls' dreams, Olivia says. "In the twenty-first century, not only do we live for sexual liberation, but

42   money is power, any means to get it. So after a while, when you start seeing the money roll in, you kind of learn to disregard everything else that comes with it."

According to Olivia, there has to be some kind of void to make these ads attractive.

> For the most part, where there are healthy families and support systems and there have been some morals and values instilled, these ads would be disgusting to teenage girls. But if there is something else going on, if they are trying to find a way to escape a situation, they would be effective.
>
> Morals and values in my household growing up weren't washed out, but it became very blurred. You are told, don't drink, don't smoke pot, but you see the pimping and all the other things going on right in your own household.

Olivia explains how the stripclub owners exploited her when she was a teen.

> I was told over and over again how much money I could make because I had a nice personality: "We can sell your pussy until the day you die if you could trust us to do that." You are hand-fed all the things that you want to hear from society, and you are hearing it from club owners and their friends. The owners know what road you are going down. They don't care. There is a sickness there. The club owners and customers are very similar. It is the same mentality. You have got to hate women on a real sick level to put their lives at risk in that way and to profit from it.

As one survivor has written: "The most important issue for the industry was that they welcomed us because of the fact that we had arrived not for who we were. We had even walked through the door on our own legs. And none had put a gun to our skulls—they hadn't needed to."[46]

Heavenly Bodies, a stripclub in Elk Grove Village, a northwestern Chicago suburb, regularly airs an advertisement for dancers and cocktail servers on 96.3, WBBM-FM (called B96), a radio station catering to

teens (featuring Madonna, Brittany Spears, and various rap artists) that
pulls in between 21 and 31 percent of the teen audience in the Chicago
market.[47] Heard on 15 April 2002, the ad emphasized girls' ability to
earn large amounts of cash for fun and independence, and provided a
toll-free number for further information. Reportedly, other ad copy
asks girls if they are tired of depending on a man for their income,[48] a
pitch that proves Olivia's point: the commercials play on girls' desire
for money and for independence from and power over men. Although
the advertisement proclaims "No nudity allowed," Heavenly Bodies
lists itself as a nude club at Stripclublist.com, an Internet directory of
stripclubs, and customers describe the lap dances there and the activities involving physical contact in its upstairs VIP room.[49]

Many girls' intimate partners also recruit them for prostitution.
Social service providers working with teens explain the role that males
play in initiating girls into prostitution and then living off their earnings. Prostitution survivor Claudine O'Leary knows all the tricks used
by "boyfriends" in what she calls a gradual process to ensnare girls for
the sex trade. If a fourteen-year-old is still at home but not in a safe
situation, she may be frequently hanging out at the mall. A twenty-
four-year-old male will approach her and over time become her closest
confidant, best friend, and ultimately her lover. It may, says Claudine,
only take him three to five days to convince the girl that her family
does not care about her. Then he will be sure to keep the girl up and
out all night, so that it will be difficult for her to return home. "Stay
with me," he says.

> The guy takes control of the relationship really quickly. He
> is going to take care of her, he buys her things, and then
> after a while he is going to say, "you owe me, you have to
> help me." Oh, if I had a dime for every time I have heard
> that story. They say, "they bought me an outfit, they buy
> me food," and then the guy says, "you owe me, what did
> you think, that was for free?"
>
> The girls don't want to lose the relationship. They've
> run away from home. They don't want to steal or shoplift
> or sell drugs, it's dangerous and violent. Selling sex appeals
> to the girls because no one is getting hurt. A lot of girls will
> say, "at least when I do this, the only person I am hurting

is myself, at least I'm making the money, it's not coming from someone else." It feels different and is more acceptable to them.[50]

What Claudine describes is the first stage of domestic violence, the "reeling in," as outlined by expert Ann Goetting:

> Typically, a woman is seduced into a battering relationship by the charming and charismatic side of a man's dual personality. That man is wonderful to her all the time at first. He comes on strong, showering her with charm and adoration. He knows what she wants and he gives it to her. It is coercion and control even then: he is reeling her in. But to the unsuspecting woman it feels like fresh, innocent, young love. The woman is thrilled and feels fortunate to have found this desirable man who is so caring. No one has ever loved her like this. She feels great and wants to preserve that feeling. Reeling-in is the initial stage of battering.[51]

Alexa Albert relates a version of the reeling in of women in her book about Mustang Ranch, a legal Nevada brothel. While working as a bank teller at the age of eighteen, Brittany met thirty-year-old Bobby. He wined and dined her, and soon Brittany was charging expenses on her charge card to help maintain their high standard of living. At the time that the credit card debt rose to $20,000, Bobby began to suggest that Brittany move to Nevada to a legal brothel. Brittany initially refused but eventually gave in when Bobby told her he would leave her if she did not. Brittany now understands that men like Bobby continue to woo other women, building up a stable from whom they profit. Staggered schedules at the brothel ensure that none of the women meet one another, although some men pit the women against each other in a kind of competition to be crowned as the main squeeze. After three years, Brittany escaped from Bobby's clutches, but had to leave all her possessions behind.[52]

Poet Maya Angelou describes a low-income version of this practice, relating how an older man named L.D. pulled the same scam on her when she was a young unmarried mother. Once he got Angelou gradually to fall in love with him, largely by playing hard to get, he

told her he had lost a large sum of money gambling. He would marry
her once he got clear of the debt, but he needed a woman who could
make some money for him quickly.

> "When Head Up had a little trouble with the Big Boys last
> month, his wife went to a house in Santa Barbara and made
> five hundred dollars the first week. In a month he was
> clear."
>
> "Doing what?"
>
> He still thought I was a square. "But I don't know if I
> could let anybody I love do that kind of business. I don't
> think my life is worth a nice woman, my woman, giving
> up that much of herself."
>
> "L.D., if a woman loves a man, there is nothing too
> precious for her to sacrifice and nothing too much for him
> to ask . . ."
>
> He pulled away and saw the tears sliding down my
> face. "What's that for? I didn't ask you to do anything."
>
> "No, I'm just crying out of joy. That you'll let me help
> you."

And so, directed by L.D., Angelou went to work in a small brothel.
Later, of course, she discovered that L.D. had many other young
women simultaneously involved in prostitution for him.

> Pity. That he thought outsmarting a young girl, living off
> the wages of women was honorable. He obviously had
> been doing it for years. He probably started in the South
> with white women, thinking that by taking their bodies
> and their money, he was getting revenge on the white men,
> who were free to insult him, ignore him and keep him at
> the bottom of the heap.[53]

Unlike Maya Angelou, the girls sometimes require more heavy-duty
coercion after the reeling in. In the fall of 2000, two men enticed a
fifteen-year-old girl from rural Alabama to go with them to Chicago
after they had promised they would let her cut a music demo. Once
there, they forced her by violence and threats into prostitution, and

she was only saved by the FBI when she was able to find a way to telephone her family.[54] Recently two Chicago men were arrested for kidnapping, sexually assaulting, and forcing girls as young as thirteen into selling jewelry and prostitution in Detroit. The arrests occurred after a seventeen-year-old alerted a security guard at a Detroit shopping center. She said she had been abducted in Cleveland and forced to perform sex acts.[55]

Sadly, research is verifying the fact that male sexual offenders possess a special ability to identify the needy and unloved, including children who have been victims before. Social service providers in the Chicago metropolitan area report that males congregate outside group homes and institutions housing girls who are wards of the child protective services, recognizing that these homes are sources of needy girls who can be recruited for prostitution.[56]

Barnardo's in the United Kingdom also notes that many of the young women being helped in its prostitution recovery programs are girls from group homes or foster care who have been targeted by pimps.[57] A pimp named Maris Malone in London was linked to twenty-two girls aged twelve to eighteen whom he recruited from those in the child welfare system. Inspector Paul Homes told BBC News: "He was extremely skilled at identifying disaffected, unhappy, vulnerable young teenage girls, most of whom were either already in the care system or on the brink of the care system."[58] U.S. experts confirm that many young pimps recruit girls out of the group homes in which they had been placed for their own safety because of sexual abuse in their homes.[59]

In 1997 Tom Leykis, the host of a nationally syndicated radio program, declared on air that women who have been sexually molested "put out" more, and he saw no reason for men not to try to determine and exploit this fact. "If you think that a woman's more likely to put out or more likely to be good in bed because she has a history of abuse, is it wrong to try to find that out and then to go for the gold?" he asked. Leykis then went on to explain his perfect calculation:

> It's a ratio. It's a mathematical formula and you express it
> in the form of a fraction and the way it works is this: On top
> of the fraction, you want a woman who has the high—the
> number on top you want to be as high as possible. You

want a woman who's the most attractive you can find. That's the top half of the equation. Bottom half of the equation? The lowest possible self-esteem. And that produces a ratio. The higher the ratio, the more you should go for it.[60]

Maggie O'Neill has interviewed Jane, who fell in love as a young woman with a man who subsequently groomed her for prostitution. Twenty years later, here are Jane's words:

> Deep inside I felt so much anger to that one person . . . he knew that I was younger . . . he knew that I was vulnerable. He was a lot older than me . . . mentally I felt that he manipulated me so the anger is to me as well for letting someone do that to me . . . When my daughter is sixteen I don't want no man to come and manipulate her . . . My anger is not because of me but at him and men like him . . . A man like that could be around when my daughter is older . . . as the years have gone on I have got stronger and stronger . . . you can't tell people it's wrong to be a prostitute . . . the authorities have failed for years . . . you can't tell people what to do with their lives, you just can't.[61]

Another expert explains how the poor are vulnerable to blandishments from males recruiting them for prostitution:

> Low self-esteem ensures that sex trade workers are easy "prey" for those who tell them what they most need to hear: that they are loved, that they are appreciated, they are understood and that they will be taken care of. No child or youth who has lived with a crippling lack of self-esteem could refuse such an apparent sanctuary.[62]

Based on her work with teens in the sex trade, Claudine O'Leary describes how prostitution seriously affects healthy adolescent development: the girls suffer from a lack of sleep, failure to eat, inability to concentrate, increased drug usage, poor school attendance or dropping out, emotional stress, and most important, increased isolation and disconnection from other outside influences that can bring in alternate ideas.[63] Commercial sexual exploitation depends on keeping the teen isolated from family and community once he or she is involved. Prostitution expert Jannit Rabinovitch explains that for adolescents this lifestyle often provides a sense of community and belonging. Owing to the isolation, however, the girls do not have access to the range of experiences that other members of the community experience, which only makes them more dependent and vulnerable than they were at the start.[64]

Recent research confirms these recruitment tactics. The boyfriend as pimp is a common theme. Over half the women in a U.S. survey considered their pimp to be their boyfriend at the time of recruitment,[65] while in the Canadian National Juvenile Prostitution Survey, 17 percent of the females indicated they had turned to prostitution to please another person who was likely a pimp.[66] Researchers in Victoria, B.C., found that women were more likely than the men in their sample to have entered prostitution through the coercive manipulation of boyfriends or family members, "suggesting that the line between boyfriend and pimp is more permeable than it is usually considered to be."[67] Chicago researchers found that 20 percent of their respondents had entered regular prostitution through the urgings of a boyfriend.[68]

Coercion also figures in prostitution entrance, although the numbers are lower. In a sample of western Canadian women, all of whom began in prostitution as teens, 19 percent reported being coerced into the sex trade by intimate partners, and in a fairly large sample of individuals in prostitution in Victoria, B.C., 12.5 percent said their involvement in prostitution had been forced.[69] Six percent in a sample in Washington, D.C., reported that they had been brought in against their will.[70]

Friends already involved in prostitution play an important role in the juvenile's entrance into prostitution, according to research studies. When Silbert and Pines asked respondents who was responsible for their being involved in prostitution, they found that in 55 percent of the cases the recruiter was already active in prostitution. Twenty-five percent were pimps, 20 percent were women recruiting for a pimp or a madam, 7 percent were women in prostitution, and 3 percent were customers.[71] Sterk found that group influences were more common among adolescents, although boyfriends also played a part.[72] In the Chicago sample, 45 percent said a friend had suggested prostitution,[73] and 30 percent in Los Angeles reported they had tried prostitution because of a family member or a friend.[74] These friends may well be in the employ of a pimp; in Chicago, one girl's former pimp approached her, offering her $5,000 if she recruited a teen girl for him.[75]

Public attention to cases in which juveniles are coerced into prostitution raises questions about whether media hysteria has led to an exaggeration of the problem. The difficulties of researching a clandestine industry make it hard to gauge the extent of youth prostitution in the United States. Recently, Estes and Weiner estimated a total of 208,278 youth under the age of eighteen not living in their own homes who are engaging in prostitution or being sexually exploited by others in the United States.[76]

But prostitution is not just an issue for runaways. Researchers recently surveyed all the 10,828 adolescents (ages fourteen to seventeen) in the public and private school systems in Oslo, Norway, finding that 1.4 percent had sold sex; among girls it was .6 percent and among boys 2.1 percent. Fourteen was the mean age for the first experience of sex sale for both girls and boys. Nor were these one-time occasions; the median number of occurrences was fourteen, and 52 percent had been involved in more than ten instances of prostitution.[77] The Norwegian teens involved in prostitution in this large sample reported higher levels of drug and alcohol use then the rest of the youth, were exposed to alcohol in the home at twice the levels of the rest of the sample, and had experienced parental breakup at higher levels. For the girls, prostitution activity was also correlated with being a victim of a serious kind of violence.[78] As these youth were all attending school at the time of the survey, the researchers believed it unlikely that this group was a permanent fixture of the organized sex industry,[79] but there was no way to know for sure what the trajectories of these young people would be.

Compounding such problems is the fact that experts believe that most of the teens active in prostitution are not visible on the street, because they are selling sex in indoor venues such as hotels, massage parlors, bars, and apartments serving as brothels. For example, in the trial of a Chicago woman named Dawn Hansel, dubbed by the media as the "Palos Park madam," a young woman testified that when she was fifteen years of age she had performed about a dozen sex acts for up to $100 a customer at a backroom bachelor party arranged by Ms.

Hansel in a local restaurant. By working for Hansel, the teen, who was said to be from a troubled home and had alcohol and drug problems, made what she called easy money: "I had never made that much money before."[80] According to law enforcement officials in the United Kingdom, two-thirds of child prostitution occurs behind closed doors, in flats and bedsits belonging to "boyfriends."[81]

We do need to know more. As Judith Levine points out in her book, *Harmful to Minors: The Perils of Protecting Children from Sex*, sexual activities during adolescence are not necessarily harmful per se.[82] But in instances in which sex and intimacy are deliberately used to coerce prostitution, and when these tactics are employed with the poor and emotionally needy, it not the sex per se, but its combination with power, control, and violence that lies at the heart of the problem for teens.

The conclusion now seems clear. Prostitution entry results from an interconnected set of factors fueled by both supply and demand. Researcher Claire Sterk's summary is a good one: "Regardless of the specific pathway the women took to prostitution, their initial experiences could not have occurred in the absence of an environment that was 'supportive' of their prostitution activities, as well as male partners who were willing to pay for sex."[83]

Social reformer Jane Addams is considered to have created a false moral panic based on gross exaggerations of the number of girls enticed and coerced into the sex industry in Chicago at the beginning of the twentieth century. Both past and present reviewers of her book, *A New Conscience and an Ancient Evil*, have found Addams's tone hysterical. In her new introduction to the work, one feminist academic asserts that the exaggerations served to limit the freedom of girls in cities to pursue professional, educational, and sexual opportunities.[84]

With its emphasis on the value of chastity, its prescription of marriage and motherhood for poor girls, and its depiction of teens as victimized urban primitives, Addams's book is certainly dated. Once past the moralizing and the objectionable stereotyping of girls in roles that serve patriarchy, however, one finds Addams describing with pinpoint accuracy the reeling in of emotionally needy girls to serve the sexual needs of men in the big city.

Addams saw adventurous girls, like Olivia, whose imaginations were starved, and who "constantly search for the magical and impossible," leading them into dangers.[85] She saw the hundreds of men "whose business it is to discover girls thus hard pressed by loneliness and despair."[86] The men assumed one of two roles, either a sympathetic older man or an eager young lover.[87] She saw a girl turning to alcohol so "that she might be able to live through each day."[88]

Addams also understood that the public allowed the sex trade to continue because it assumed that the girls had decided on this life course.[89] The uninterrupted existence of prostitution throughout history reinforces public indifference:

> However ancient a wrong may be, in each generation it must become newly embodied in living people and the social custom into which it has hardened through the years, must be continued in individual lives. Unless the contemporaries of such unhappy individuals are touched to tenderness or stirred to indignation by the actual embodiments of the old wrong in their own generation, effective action cannot be secured.[90]

Rather than viewing Jane Addams's book on prostitution as an interesting museum piece, we should recognize that it provides critical historical evidence that the enticement of poor and needy girls has not dramatically changed over a century in Chicago. Addams cautions us not to let the historical persistence of prostitution paralyze us into inaction. Were she still alive, Addams would surely say that now, more than ever, we owe it to these girls to determine just how many are present in each of our communities and to make a commitment to help them.

CHAPTER THREE

Stripping

The man who is really virile, who is a person of power,
never fears any accession to power on the part of a woman.
But all those who are not indulge in anti-feminism.

— REBECCA WEST, "The Lamp of Hatred"

To work at the stripclub, Olivia had to lie about her age. Initially, the
sixteen-year-old girl believed she was hired to dance at the facility.

> I really thought of it as a dancing job. Within thirty days I
> found out the real dynamics of these clubs. I thought I was there
> to dance. I remember my first routines. The older dancers must
> have thought, she is some joke, she will learn real quick. I did
> all these modern dance routines, and I really thought I was hired
> because I was a good dancer. You find out it has nothing to do
> with the dancing, or whether or not you can dance. It's your
> willingness to take your clothes off, to be seductive. The alcohol
> helped me to enjoy that part of it because I saw the rewards.
> The alcohol helped me to get through it, the money reinforced
> the benefit of it. I said, this is the easiest money in the world.

For the first year Olivia didn't turn any tricks and was not aware there
was prostitution going on in the club, but the wooing process had
begun. She danced, she flirted, and she got customers to buy drinks.
Selling the drinks was where the real money in the clubs was. The

more drinks the girls and women got the men to buy, the more money
the strippers made. The job was mostly eight hours of hustling drinks.
And Olivia had to endure considerable verbal abuse.

> The verbal abuse from the customers was continuous. "I'd love
> to have my tongue inside you, I'd love for you to sit on my
> dick." It didn't take long for me to be gritting my teeth and
> pasting that phony smile on my face. There was a shift in my
> attitude. These guys are here, and I'm just a piece of meat up
> there.

In the course of an evening Olivia also had to worry about the physical
contact with the men, the buttocks smacking and the fondling.

> They reach up and put money in your G-string, and they ram
> their fingers into you. A lot of groping. Within thirty days the
> awful reality sets in. There are 50,000 hands touching me, you
> begin to feel dirty, the guys are smelly, they are usually drunk.
> Some of them sit and drink so much until they are physically
> sick. Even talking about it now, I can still smell them. That is
> the most disgusting part. They were animals.

So why did she stay at the club? It was a combination of the money
and the glamour. The teen-aged Olivia and a girlfriend shared an apartment.

> Life was just one big party. You go places. My girlfriend and I
> went to the Bahamas, we went to Jamaica. We ate out, I bought
> clothes, always lots of clothes. Costumes at $1,500 each. You
> want the most glamorous. I helped my parents out a bit here
> and there. The money really flirts with you. It is very seductive
> at sixteen, especially. This is such an easy way. Can I deal with
> this?

For Olivia, alcohol became the way.

> It is a myth that any woman can get up there and do that and
> not have something in her. It doesn't have to be hard-core drugs,

> but you have to take something to help you deal with it. Alcohol
> is probably the easiest because it is so accessible in the clubs.
> Before I got to work, I would drink anywhere from a pint to a
> fifth. I found out that a couple of drinks would take off the
> nervousness right away. I then had the courage to get up there
> and take my clothes off. I was able to disassociate totally,
> totally. I did not have to be presently there, but I could do
> my job.

Olivia says that her parents never had any comment about her stripclub involvement. She only heard from them when they wanted some money from her. Alta, Olivia's older sister, remembers the time well: "She was out of the house, she was really having a good time. A great time. Not having any responsibility. She was beautiful, just beautiful. She was on her own doing things with friends and it really was like life was one big party for her."[1]

On one level, the job remained attractive. Olivia admits now that she enjoyed all the attention from the men. She spent a lot of money on costumes. Her self-esteem rose. Stripping met her needs at the time for "validation, as sick as the validation may be." Trading on her extro-verted personality and strong verbal and communication skills, the whole set-up gave Olivia a sense of power, although now she sees it as a false sense of power.

> For the first time in my life I felt that I was in control of my
> life. I had money, I could shop when I got ready, stay any place
> I wanted to, get an apartment here or there. You think, it is a
> sense of independence, but as it continues, it becomes a total
> dependent way of life.
>
> When I found out what was involved, I weighed the worst
> of two evils. I can continue to do this and support myself,
> regardless of what I have to go through, or I can try to do
> something different, but not make as much money.

Olivia recognizes now that stripping met some underlying deficiency.

> It met some need that I was not even aware of at the time. I
> had no idea that I had other needs that were being met or even

needing to be met. I was really caught up in it. I had control of
these guys, I could make them eat out of my hand. And the
beauty of it, the wearing of the pretty costumes. The changing
of my name, I could be anybody I wanted to be. I did it for so
long that I began to really forget who I was. I didn't use my
real name for years. Every place I was I changed my name. It
is a great way of escaping you in life.

So Olivia made the fateful decision to stay in the business. And her
alcohol consumption increased. She began to drink throughout the
entire night. Sometimes she drank so much that she had blackouts and
had to be awakened in the dressing room after she had missed her
dance set. Or she would be found with her head in the toilet, violently
vomiting. The majority of the girls and women in the club drank to
excess like Olivia: "It is impossible to do these kinds of acts and be
treated in that manner in the right state of mind."

And slowly but surely, Olivia began to be enticed into doing more
at the club. "They lure you in phases. I was very uncomfortable with
it, but I was zapped into the glamour of the whole lifestyle."

The club featured lap dancing, which involves "grinding" in the
lap of a clothed man, and table dancing, with a naked dancer standing
atop a four-foot high table and gyrating while the men encourage her
to "bend over" and "shake your tits." Olivia was sometimes asked to
dance in a private room while a guy masturbated. No physical penetration occurred, and Olivia made $1,000, a lot of money for fifteen
minutes.

Slowly you are lured into doing more. Each step, there was more
involved, and more money involved, and more drinking, drinking
was almost around the clock by this time. It was pretty disgust-
ing, but alcohol cured it for me. When I'd feel a moment of
disgust, I'd drink a little more and I would get less inhibited, it
didn't seem as bad. If I woke up and thought, oh my god, I did
this in front of people, I gave a blow job in front of six other
guys, for a minute I would feel really bad about it, but again,
I rationalized it a lot. I made it make sense. You make sense of
the world around you, and that is what I did. You say, at least
I got the damn fool's money.

The club owners and customers exploited the teenaged Olivia, who yearned for approval and validation and worked so hard to please. Sensing her vulnerability, the owners and customers worked it to their advantage.

> When the guys said they really liked me and would ask for me,
> I was their regular girl, I felt they did really like me. I realize
> now that the guys had been coming there for years, and they
> knew how naive I was. I really believe that they totally took
> advantage of how naive I was.

At the same time, the club also became a social support network.

> When you want to belong, you fit into what is going on around
> you, and when I looked around, this became a little family.
> After the club closed, you went out and partied with the club
> owners. You wind up getting smashed, and you are up on the
> tables dancing for the club owner and his friends. The owner
> really wants to keep you if you are a moneymaker, so he invites
> you out on his boat. At my age and with my background, this
> is great. You wound up with the club owners until eight or nine
> o'clock in the morning, and you went home and slept. You kind
> of disassociate yourself from anything outside of that lifestyle,
> because your hours are abnormal. Most people that I would have
> known before are not the ones that are going to get up at two or
> three in the afternoon, and that is when your day starts.

The club managers, explains Olivia, were manipulative. For the most part, they got the girls to do what they wanted by being nice, but when that didn't work, as in domestic violence, they switched to intimidation and threats. Olivia saw girls being slapped if they didn't do what the manager required. The manager would withhold the money Olivia had earned until she took care of a customer he assigned to her.

> You have to be really sharp to catch their game. Initially they
> very much come on to you that this is all in your best interest.
> But they weren't the fatherly figures looking out for their girls.
> They're protecting their own interests.

In all the years, I met only a couple of good guys. One
manager used to tell me, "Olivia, you should be putting money
away." He was also the only one who mentioned the amount of
alcohol that I drank: "Olivia, don't you think you are hitting
the stuff a little heavy every night of the week?" No one else
would say that, and he was one of a million and not the norm.

Over time the party began to wind down.

Eventually you feel the self-loathing and the shame. Jacking
these guys off, I'm letting them spill on me, I'm sitting on their
laps, they are breathing on me, you can feel their whiskers
touching you when they put their face close to you. It was
totally against me morally; somewhere deep inside, I felt it was
wrong. I knew it was. I began to see myself: oh my god, you
will do anything, you will let guys do anything. The drinking,
the drugs help you find a way to feel better about what has
happened to you and what you are doing to yourself. There are
glimpses of yourself that frighten you, that tell you this isn't
right, you shouldn't be living like this, and you feel sad for a
minute. But if you drink enough, or get enough in you, you can
push it far, far away.

Ultimately, the sex became humiliating for Olivia.

I definitely felt degraded most of the time. I showered, I washed
over and over because I felt unclean. You feel so degraded doing
some of these acts or even accepting being talked to in that
manner. You know it is wrong, but there is nothing else you can
do about it.

∽

Throughout history, girls have experienced the same initial feelings of
power as did Olivia when trading sex for money. As revealed by a
recent biographer, French novelist Marguerite Duras was, like Olivia,
involved in prostitution as a teen because of family influences. Her
father was dead, and Duras's mother barely eked out an existence in
Indochina after the entire family fortune disappeared into a failed salt

mine. Duras told her biographer that her family had maintained absolute control over her. Her mother encouraged Marguerite to drink until addiction resulted, and both her mother and brother regularly and brutally beat her, telling her she was a good-for-nothing failure, so ugly that she put men off and would have to accept being an old maid. In her diary Duras wrote:

> The difference between my mother's and my brother's beatings was that the latter's were much more painful and difficult to take. Every time he beat me, I'd reach the point where I'd think my brother was going to kill me, and when anger would give way to fear, fear that my head was about to be separated from my body and roll across the floor in fear that I'd end up going crazy.[2]

Since it soon became clear that Marguerite had no real choice, she gave in to her mother's wish that she earn needed money for the family through a love affair with an affluent twenty-five-year-old Chinese man named Leo:

> Marguerite was for sale. The brothers had no intention of working for a living and as far as the mother was concerned, it was normal for a daughter to leave home in return for a large cash payment . . . Marguerite was trapped. She felt it was up to her to save the family from destitution. It was something she could do.[3]

Egged on by her mother and brother, Duras eventually agreed to a love affair in exchange for a great deal of money from the older man. After a thorough investigation, her biographer has concluded that this story was true. What could it have been like for the young girl? Her biographer gives us this passage from Duras's diary in which the girl describes the first kiss like a rape:

> He caught me off guard. I cannot describe how repulsive it was. I hit out at Leo, spat, wanted to get out of the car. Leo didn't know what to do . . . I kept saying, it's over, it's over. I was the very personification of revulsion . . . I had

> to keep spitting, spat all night, and again the next day
> whenever I thought about it.[4]

The affair slowly continued. Marguerite inured herself to Leo's caresses because of the power the situation gave her over her own family members. At school Marguerite boasted to her friends of leading a double life. Nor did she ever think to seek help at school, because once the teacher in charge had locked her in his office and tried to kiss her.[5]

Many years later, Marguerite turned this real-life episode into literature with the publication of The Lover in 1984. But in the novella Duras adjusted the story by eliminating the mother's role in the affair. In this way, explains her biographer, Marguerite obliterated the shame of the mother selling her own child and erased her own victimhood.[6] In the fictional account, Marguerite is the independent protagonist and not her mother's stooge. Writes her biographer: "The Lover was her revenge. She eventually turned an abject story into an erotic tale and happily pocketed the money. Honour had been satisfied."[7]

In transforming the story Duras described in an unforgettable way how young girls can exert power through their own sexuality, surely a depiction of her feelings during her own very real affair and those familiar to girls in prostitution today:

> From the first movement she knows more or less, knows
> he's at her mercy. And therefore that others beside him
> may be at her mercy too if the occasion arises. She knows
> something else too, that the time has now probably come
> when she can no longer escape duties toward herself. And
> that her mother will know nothing of this, nor her
> brothers.[8]

Yet at the same time, Duras's heroine feels desire toward this man. This potent combination of power-seeking and desire is one that her lover recognizes. He says the girl will deceive him and all the men she will ever be with.[9]

Critic Vivian Gornick agrees that The Lover illustrates how girls use male lust to achieve missing power: "Desire, she can see, is her ace in the hole; the place where she understands deeply the instrumental nature of human relations. This understanding will become her strength, her armor, her revenge, her ticket out."[10]

And another critic makes a connection with the girl's childhood: "she begins to recover from the damage of a brutalizing childhood. The man is exquisite, his reverence extreme. For Duras, it is he who is broken by love and she who is healed."[11]

❧

In January 2000 David Sherman, a former manager of various strip-clubs, presented testimony to the Michigan House Committee on Ethics and Constitutional Law, providing a unique insider's view of the stripclub business. Sherman's account fully revealed how stripclub owners and managers shamefully manipulate needy girls.

Confirming Olivia's experiences, he stated that girls have to be lured first into dancing, and then into prostitution at the clubs. The money, Sherman said, is not as important as the attention and praise. "It becomes as important to them to hear how beautiful they are 200 times a day as it is to actually make the money from the dancing."[12]

> Because of the use of drugs to medicate what they do and hearing how beautiful they are all the time, they soon experience what I call "BDA," Basic Dancer Attitude. This is when the dancer thinks that no matter what friends, children, husband and families think about her, it doesn't matter. They can all be replaced because all of the patrons around her find her attractive, beautiful and idolized. Now, the dancers are truly caught in the "adult scene." With friends and family gone from their lives, they exist alone in this dark subculture of sex, drugs, alcohol and prostitution. All of this perverse living, to the dancer, is now just part of her normal lifestyle.[13]

As the dancers age, explained Sherman, they can no longer keep up with the younger girls, and most of them have to survive in other more violent and degrading prostitution activities.

> They become society's throwaway people. People used up—degraded, abused, and even sold by the people who

own these establishments . . . Sadly, these young ladies over time, little by little, become manipulated, controlled and finally destroyed by a world that our communities have closed their eyes to.[14]

Sherman provided an outline or blueprint for the manager's enticement of the young girls. First, he said, the manager must require the staff and management to treat the recruits, initially hired as waitresses, "as if they were long-lost friends." After a few weeks, the manager asks the girls for a favor: They are short that night, could they help out by stripping? According to Sherman, the girls, now used to the environment of nudity in the club, are usually "intoxicated" with being onstage. The manager, he explained, may have to take a girl out to dinner and get her under the influence of alcohol before she will agree to disrobe. Afterward, the experienced dancers will welcome her, telling her how beautiful she is and how much money she will make.[15]

Sherman also explained how managers instruct the girls to develop regular customers; since these are men who believe the girls actually care for them, they will come back on a regular basis, guaranteeing the club a regular clientele. One of the manager's roles is to train the girls to "prey" on these men in this way.

> Soon the dancer starts running around with the more hardened and seasoned girls, and they realize how much easier this job is being drunk, high, or more often than not, both. By now she's working until 2 a.m. in the morning, staying out all night partying after work, and then grabbing breakfast with the girls. They wake up, go to work, and the cycle starts all over.
>
> They are deep into the club scene and on the road to hard times and self-destruction. At this point, school, family, and friends as well as everything else they once had faded into a world that no longer exists for them.
>
> As a manager, at this point anything you say, ask or demand of the girls will gladly be done because the club is now their home . . . the club manager has total control over what's going on in their lives. The girls will even put up with degradation, verbal and emotional abuse and everything else the manager wants to do.[16]

Sherman's frank description of the enticement and subjugation of teen girls goes a long way toward answering the question of why girls like Olivia don't just leave the stripping business. The large amounts of money for a teen, the clubs' deliberately close and claustrophobic atmosphere, and the adverse effects of alcohol and drugs all serve to bind the girl to her milieu. One survivor of prostitution aptly described the syndrome as a "closed circuit:" "because it is not a job you can go out and admit to the world . . . you have the friends you work with . . . and they become the friends you go out with . . . so in the end you stay within the circuit."[17]

❧

Usually stripclubs operate legally, with various forms of illegal prostitution activity on offer to the customers in back rooms. Other sex trade activities are incorporated in health clubs, saunas, beauty salons, massage parlors, and restaurants and bars, which may also have back rooms for prostitution use. Even more clandestine are the escort services and brothels operating out of private residences. Only 10 to 20 percent of prostitution activities are thought to involve street prostitution.[18]

Women of color appear overrepresented in street prostitution and less active in indoor venues, in which the demand for White or biracial women prevails and forces a higher price tag.[19] Gloria Lockett, one of the few women of color to speak out about her experiences, confirms the racist nature of the male demand: "For the most part, white prostitutes work inside."[20]

Significantly, a great deal of local variation exists within stripclubs. A recent survey of the sex trade industry in the Chicago metropolitan area located twenty-five clubs with exotic dancers or stripping, and another twenty-seven clubs that featured dancers occasionally for special events.[21] In contrast, Raymond and Hughes found that New Jersey has more stripclubs (known as go-go or juice bars) than any state in the nation, with over 300 in the urban areas. Some are locally owned, and others are said to be under the control of Russian businessmen, many of whom may be members of Russian organized crime networks.[22] In fact, law enforcement agents report that organized crime groups control, finance, or back 76 to 100 percent of the sex enterprises in the Northeast, metropolitan New York, the Southeast, and metropolitan San Francisco.[23] The publisher of the "Exotic Dancer Bulletin" estimates that there are now 250,000 exotic dancers in the United States and that the number of clubs has increased by more than 30 percent since the late 1980s to a total of approximately 2,500.[24]

Despite significant evidence to the contrary, the stripclub industry encourages the public to believe that stripping involves very little violence, abuse, or actual prostitution. In this campaign the owners and managers have received assistance from stripping proponents like anthropologist Judith Lynne Hanna, on the faculty at the University of Maryland, who has testified as an expert witness and filed briefs on behalf of exotic dance clubs around the nation. Hanna's position is that exotic dancing is movement that communicates the beauty of the body and the notion of the desirability of the female in an art form that is only pretend, acting, and play.[25]

Although stripping, according to researcher Melissa Farley, has greatly changed over the years, the public has not caught on to the transformation of the business. Historically, there once were gentlemen's clubs where only dancing occurred, but she asserts that "physical contact has now escalated. Now you can buy a table or a lap dance. This is socially normalized prostitution."[26] Olivia's involvement in exotic dancing occurred more than ten years ago, but routine physical contact between customers and exotic dancers has only increased since then in most U.S. stripclubs.[27]

Kelly Holsopple, a survivor of thirteen years of stripping, has described what is now expected in stripclubs:

> Stripping usually involves prostitution, and always involves sexual harassment and abuse. Women are expected to climb on small tables or couches and display their genitals, often within inches of a customer's face. At more and more clubs, women are expected to straddle a man's penis during a lap dance until he cums in his pants. Women are continuously called cunt, whore, pussy, slut, and bitch by customers and management alike. . . . Customers spit on women, spray beer, flick cigarettes, and shoot water guns at them. Performers are pelted with ice, coins, and trash. Some women have been hit with cans and bottles thrown from the audience. Customers pull women's hair, yank them by their arm

or ankle, and grab their breasts, buttocks, and genitals. Women are commonly pinched, bitten, slapped, punched, and kicked. Men often expose their penises and try to stick their fingers, money, or bottles into women's vaginas.[28]

Two recently published books by ex-strippers, although seriously compromised by false publisher advertising,[29] corroborate Olivia's observations and confirm the blurring of the lines between exotic dancing and prostitution. Lily Burana (not her real name) was involved in stripping on and off for about six years, beginning at the age of sixteen when a friend repeatedly urged her to join her in a New York City peep show. Five years after she had left to begin a career in journalism, she decided to return to stripping in several U.S. locations and described her experiences in a 2001 book.[30] Surprisingly, she failed to write anything at all about alcohol, drugs, or prostitution in stripping, an omission that seriously compromises the book as a complete portrayal of girls and women in the stripping industry.

Burana has subsequently dealt with these issues in discussions about her book. In responding to a question about drugs in an interview posted at a book review Web site, she replied that "Drugs, well, yeah, drugs are also a constant in stripping":

> Since a large part of making money is sitting with the customers and sharing a drink with them, it's reasonable to expect to have upwards of five or six drinks bought for you a night. I didn't drink when I worked, or get high, simply because it was too scary to be f*cked up in that environment, and I never felt it would help me relax or be more efficient. But I did know women who simply needed the drugs and alcohol to keep working, to stay awake, to keep making money.[31]

As for trading sex for money, in the same interview Burana admitted its constant presence in many clubs: "Some clubs are notorious for allowing prostitution on the premises, which puts everyone at risk for arrest." Burana explained that she could count on one hand the days/nights she worked when a customer did not proposition her, even when the club did not condone prostitution.[32]

On her 1999 journey, Burana did not want to become involved in any activities in which men would have the opportunity to touch her. Finding clubs throughout the country that did not allow customer contact proved extremely difficult.

> Stripping didn't used to be so touchy-feely, but in the past ten years, it's become a full-contact sport . . . if increasing contact is the trend, I worry what the next generation of strippers will have to do to keep up. It's hard enough rearranging your psyche so you can comfortably work half-naked in front of strangers, but touch is something quite apart. Touch changes everything.[33]

Aiming for clubs that did not get more extreme than table dancing, Burana found that this guideline eliminated a large percentage. As a result, her tour of clubs across America describes conditions in only a small segment of the stripping industry, a fact not acknowledged by the book's publisher in its marketing. Now and then Burana stumbled upon and observed today's more typical club scene that involved lap dancing:

> I'm having trouble here. I fix my gaze on Stormy, trying to imagine myself doing what she's doing and I can't. I envision myself on all fours on the stage, sliding my knees around either side of a man's head and feeling his whiskers tickling my inner thighs. I shudder at the thought. . . . What is it like to go home after spending the night bouncing your crotch over the faces of people you don't know? How long does it take to settle back into your body, because you'd have to go pretty far away in order to be that exposed for that long, wouldn't you?[34]

Even within this tamer part of the stripping industry, Burana describes both what she calls the liberating and the degrading aspects of stripping. She admits that as a teenager, and even now, there was for her something thrilling about stripping because it broke a very serious taboo, which was scary, "but in a small, sleazy way, it's exciting too." When she first started, Burana said, she felt more in control of her life than she had in months.[35] During the course of her later journey, Burana continued to experience the stripper's high:

> I don't know if it's skill, comfort, risk, disassociation, or a combination of them all that, in rare moments, makes stripping seem like a borderline ecstatic state. But I know I'm having one of those moments now. When it just feels right. Righteous. At times like this, I can believe that I have all the hearts in the room gathered into the palm of my hand. I will never get old. I will never know harm. As long as I stay on this stage under the benevolent auspices of darkness, everything will be okay. . . . That rush. That blue bolt high. It's like I'm suspended in a narcotic bubble, yet I'm more fiercely aware and alive than I've ever felt.[36]

Celebrating what she calls a "communal group high" that gets created in a club on a really good night, Burana proclaims, "It's . . . like cruising this exciting rock'n'roll vibe."[37]

Later on, however, Burana is forced to conclude that "stripping still won't parse as benign."[38] She outlines the downsides of stripping, although interspersed with the more liberating aspects in a way that undoubtedly mirrors the power/abuse confusion the strippers experience. The constant disassociation and what Burana calls "stripper fatigue" take their toll:

> That permanently shell-shocked look. That inability to dedramatize and get life on track. Another surgery every few months, a different hair color. Crazy boyfriends or girlfriends yelling or whining or hurting or cutting down and spending all the money. A life small as a mouse/insect/penny and self-hatred wide and deep as the sea.[39]

At the end of her book, as Burana is permanently leaving stripping, she gives away her costumes to a teen stripper whom she calls Autumn. Burana looks at the girl and wants to tell her: "You've got a hard road ahead of you." She realizes that Autumn is in "the invincible period" where "she is over her nerves and the money is so good that everything seems like a lark."

There is nothing to be said to a girl in that place.
I know.[40]

Like Lily Burana, Elisabeth Eaves is a stripper turned journalist, and like Burana, she is White, blond, good-looking, and from a middle-class household. Her 2002 book describes the one year she spent in the Lusty Lady, a Seattle peep show, in which the women stripped and simulated sexual acts while the men, separated from the dancers by a pane of glass, watched and masturbated. Later, Eaves performed for three nights at a lap dancing club, but, unable to maintain the activity without recourse to drugs or drink, she quit.

As honestly as she can, Eaves explores the attraction the stripclub held for her, and her story proves similar to Olivia's. From young adulthood on, she strove for independence from men: "The power was exhilarating . . . Admiration from many meant no single one could make a claim on me."[41]

Because she needed to be independent, Eaves had ended every relationship with a member of the opposite sex when it became too established.

> I was taking back what should have been my own, freedom
> from a sense of menace. I was even feeling vengeful, glori-
> fying in the fact that they were down there, trapped in their
> little boxes, and I was above them in every way. They were
> a substitute for every man who had caused me fear.[42]

Eaves also gloried in being the center of attention, and she was also "thrilled with the deviant status, the double life" that stripping gave her.[43] To become independent by using the power she had over boys and men filled a real need for her at the time.

> Looking back, it seemed as if the Lusty Lady's mirrored
> boxes had contained me like a chemical reaction in a test
> tube. There had been no place else to put the volatile mix
> I had inside: desire and vanity, seductiveness and anger,
> exhibitionism and self-consciousness. Stripping, in retro-
> spect, looked like a much-needed outlet.[44]

·

Ultimately, Eaves succumbed to the enticement to work in the club's booth, in which the customer can talk with the dancer through the glass and request and pay for special moves. Since booth dancers could earn as much as $90 an hour, the money was hard to resist. In the booth, customers asked Eaves to perform certain acts, such as using dildos or other sex toys or urinating. To remain in control and turn such requests down, something that many of the women in the club were unable to do, was vital. Nothing in the set-up kept the men from crossing over the line, further blurring the demarcation between stripping and prostitution in the booth; there would be more money for meeting the requests from the men for outside "dating."

> Because of this, my boundaries became more ironclad than ever. They had to be, or I would have been pushed until I had lost any sense of where the men stopped and I began. The customers would always test how far they could go because they, too, were off the map. I wasn't in the category "girlfriend" or "wife," characters they thought they knew. I was "stripper," a creature who did sexual things for money, and if I didn't tell them what the limits were, nobody would.[45]

What the men desired out of the transactions at the Lusty Lady was fairly obvious. First and foremost, they wanted to masturbate in the presence of naked women. But that was not enough; Eaves says that the customers also required the women to be turned on to them, to have orgasms. Did they want to please the women, or was it a sort of conquest? asks Eaves. "At work my impression that men, like women, were aroused by causing arousal was confirmed. Our job wasn't just to be naked, it was to look and behave as though the customers really turned us on. For a convincing performance, men were willing to pay."[46]

The men were also interested in peering into the women's intimate parts.

> These men wanted, simply, to see more. More body, more tongue, more tit, and especially more pussy, as deeply as they could behold. Sometimes I laughed out loud at this.

> More was never enough. You could have your labia nearly
> planted against the window and they still made "spread it"
> motions with their hands, bending and peering to get a
> better angle. There was one stage regular who always came
> equipped with a flashlight. What did he think he would
> find?[47]

Specific fantasies interested some men, who asked the women to play-act being schoolgirls who were shocked by the men's nakedness and then turned on by their own desires. Sometimes the fantasies involved coercion of schoolgirls, with the customer playing a teacher with the power to force sexual compliance. Eaves says the dancers wondered about what they were doing.

> Sometimes I thought we did a service to society in there,
> keeping potentially dangerous appetites locked up in a safe
> environment. But then maybe we just encouraged them. Or
> as Kim, an expert booth performer, had once told me, "I
> am hopeful that it's a safe redirecting. I am not one hundred
> percent confident."[48]

And, finally, large numbers of the men masturbated while they fantasized about humiliating the women. "It was true that hundreds, perhaps thousands of Lusty Lady customers enjoyed getting off while imagining coming on someone's face."[49]

Several years later Eaves did a short lap-dancing stint at Rick's, a Seattle establishment like most of the stripclubs in that city, where lap dancing had replaced the now passé table dancing. Only one stripclub in the Seattle area at that time forbade lap dancing. Drugs dominated the dressing room at Rick's; one dancer sold pills and pot, and girls smoked from a pipe that looked exactly like a lipstick tube.[50] Eaves soon found that she could not continue at Rick's:

> I couldn't lap dance. It was a physical action too intimate
> to do with anyone but a lover. I was violating my own ethic
> about sex, namely, that I should only ever do it because I
> had the desire. . . . If I continued to lap dance, I would have
> to disengage. I would have to keep my mind on the money,

unhook body from thought. Through all my stripping, my boyfriends, my role-playing, and my different lives, I had never lost hold of the person at the center of it all. But lap dancing, if I continued, would force a split. I had found my edge.[51]

Eaves observed the sexual activities occurring on the back benches. She saw women giving hand jobs. Some did it on their knees, between the men's legs, while others straddled the men. One bouncer said he had seen a woman having anal sex with a customer on the back bench. Dancers told her that they were expected to grab crotches during lap dancing now. The boundaries between stripping and prostitution were effectively dissolved.[52]

At the end of her journey, Eaves concluded that "stripping did more harm than good." Like Olivia, she came to understand that stripping represents a battle for power and control between men and women:

A stripper can be a feminist, if she is one who wants revenge on men or their total exclusion from her life.

In the long run hostility and exclusion were not what I wanted. So I had to consider the effects of stripping, not just on me but on men and women in general.[53]

Interacting with men at a stripclub involves a power game that the women win because they take the men's money while pretending to be adoring or turned on, writes Eaves. As for the men, stripping reinforces the general societal idea that women can and should be bought, while emphasizing the importance of women's appearance and behaviors that she came to believe were simplistic and harmful to healthy relationships between men and women.[54]

The on-line recommendations of men who pay for sexual services graphically illustrate the prostitution opportunities currently available in today's stripclubs. Alt.sex.services, which archives its material on a Web site called "The World Sex Guide," provides comprehensive details about paid sexual activities in every country in the world. Patrons rate both indoor and outdoor sites, describing the attractiveness and compliance of the women. The men's reports paint an up-to-date picture of prostitution activities occurring in many stripclubs in the United States.

For example, the information posted about stripclubs in the Chicago metropolitan area makes clear that some establishments offer nude dancing but "no touching opportunities." In others, however, the back rooms are available at various prices for different sexual activities. Consider this description of the activity on offer in a Gary, Indiana, stripclub:

> No cover charge but the drinks are cheap. . . . As soon as you get your drink and sit down one of the girls will come up to you and start some small talk. About one minute into the conversation the barmaid comes over and says, "You can buy her a drink for $10 or get a dance for $15?" . . . If you like what you see opt for the dance. You go back into this room in the back of the club and wait for the next song to start. . . . Once the song comes on she will mount you and begin the dance . . . and if she really likes you she will let you finger fuck her right there! This one broad had her hands in my pants while I was fingerfucking her. She almost riped [sic] my dick off![55]

Dances were available for $50, $100, or $150 in another club in Cicero, Illinois. For $50 the man gets a private dance for fifteen minutes that takes place in an area with a table and chair covered by a seethrough string curtain in a short hallway where "no sex, but a feel up can occur." In a $100 dance, the man goes a little farther back in the hallway to a mirrored bench area that is more private and where twenty-five minutes of sex can occur, although a barmaid walks by every ten minutes. The $150 dance, lasting about thirty-five minutes, takes place in a room with a door, affording greater privacy. The author tells his audience, "You can do a lot in the $100 dance, and even have a little fun in the $50 dance . . . if you know what you're doing." This Baedeker guide to the stripclubs of Chicago advises the men to "make everything clear before you even go back. Some of the girls will let you suck their tits . . . and some of them will put prices on different parts of their body—like total bitches. Ask around . . . ask guys who look like they go there a lot."[56]

At Stripclublist.com, an Internet directory of approximately 5,500 clubs in one hundred countries, browsers can read current customer comments and dialogue, organized by geographical area and club. "Superfriendly and serious contact in the VIP room, a little on the rough side, which I really dug," or "In the private room she offered to 'rub me out' for some extra cash," are typical of the comments of customers in the Chicago metropolitan area who are letting others know what is on offer, despite the illegality. Visitors to New Jersey stripclubs commented, "Some will go the extra mile upstairs"; "lots of contact"; "They don't have a lap dance area, so the girl will turn around and rub her butt against your crotch"; "A lot of grinding was going on, and touching is ok. Will return!!!"; and "All black dancers. Pretty and friendly. Touching is allowed." Even more chilling are comments about women from eastern Europe, eastern European blondes, and Czech women with heavy accents, raising suspicions that these may be poor and vulnerable women trafficked from Europe, as well as indications that some of the dancers may be very young: "Stacy was nice but a little childish."[57]

Private upstairs rooms in stripclubs have even figured in litigation around the Americans with Disabilities Act. In the summer of 2002, quadriplegic Ed Law sued the West Palm Beach, Florida, Wildside Adult Sports Cabaret because the area where private lap dances were performed was up a flight of stairs and inaccessible to him. The club's manager responded that the man could receive a lap dance in the main area, but Law wanted the opportunities that everyone else had.

> I saw that other guys getting lap dances took their chicks into this room where they could cool out on recliners in private. I said to my friend, "I don't want to be out here, looking like a spectacle. I want to go in that room." But the girls go, "I don't know how we're going to get you in that room 'cause there's steps."[58]

In January 2001 prostitution survivor Claudine O'Leary visited a well-known northside Chicago stripclub, accompanied by a former stripper and her male friend, who had formerly patronized these clubs. On this late Thursday evening, about fifty men were present or entered the club during the two hours the three were there. Because no alcohol is

served in the club, the women are allowed, under Chicago's ordinance
regulating exotic dancing, to strip to the nude during their dances.

Seventeen young women circulated about the club floor offering
dances to the men at $10 a song. Many of the girls put on a happy
face, but some had no expression at all, even while soliciting dances.
Claudine observed that the girls came very close to the customers;
women placed their breasts or buttocks within an inch or two of the
men, dropping their hair over the customers' heads and placing their
hands on the customers' shoulders and legs. At different points the
women would disappear to the dressing room when feature dancers
appeared. One of these was a well-known porn starlet who put on a
nude-colored thong during her third song. She went from man to man
sitting around the stage and pushed their heads into her breasts,
wrapped her legs around their heads with her vagina in their faces,
straddled them from behind, and simulated oral sex until she had made
her way around the room.

Claudine noted that there were rooms upstairs that they were not
able to visit, to which dancers escorted men if they wanted to pay for
a "private dance." She and her companions did observe dancers leading men out of the club area. Claudine's friend observed that the
women were far closer to the customers than she had ever been as a
dancer. Both she and her male escort remarked that they had never
been in a stripclub sober before, and as a result, the experience that
night was extremely difficult for them.[59]

CHAPTER FOUR

Shooting Up

> . . . for we never would have succeeded in getting through
> our childhood if we had not cultivated the art of ignoring
> the unpleasant till it was forced on our attention.
>
> — REBECCA WEST, *The Fountain Overflows*

After a while the alcohol stopped dampening Olivia's feelings of loss of self-respect. She had started spending time with a fellow stripper in her apartment. One night Olivia caught her friend in the bathroom with a syringe in her arm. That was the first time Olivia had ever seen anyone injecting drugs. Of course she had heard about it. When Olivia asked her friend what she was doing, she said, "I do this because I hurt so bad inside." Olivia remembers looking at her friend and saying, "I hurt bad inside me too. I thought no one else felt that way."

So Olivia tried heroin, too. Her friend injected her.

> It was the greatest feeling. It is so warm, like a warm glow of
> contentment that comes over you. The rush is what I would
> describe as the world's greatest orgasm, one that you should
> never have experienced, and I think that I spent the next eighteen
> years chasing that first feeling. Non–drug users will never know
> that euphoria, and therefore they would never chase it. It gives
> you the understanding of how people could actually kill for that.
> You don't ever want to give up that feeling. It does actually take
> you away from any normal problems, fears, and insecurities

*that you ever have, it is just a sense of well-being that you did
not know existed. It was a state of euphoria that I should never
have experienced.*

*It hits you so fast. The first time you go to a place that
you have never been before, and the sensation from that keeps
you chasing that feeling. You never get that feeling again, no
matter how much you take, because that was the initial introduction. It comes close and the intensity is there, but you don't
feel it like you did the first time. But you chase that for years.
You want that feeling.*

After the first injection, Olivia clung to her friend, who continued to
inject Olivia for about a month until Olivia learned how to do it herself. "I didn't let her out of my eyesight, because I wanted more and
more every chance we got." Olivia was seventeen years old.

*I know now that I don't need to be elated or depressed. There is
a balance. I was very hurt emotionally for a very long time
throughout childhood and had learned to repress it enough to
cope. I was functional, but when you realize how attractive
heroin was to me, you can see the vastness in between. If your
life is pretty normal and there are only the minimal ups and
downs, you have no reason to experiment or try to find something externally to feel better, you already have a sense of well-
being. Obviously mine was shattered through whatever circumstances.*

Once she was on heroin, Olivia turned to actual prostitution in the
back rooms in the clubs; thanks to the drug, her inhibitions were so
lowered that she "simply didn't care anymore." The club manager sold
the back room as something special: he was choosing Olivia to turn on
a particular customer in the club or at a private party. There were no
holds barred in the back rooms. The women did what the men wanted,
including sexual intercourse. The back room was also the site of a lot
of violence.

*This is where you would get the guys who would want to burn
you with cigarettes. Sometimes in a frenzy, but some just do it*

as a kind of humiliation to degrade you. You try to resist it,
but you get grabbed and held, you're half-drunk anyway, these
guys are always bigger and stronger than you, and you walk
away with scars and marks on you.

I remember another girl in the next room was getting
choked, and they ran back there and they kind of coddled the
man, saying come on, you can't play that rough. If you thought
you were going to be killed, you would really have to make a
scene. But scenes were not good, because you wouldn't be around
much longer if they had to come to your aid. I screamed like
that once when my hair was pulled back so far that I thought
my neck was going to be broken.

For these indignities the club owner paid Olivia $200 or $300 per
encounter. Today Olivia wonders how much the customers had paid
the management.

Before going to the club, Olivia would have injected heroin twice
and would have drunk a fifth of vodka, and during the evening she
sipped champagne with the customers. As long as Olivia could function and for as long as she was useful, the managers paid no attention
to her use of substances. Through heroin Olivia created a totally escap-
ist world. Every night she changed her name and donned a different
costume.

I became someone different, it was a whole fantasy thing for me
in the club. If customers got rough, or whatever would happen,
I would pretend it didn't happen, and not face it at all.

It is kind of like you are out of your body watching some-
one else do this. At the time, you don't feel, but the next day,
always before I reached for the first drink, I would get glimpses
of whatever it was that happened, and right away I would want
that drink. If you look at it like it was two different persons,
then you don't have to accept responsibility for your actions,
you don't have to really face the shame of it, I let this guy do
this to me. Or, I could have gotten killed last night. You don't
have to be reality-based. In the beginning use of the heroin, it
was like you were on cloud nine. A couple of times I had bruises
from the guys, so there were some actual intimations that some-
thing did happen. But then you numb out again.

Olivia was able to disassociate during the sex acts, but she could not obliterate everything.

> Some of the things you can't blank or numb out are some of the
> smells. Even talking about it sometimes, I can still smell the
> men. I realize how disgusted I must have been at the moment,
> and how I was able to disassociate totally, totally, and the
> longer I did it, the worse it got.

Eventually, in an eight-hour-night's stint in the stripclub, Olivia was involved in real sexual activity in the back room with six to eight men, two or three of whom would be violent. With "other stuff," it could be seventy-five to eighty customers a night. There was lap dancing, table dancing, letting the men talk dirty, spanking them, being spanked by them, giving blow jobs, or letting men masturbate between her breasts. Part of the job involved being grabbed, pinched, spanked, having fingers or objects put inside her, and being called offensive names. And, although all the sex was supposed to be negotiated, part of the job was putting up with unwanted sexual acts, such as masturbation, exposure of the penis, and having one's sexual parts grabbed.

Because the club's main goal was to sell large, expensive bottles of champagne, it used the women to create the necessary atmosphere for liquor consumption. The publicity-adverse clubs did not want any violence, but it was "a rugged game" because there was always an element of danger with men who were inebriated.

> You would tease some guys to buy some more champagne, and
> they would grab your hair and twist it around, and you would
> hold your breath and pray that the waitress would come back.
> Some of these spots were placed far back out of sight. I remember
> one time really fearing that if this guy had a knife in his pocket,
> he could slit my throat, and they would just find my head lying
> there.
>
> You never knew why he would grab your hair. No idea of
> what he is thinking or feeling or wanting. It was part of what
> he was paying for. Now that I think about it, what angers
> me the most is that you could not retaliate, even to throw a
> drink in the customer's face or even spill one on him. It's a guy

who is spending money. You put up with it, or you would lose
your job.

  And another part of the job was pleasing the manager so
you could keep your job and get extra jobs, such as bachelor
parties. Eating out, partying with the owners, so that you could
stay in good with them.

Supposedly men use women in prostitution because they lack sexual
partners or have intimates unwilling to undertake certain sex acts. Olivia's view of the men in the clubs is starkly different.

  I don't believe that it was the acts of sex that their wives
wouldn't do. I believe it was whatever in life they have been
through, they wanted some way to act it out or give it back.
These are women who were vulnerable or put themselves in com-
promising positions to be abused. It is total abuse, and they are
willing to pay to abuse. The guys come in and pay $200 or
$300 just to call you a bunch of bitches, or a black whore, or
a black bitch. They figure that because they pay for it, they are
entitled to talk to you that way.

Olivia remembers the contempt the men acted out.

  Wanting to tear your clothes off you, saying things like "you
bitch, you are nothing but a slut," wanting to fuck you in your
mouth. It is not for the orgasm as it is the acting out itself. It
gets them real excited, you can see the look on their face, you
can see the actual hatred on their faces. You can see it, and you
can feel it in their touch. They are caught up in that cycle of
whatever anger or hatred they are feeling, and they cannot control themselves. And they feel justified because they give you
money.

And the racism in the clubs was pretty blatant. Out of fifteen girls in
the club, Olivia and another biracial girl would be the only women of
color there. The customers were 95 percent White.

  I was exotic, something different and there were customers who
would really gravitate towards me because they would call me

> "Black bitch" or "Black whore." I was something they would
> never go in certain areas of the city to pick up, but they felt
> safe enough to do it in the club. It was part of the sexual charge.
> They were with someone different than they had at home, or
> different from anything they had ever been exposed to, part of
> their fantasy world. They probably always wanted to say that.
> They were pretty sick customers, if you think about it. Why
> else would they do that?

Olivia believes that most of the customers accepted the myths of the
sensuality of Black women. But because of the men's racism, they
weren't really comfortable with dark-skinned women. The biracial
Olivia fit the bill exactly.

> He can abuse a Black woman because he has no respect for her,
> in comparison to a White woman who is his wife, sister, or
> mother. He's free, he would feel more comfortable to act out
> sexually with me because he doesn't owe Black women anything.
> And as a Black woman, I'm reinforcing what he already thinks
> of women of color. There are very few boundaries that you can
> set once you put yourself in that position.

Blue-eyed blondes were the other desirables in the club. Here the stereotype was of the dumb blonde. Olivia says she knew many girls and
women whose whole image was to look like Marilyn Monroe: "And
they made a lot of money playing that role." And last, there was the
baby doll: "In any stripclub there is always someone, no matter what
her age, dressed as a young girl with the petticoat dress and ponytail.
For some reason this is a big turn-on. You tell me. What is missing
here?"

Clearly the sexualized racist epithets were intended to be abusive,
and, like the violence, were the men's tools to hurt and oppress Olivia.
The verbal abuse began to take a toll.

> It definitely plays a big part in damaging you totally. I don't
> care how strong psychologically a person is, you can only be
> told something so long. The skin gets thin. You don't realize it
> until you come out of that lifestyle, when you really begin to

*go through therapy or take a look at rebuilding your life. Then
the impact of this finally hits you.*

Olivia knows now that she would not have been able to survive it
without the heroin.

> *If the impact of all this had ever come down on me, and I had
> not had enough drugs in my body, I probably would have killed
> myself, I know I would have. I have been very close many times.
> Out of shame, out of disgust, just feeling humiliated, dehuman-
> ized. Aside from the violence, the dignity of the human is gone.
> That guy just pissed on me. What kind of person am I? What
> have I become? You lose you. Did I make enough money for the
> boss at the club, did I please the trick so he will come back and
> see me again? You did it to please.*

By disassociation through alcohol and drugs, and through the fantasies
of pretending she was someone else, Olivia left her true self behind.
While in stripping, Olivia never used her real name. Frequently changing her name enabled her to put behind her what she had done under
another identity.

> *I wanted to separate Olivia from all the things I was doing. It
> was a way of being able to stand that I was doing something
> that Olivia knew was wrong. I needed to keep some part sepa-
> rate.*
>   *If I didn't like what I had to do with the last trick, the
> next time I could change my name and pretend to be someone
> else. You can lie to yourself so much that you start to believe
> your lies. Some sixteen- and seventeen-year-olds starting in
> these clubs never have a clue of who they really are.*

It was "wrong" to Olivia not because she was trading sex for money,
but because of the nature of the sexual acts that she was asked to perform. "I felt bad and ashamed of what I was asked to do, but I continued to do it. There was no loving or caring at all. It was degrading
sex." What Olivia now expects from relationships, including sexual

ones, was missing—the honesty, caring, respect, and mutual consideration that are an important aspect of emotional and physical intimacy.

Today Olivia is well aware that stripclubs are part and parcel of prostitution. "You can't stay there without getting involved in prostitution. The stripclub is the entryway to prostitution. It was like that ten, fifteen years ago, and it is like that today." She also rues the glamour image of the stripclub promoted by the prostitution industry to lure teens into the business. "The people who have never done it, they make it look like it is so glamorous. They show the outside all painted up, but inside the woman is dying."

Researcher Melissa Farley quotes one prostitution survivor on stripping: "It is a process. The first year was like a big party, but eventually progressed downwards to the emptiest void of hopelessness."[1]

Olivia spent seven to eight years in stripclubs. Looking back on it now, she sees that it was "a slow suicide. . . . Thoughts of getting out did not cross my mind. By the time I actually thought to stop, I was so worn out."

಄

Wendy McElroy, an advocate of legalizing prostitution, criticizes most of the research on violence in the sex trade because she asserts that it has only surveyed street prostitution, where she admits abuse is rampant. Although she claims that abuse is uncommon in off-street venues such as escort services and stripping,[2] a mounting body of research data about inside prostitution venues disproves her assertion.

Former stripper Kelly Holsopple's survey of eighteen White longtime dancers (who spent an average time in dancing of six years and seven months) in stripclubs in the Minneapolis/St. Paul area found that all the women had reported being propositioned for prostitution in the clubs.[3] One hundred percent of the dancers also stated they had been physically abused in the clubs, ranging from three to fifteen times, with a mean of almost eight occurrences in the course of their involvement in stripping.[4] Sexual abuse also happened with frequency, connected mainly to lap dances: "That's the first thing men try to do when they get close to you and always in a lap dance."[5]

Forty-four percent of the women reported that the men had threatened to hurt them, with a range of three to 150 such threats during their stripping involvement. As one explained, "When I wouldn't let a customer grab on me, he would call me a bitch and threaten to kick my ass or rape me."[6] Sixty-one percent had experienced attempted vaginal penetration with fingers (39 percent successful), 33 percent had experienced attempted anal penetration with fingers (27 percent successful), 33 percent had experienced attempted penetration with objects (11 percent successful), 28 percent had experienced attempted forced masturbation from customers (27 percent successful), and 17 percent had experienced attempted rape (11 percent completed).[7]

All the respondents reported verbal harassment, most of which involved being called degrading names. Corroborating Olivia's experience with the men who frequent stripclubs, the women in Holsopple's study asserted that many of the customers are drunk and exhibit negative attitudes toward the women: "They smell so sour, they breathe very heavy and kind of wheeze when women are near." "They are weak abusers who love to subordinate women and girls to feel like a man." "I am repulsed by the sight, sound, smell, and touch of them." "Moreover," concludes Holsopple, "they perceive that customers are out of control, have power and abuse problems, and will do anything to degrade women because they hate women."[8] As reported by the strippers, some stripclub owners, managers, and staff expect women to masturbate them, and some force intercourse with them.[9]

Women in Chicago involved in activities such as escort services, exotic dancing, and prostitution in their own residences reported experiencing violence and abuse from customers in significant amounts. For example, 21 percent of women in escort services stated they had been raped more than ten times—the same percentage as for women in the streets—and 11 percent five to ten times. Approximately 29 percent of the women in escort services reported that fingers or objects had been put inside them ten or more times, and almost a third had been slapped, had their hair pulled, and been spanked ten or more times.[10]

As for strippers or exotic dancers, 7 percent reported rape more than ten times and another 7 percent five to ten times. However, almost 12 percent said they had been threatened with rape between five and ten times, and almost 19 percent had been threatened with rape more than ten times. Almost 19 percent of the strippers had been threatened with a weapon between five and ten times, the same number had their hair pulled or been pinched and spanked ten or more

times, and 23 percent reported ripped clothing ten or more times.[11]
Customers perpetrated most of the violence against women in exotic
dancing: they were responsible for 30 to 100 percent of all acts of
violence in this prostitution venue, including all acts of sexual violence.[12]

As it is unlikely that guns or knives would be drawn on the open
dance floor, researchers point out that the primary sites of violence and
abuse are the back rooms, where some customers attempt to obtain
more than the women want to deliver. These data indicate the difficulty some women have in controlling some customers, especially
those who may be inebriated.[13]

A recent study of violence undertaken in three United Kingdom
cities with 115 women in outdoor prostitution and 125 indoors (in
saunas or flats) corroborates this finding. Outdoor women were
younger, involved in prostitution at an earlier age, and experienced
significantly more violence from their clients than those indoors (81
percent compared with 48 percent), but the amount of the violence
indoors was not insignificant. Women outdoors most frequently reported being slapped, punched, or kicked, but those indoors cited attempted rape more frequently.[14]

In one of the few projects to research massage parlors, women in
Australia said they were vulnerable to unwanted sexual advances and
rape, although those in legal brothels said they felt safe. Women in
massage parlors believed they had little real control over the sexual
encounter with the client. One explained, "Sometimes they want to
touch. I can't say no all the time, otherwise I'm not going to get work.
I have to sometimes. . . . I've only gotten scared a couple of times, not
many times, when I thought that my life was being threatened."[15]

One expert discovered a booklet for call girls in London that rec-
ommends having mirrored walls so they can see whether a customer
has a knife behind his back. When she appeared on a radio program in
London with a woman in escort services, the woman expressed fears
that her next client might kill her, now that her Alsatian dog had died.
Considering the mounting body of evidence about violence in more
upscale prostitution venues, she concludes:

> But somehow this rather convincing evidence that prostitu-
> tion is not just an ordinary job gets ignored by those who

want to see themselves as socially progressive. A determined avoidance of the facts of prostitution is part of the
present determination by many social liberals to see prostitution as a fine job for a woman, but one which they would
never, ever, wish to do themselves.[16]

Maticka-Tyndale and colleagues interviewed thirty exotic dancers in
ten clubs in southern Ontario, Canada, confirming the association of
physical assaults and unwanted sexual contact with lap dancing and
with venues featuring private booths and back rooms. Respondents
reported that managers in some clubs threatened them with job loss if
they did not lap dance and repeatedly pressed them to do so. Ever
present were unwanted sexual contact and verbal harassment:

Women spoke of having their breasts and genitals touched,
and of men "poking" fingers inside them or licking various
parts of their bodies, including their genitals. . . . "It was
like [you're] a cow, as if you're mechanical. They just assumed that they could do things. And when you bend over,
they could poke their fingers in you."[17]

As a result of maintaining a different and separate dancer identity,
persistent and long-term disassociation resulted for some. One woman
stated: "It makes you feel like you're losing your mind," while another
explained, "I turn into a totally different personality. . . . And it's
getting to the point that it's really hard to find Jane again. I'm becoming this other person totally."[18]

Jennifer Wesley, who interviewed nine current and eleven former
strippers in a southwestern metropolitan area in 2000, found that the
dancers took as a given the physical violation of their bodies. One
dancer's comments were typical: "Guys in the club grab your butt,
grab your boobs, touch your leg. I got grabbed all the time. Guys
would do rude things but figure it just comes with the territory. You
don't like it, but you deal with it. To make money."[19]

Wesley found that stripping gave the dancers a much-needed
chance to assert power: "The women derived a sense of power from
the ease with which they convinced men to pay a good amount of
money for a glimpse of their bodies and a few moments of their time

and the way they could command the customer's attention and adula-
tion."[20] The money they earned also signified power and achievement.
One woman, Paula, recognized her need for attention:[21]

> It's also kind of an ego thing . . . I had a guy actually bow
> down on stage and kiss my feet. As if I were a god. And I
> know these men are so enchanted by the idea of me. That
> they're going to go home smelling their shirts, laying [sic]
> in their beds next to their wives, thinking of me. Being at all
> the foster homes I've been, something I've always wanted is
> to be remembered. Now it's my chance to get even.[21]

Vacillation between feelings of power and vulnerability was, however,
frequent because the dancers could so easily lose control of their bodies
while stripping. The customers, said Wesley's subjects, felt entitled to
the women as sexual objects and acted accordingly. As the words and
actions became abusive, the dancers felt violated because of their powerlessness over the situation:

> Sometimes guys will push the limit and say really nasty,
> vulgar things, and you're like, you want to cry. You want
> to be like: Why do I feel I have to do this, I'm the one who
> got suckered into this, I'm the one who's losing here, I'm
> losing a piece of me every time I do this.[22]

Although the dancers made efforts to stay in control, their attempts
were constantly undermined by assumptions of entitlement. Wesley's
respondents did not like the abuse, but like Olivia, they put up with it.
Wesley concluded that "The sexualized body becomes both the source
of power and the root of powerlessness for the dancers, and they struggle to negotiate these contradictions."[23] Many women confront this
dilemma, but for strippers, "these negotiations and resistances were
confined to their bodies, instead of being broadened into other con-
texts of existence."[24]

Carol Rambo Ronai, who herself stripped between 1984 and 1985
and later returned to stripping in 1987 in Florida solely for the purpose
of research, writes that although customers were allowed to touch only
the hips, back, and outside of a dancer's legs during a table dance,

"Many men tried and some succeeded in doing more."[25] Illegal sexual activity (hand jobs or oral sex) did sometimes occur. More common were body-to-penis friction and masturbation: "The most frequent form consisted of the customer sliding down to the end of his seat, spreading his legs, and pulling the dancer in close to him where she could then use her knees discretely to rub his genitals while she danced."[26]

When a customer violated rules by putting fingers inside the dancer's briefs or touching her breasts, the woman would dance away from him to escape his wandering hands. This maneuver was tricky, because the customer always attempted to get more than was allowed, and the dancer needed to keep him in line without turning him off.[27]

> The negotiation process we have described then is a case study of exchange between those differentially empowered. As in other occupations in which a person's job requires emotional management, stripping has high emotional costs. . . . Stripping, as a service occupation, pays well, but costs dearly.[28]

Although alcohol and drug addiction may occur at more severe levels for women in prostitution on the streets, that does not mean that many women in indoor sex trade venues, like Olivia, are not plagued with these issues. Indeed, research with women in off-street sex trade sites discloses serious problems with substance abuse.

For example, in a Chicago study, every respondent involved in escort service prostitution stated she sometimes used drugs or alcohol, and only about 5 percent of women in exotic dancing said they had never abused these substances.[29] Almost 43 percent of the women stated they used the same drug more often while in escort services, and 46 percent reported they took more drugs more frequently. About 11 percent said there was no change, less frequent use, or fewer numbers of drugs, but not outright cessation. In stripping, about 19 percent reported some decrease in frequency or number of drugs, while the rest stated they used drugs more frequently or more drugs more often.[30] Women operating out of their own residences more often reported taking more kinds of drugs during this activity. Otherwise the pattern was similar; only 4 percent never used drugs, and 4 percent did cut back by taking the same drug less frequently.[31]

Strippers in the Chicago sample provided examples of substance abuse that began after they started performing. "I never used drugs while growing up, but started smoking marijuana and drinking after I began stripping" (a twenty-four-year-old). "I had never gotten high until I started live sex shows. Then I drank so I could perform" (a twenty-nine-year-old). Another twenty-nine-year-old in live sex shows stated she started using alcohol, drinking two shots per show, after she began participating in the activity. A twenty-four-year-old exotic dancer "started drinking just to dance." One stripper, who stated that she did not engage in prostitution herself, remarked that most of the girls she knew in the club "live in hotels, have a drug habit, a pimp, and turn tricks." She herself just danced. "I was raped when I was young, and by the time I became involved in dancing, I had set certain boundaries."[32]

Maticka-Tyndale and colleagues also found that many women reported using alcohol and, less often, other substances to make it possible to continue dancing in the clubs. One woman admitted she typically consumed between five and nineteen drinks each evening shift. All reported drinking alcohol before their first stage performance, and for some this dependence on alcohol continued for an extended period or throughout their dancing. But not all kept up the drinking; believing that alcohol would compromise their safety, some stopped its use. Marijuana was the most common illicit drug used to relax the dancer as an alternative to alcohol.[33]

Holsopple corroborates the reliance on alcohol in stripclubs:

> The greatest response to questions regarding preparation
> for work was "drink." Women drink while getting ready
> to go to work, and they drink while doing their hair and
> make-up in the dressing room. Women who work at nude
> juice bars that do not serve alcohol or at bars that do not
> allow women to buy their own drinks report that they stop
> at another bar on their way in and "get loaded."[34]

Researchers with women in brothels and escort services also discovered reliance on drugs and alcohol. Lever and Dolnick found that 21 percent of women in their escort service sample drank alcohol before the dates or tricks, and during the dates the women consumed alcohol with the clients 18 percent of the time.[35] Half the brothel workers in a research project in Australia reported current or recent injecting drug use. In only a few cases had heavy drug use preceded a woman's involvement in the prostitution industry.[36] Women in indoor sex trade venues in the Netherlands in 1990–91 were often under the influence of alcohol and drugs; 90 percent of women on the streets were sometimes under the influence of drugs, but 87 percent in clubs, 78 percent in brothels, 81 percent in window prostitution, and 67 percent in their own homes said they sometimes were.[37]

David Scott, who labors to present a balanced view of stripping based on observations in a Las Vegas club, appears to have completed his research in a venue with no visible prostitution activities. All the Las Vegas strippers he observed "were stoned on something, be it alcohol, marijuana, hashish, or cocaine." Heroin is not a stripper's drug, he says, because

> it works against the principle of motion. In this medium numbness does not work as well as dreamscapes or crystalline energy rushes. . . . Although there is the odd teetotaler among them, for the vast majority of strippers, sweetening the experience with something or other has been, since day one, a means of coping and probably a means of forgetting certain things.[38]

On the Internet, men's recommendations and ratings about escort services often mention women's drug problems. Consider this write-up on "Liz":

> She is one of the best dates I have ever had. She was truly into her work and never rushed me or made me feel less than a real date. She is a voluptuous figured woman just as she advertises. Her face is just as beautiful as Liz Taylor ever was. Finding a consistant [sic] escort is very hard these days of drug addicts etc.[39]

An escort service owner interviewed by researcher Norton-Hawk said she knew that some of her employees broke her rules prohibiting drug use. Most, she thought, took diet pills or sedatives, which the customer was less able to detect.[40] And although no-drug policies are common-place in indoor prostitution, a substantial number of the women in these venues in a Victoria, B.C., study reported problems with drug and alcohol addiction. Some explained that they were able to hide their drug use from the management, but in other cases concealment was unnecessary because the owners seemed totally unconcerned. One woman described some agencies in which the girls "just look haggard. You can tell that they're doing drugs and they're not supposed to."[41]

All in all, these data would caution against making blanket statements that violence and alcohol and drug addiction are not associated with indoor prostitution. Indeed, some researchers believe that off-street sex trade venues are more dangerous for women: those involved in clubs, massage parlors, brothels, and pornography production may be even more isolated and have less control over the conditions and situations in which they are active than women on the streets and, as a result, may face greater risk of exploitation.[42]

Some of the overall danger results from management's failure to protect women, a topic that has received surprisingly little attention. In a recent Victoria, B.C., study, for example, the indoor prostitution venues operated like sweatshops, with managers taking most of the women's earnings and trying to increase profits by maximizing the number of customers. The madam/boss sometimes failed to shield the women from aggressive clients or was reluctant to intervene for fear of police involvement that might result in closure of the business. One woman complained, "There's a girl that has been sodomized in a hotel room and . . . the agency sends another girl out and another girl out and the same thing happens and happens."[43]

David Scott recognizes the upside of stripping and its attraction for girls like Olivia: "It's the buzz of showbiz, the pizzazz, the snap and sizzle of life after dark, the glitz and the gusto: it's all of these, but with an extra twist. This is a life whose sails are set for commotion."[44]

But Scott also observes the downside. He writes of women on the floor with their legs spread open, with men sitting on the stage trying to roll quarters into their "coin slot." Customers pelt the dancers with ice cubes, French fries, chicken bones, prophylactics, glasses, and ash-trays. Because of the amount of alcohol being consumed and the nature of the club activities, a menacing atmosphere prevails.[45]

Most strippers come into the business, he concludes, "in a state of need. They are often naive young women, disconnected and lonely, who are grateful for the opportunity to work. From the first moment they are in a position of indebtedness."[46]

"It is not a form of entertainment," says Olivia today with a heavy note of finality. "It is sold as a form of entertainment. There is nothing entertaining about it."

❧

Like Olivia, academic Lillian Faderman possessed a sexual magnetism that she used periodically to make money as a teen. Nude modeling and stripping continually brought her to the edge—to prostitution—but each time she stepped back from the brink. Faderman's mother and aunt, survivors of a Latvian family destroyed in the Holocaust, raised the girl, but their sweatshop labor and her mother's mental illness trapped Lillian in poverty and limited her opportunities. Olivia and Lillian chose the same path to advancement and escape from dysfunctional families. Faderman's autobiography clearly delineates the attractions of stripping and modeling for needy girls, but it also illustrates the thin line between these activities and prostitution.[47]

Why, then, did Olivia step over the line and Lillian not? This author posed the question directly to Faderman. In the end, she responded, it was her family that held her back: "I was all they had left, I was a remnant, the only one in my generation from their slaughtered family." Faderman also points to the luck of having social worker Maury Colwell come along at the right time in her life to show her another way to success through higher education. But concedes Faderman, "It wasn't always simple. Even as a student at Berkeley I was tempted right after I thought I was safe."[48]

Luckily, for Faderman, there was a warning bell every time she got close to succumbing to the lure of prostitution:

> I am in danger, I thought on the ride down from the Holly-
> wood Hills. I am on the verge of going out of control. . . .
> There's a bogey man lurking in wait for me out there . . .
> and if I don't stop placing my naked self in full view, one
> of these days he'll surely pounce and drag me off to the fate
> prepared for girls like me.[49]

Unfortunately, no such warning bells ever sounded for Olivia.

CHAPTER FIVE

The Street

The procurer is an immutable specialized type, whose energy has been concentrated by degeneracy into an insensi-
bility to the fine things of the flesh and the cold execution
of premeditated villainies. We have a right to protect ourselves from his talents. His existence is a riddle, and he
might as well solve it from behind prison bars.

— Rebecca West, "Battle-Ax and Scalping Knife"

Olivia's heroin use increased over time, and after a while she wasn't
shooting up to get high—she was using so she wouldn't get drug sick.
In other words, she became a maintenance user, injecting nine or ten
times a day, getting enough drugs in her so she could function. The
fear of being drug sick would propel her to the next fix.

*Without heroin, physically you want to vomit, you have no
control over your bowels, there is this acid bowel taste that
comes up in your throat, your skin crawls, you have goose
bumps all the time, you are constantly cold, you shiver, you are
nauseous, the smell of food will really make you throw up.*

At the time heroin cost $20 per bag, which would maintain her for
about two hours. The need for the next fix made it difficult for Olivia
to continue in the stripclub. Drugs were absolutely forbidden there,
and the club owner or manager would seriously beat women for in-

fractions. Because she could not wait that long for the next injection, it came to the point where Olivia could no longer sustain the club's full eight-hour shift. As the tracks on her arms started to become visible, it was also becoming more difficult for Olivia to conceal her drug use. She began by making excuses to leave the club to go off with different tricks.

Olivia started her new activities downtown on Rush Street, near a hotel in which accommodating bellhops would connect her with hotel customers who took her to their rooms. The number of customers she saw a night depended on how many well-paying men she met and whether she could rob those who had money.

> I was involved night and day, there was no standard, six, eight, twelve, fifteen men, depending. It rapidly went downhill after the first three weeks. You expected violence any time, and you're scared of it at all times. For the most part I tried to be as quick as I could. I did blow jobs a lot, I did not do penetration sex a lot. I would steal from the guys, I was real good at it. I needed to get a fix, and I didn't want to have to come back out right away. You begin stealing because you don't have the energy any more to turn a date. You don't want to lose the time. You can't tolerate the sex, you need to get high. That's when I got stabbed, stealing.

"Strych," short for his longer nickname "Strychnine," was Olivia's drug supplier. He lived in the same building she did, and he started bringing clients to her. In the beginning, Strych wasn't using hard drugs, just marijuana and alcohol. Olivia lost her apartment when she couldn't continue in the clubs. So she teamed up with Strych, who would help her ply the streets, a territory he knew well.

"I had a great fear of going to the streets," Olivia says, "That wasn't how this had started out. It was a down-spiraling of the drugs that forced me to the streets, it wasn't a real choice. Strych helped me to get set up in the streets." Soon Strych became Olivia's intimate partner and who began to live off her earnings. He was six foot three inches and about 230 pounds. People on the street feared him. He was known to be quick to anger and fueled by alcohol, quick to fight. Plenty of men on the streets looking for money to buy drugs would beat women like Olivia who didn't give their money to them. But because of Strych, no one harrassed Olivia in this way.

In actuality, Strych did nothing to protect Olivia—only his reputation helped her. He was always there when Olivia got into a car and when she came back. But that was not to watch out for Olivia; that was to protect his money.

> If I had not showed up, he would have picked up the next hooker and sweet-talked her into it. He was not there for protection, he was waiting there for money to get high. It is such a myth about women who have guys working the streets—they're not there for the women's protection. At the time I thought he cared about me.

Olivia soon turned Strych on to regular heroin use. She made the money for the two of them to get high. Olivia's new partner had an apt nickname. Strych became Olivia's violent abuser: "He broke my ribs. I had black eyes all the time. I got hit on the back. I got stomped. He wanted sex, but after a while neither of us really cared about the sex."

Olivia was with Strych for about eight years. His violence was all about control. He was jealous of the customers if she stayed with a trick too long, or she didn't want to go back out and that meant that Strych would have to hustle for them both to get high. Like a lot of batterers, he would tell Olivia she was nothing but a dope addict or a whore, and nobody else was going to want her. "I really thought that," Olivia remembers. "I thought I should be gratified that he would put up with me."

> I had this false sense of being protected. He was known to be very dangerous, so I didn't get robbed a lot and didn't get bothered a lot, everyone knew. Another false sense of esteem—I was his woman. A sense of belonging. The intensity of the violence was much confused with love or trying to please him.

When they were drug sick or when they were short of cash, the violence was always worse. Olivia began to fear Strych more and more.

> I remember being really fearful of him. He scared me. I've had
> broken ribs. He threw an ashtray at my back that caused dan-
> gerous fluids to form on my kidneys. I was hit by him with
> baseball bats. I've been beaten on the street, just totally degraded
> on the street.

Olivia's sister Alta vividly remembers Strych:

> Strych was a great big guy, probably twice her size. He
> was such bad news. Olivia seemed terrified of him. But she
> wouldn't talk about it. She wouldn't leave. He was control-
> ling her so much. But she didn't seem to mind it, which is
> typical of domestic violence. Violence to Olivia was love.
> The black eyes, the bruises, the thumb that had been almost
> cut off. I thought she was going to end up dead, and there
> was nothing I could do to stop it.[1]

By midnight Olivia would have usually made enough money for a
heroin purchase and to rent a hotel room for her and Strych for twenty-
four hours. At about three or four, she would need another hit and go
back out again. The hotel room was just the place to get high and to
drink in. Eventually, Olivia would traffic with twenty to twenty-five
customers in a twenty-four-hour period.

When a customer approached in an automobile, Olivia would bar-
gain for the price before she got into the car or soon afterwards—the
customer always had to pay ahead of time. Olivia would then tell the
customer where to drive, usually over to the lake if she was up north,
where there were many underground self-parking garages open
twenty-four hours a day. She would try to find someplace close, with
the average length of time for the encounter at ten to fifteen minutes.
If the customer wanted to get a hotel room, Olivia would always try
to steal from him because she would know he had money stashed
somewhere. And always there was violence.

> I've jumped in cars and had guys put a gun to my head many
> times, scars where I've been stabbed. A lot of times the guys pay
> you, allow you to give them a blow job, and then pull a knife
> on you, take their money back, and kick you out of the car.

> Some guys do it for fun and put a gun to your head, click it,
> and there are no bullets in it, but you don't know that. [For]
> the majority of the violence on the street, you are alone. You are
> truly alone once you get into the car.

A great deal of the violence occurred when customers took back the money after a sex act. Alone in a man's car in an isolated spot, Olivia was always vulnerable. Several times a month, customers would threaten her with a knife as they took back the money. One time a customer badly slashed Olivia with a knife out of the blue for no apparent reason. He repeatedly gashed her as he hatefully exclaimed, "You bitch!" Other customers would pull her hair back with brutal force during encounters. Olivia was always in a state of anxiety or panic because she never knew when violence would break out.

> You're giving a blow job, and all of a sudden he is ramming
> your head against the car. He rips off your clothes, or tells you
> to take your clothes off and pushes you out of the car and laughs
> as he drives away. You are lying there, and part of you is
> grateful to still be alive. You act like you don't really care that
> people see you. It's broad daylight, and you pretend to be invisi-
> ble. You really have to convince yourself that this really didn't
> happen, because you know that you have to continue to do this.
> Otherwise you would either kill yourself or go crazy.
>
> Verbal abuse, pretty inhuman, accompanies this. Even
> when you are high, it takes a lot of energy and effort to wash
> that out of your consciousness. You continue to get high to try
> to make it disappear, or try to pretend that you are not the
> person that just went through that.

Out of fifteen customers a night, Olivia says that about half would perpetrate this kind of violence. "When it happened we always said, 'It comes with the territory.' It shouldn't come with the territory. No one has a right to do that."

Rape also became almost normal.

> Rape: you accept it, it comes with the territory. Numerous
> times a guy picks me up. He knows a place to park, and you get

around the corner and there are two other guys—and you know
you are going to be raped. Or he pulls around for you to do a
blow job, and in jump two or three other people. Gang raped,
over and over, generally in the car. No pay. Then you are just
left there, and you just pray you won't be hurt.

This kind of scenario occurred four or five times a month. One episode
involved three men who blindfolded Olivia and took her some distance
away. "When they got tired of me, or of smoking weed, they blindfolded me and dropped me on the South Side at the el station. Disassociating for four or five hours. That was one of the worst times."
    Even if it wasn't rape or gang rape, the sex could often be violent.

You could feel the harshness, you could read the facial expres-
sions. You can have sex with one guy, and it can feel like you
have had sex with three. You put up with it. Most of the time
I was too high, and I didn't feel the effects until after I got up.
It felt like your body has been run over by a truck at times.
And this has nothing to do with what it does psychologically.

Customers have grabbed, bitten, slapped, punched, pinched, kicked,
and spanked Olivia, cut or stabbed her with a knife, burned her with
cigarettes, and threatened her with weapons.

Some of these guys could well be rapists. They figure that because they pay for it, they are entitled to talk to you that way.
I think that the women in the streets are the target of everything
that has built up inside them. It is not a romantic affair. It is
very degrading. With a person that I love, I would not allow
him to talk to me that way or allow him to do these things to
me. It makes you stop and think about it. Where did all that
come from? It was a hatred of women. Rape at a different level.
    They know they can do this. They come out on the streets
looking for a target. They don't go and pick up a girl in the
office and pull this. They don't look at us as human beings.
You're out there, you get what you deserve, is their attitude.
That is what they are looking for, women to do this to.

Olivia was extremely well paid by mostly White customers for the "crazy stuff"—letting men urinate on her, urinating on them, spanking them, being spanked, choking them. Most of the encounters, though, involved a quick sexual act in the front or back seat of the car, during which Olivia would assume the different positions requested by the customer. Sometimes she felt like a contortionist. Removing her clothes would cost the customer more money.

> There was nothing cherishing or nurturing about the acts that I was asked to perform, or not even asked, applied on me without my consent. You don't want the rest of the world to really know how bad it is until you come out of it, because you couldn't live with yourself, you would commit suicide. I have left tricks and wished I was dead. I could get high enough to act like it didn't happen afterwards, but I have actually left thinking, I wish I could kill myself. If it was brutal enough, I wished the guy had killed me, because it is so hard to face yourself afterwards.

On the street, Olivia lived in fear on a daily basis. She was afraid of being drug sick, terrified of Strych, anxious and fearful of the customers, and frightened of police officers who would demand sex or could be violent. Today Olivia finds it unpleasant and difficult to talk about these car encounters. Nor does she remember a lot about it. Perhaps the worst memory is the smells of the men: their body odor could be overpowering and stayed with her after the encounters. Many men had bad skin conditions as well.

> You keep saying, after you get through this you will have enough money to get high. You disassociate enough to get through it, and you get out of the car wishing you were dead and that this wasn't really happening to you.
>   I remember throwing up many times, gagging, trying to give a blow job. I had a hard time separating out, whether it was the act itself, or whether I needed drugs. It got to the point that I disgusted myself with what I was doing.

Seventy-five percent of the men seeking sex in that North Side neighborhood were White, but the majority of the women selling sex were

minorities, most of whom were strung out on drugs. The racial epithets were as prevalent as in the clubs.

Olivia tried the best she could to reduce the amount of violence
she faced on a daily basis. For instance, she seldom accepted African-
American men as customers because she found them stronger and
more aggressive.

> That kind of backfired on me too, because what I found out was
> that most of the sickos on the streets were the White men, the
> brokers, the executives. Those were the ones with the suits on,
> and you get in the car and they put this razor to your throat.
> Or they say how you remind them of their mother and ask you
> to do all these crazy acts and lock the doors. In the state of mind
> that you are in, under the influence of drugs, it is pretty hard,
> but you do the best you can. You try to learn to rely on your
> instincts, but we are talking about a lot of sick men out there.

The men's appearance and color enabled them to pass as benign, making it difficult for Olivia to avoid choosing them, and facilitated her
abuse. Although the women competed with one another for customers, they did watch out for each other, sharing information: look out
for a car of a certain color, a certain van; someone was brutalized the
day before; someone crazy is on the rampage.

"For as little communication the women on the street had with
one another, we did try to have a kind of internal safety communication," Olivia recalls. "I guess it worked, I survived it. I carried a knife.
I pulled it a couple of times. I never used it. I don't know if I ever
could."

Later on, the routine went like this: Olivia and Strych would take
a cab to the West Side of Chicago to buy the heroin. They would find
a place to get high and then take the el back. Six hours later, they
would do the same thing. Night blended into day, and day into night.
They slept three to four hours at the maximum, sometimes in the park
during the warmer months so they would not need to spend money
on a hotel room. Sometimes they bought little junk cars and would
sleep in them. Only occasionally would they stop to eat.

Toward the end of her eleven years of street prostitution, Olivia
was involved in a peep show for about four to six months. She didn't

stay long because the money wasn't good. Olivia found the experience much more degrading than turning dates on the street.

> You feel really used. There is glass in front of you, and when
> you dance you feel like a caged animal. I know how the animals
> in the zoo must feel as people walk by gazing at them. You can't
> hear anything, but you see the gestures and the facial expres-
> sions, more so, because when you are actually with the customer
> you can close your eyes. It is knowing that they are on the other
> side of the glass jacking off. Emotionally, it had more wear and
> tear for me than the actual physical dating.

Olivia's life took a large toll on her family. As the years went by, she became more secretive. Sometimes she would call her family and say she was in trouble and needed help. Alta and Olivia's mother would go to wherever she was, but by the time they got there she would refuse to open the door, or she would say, "Things are okay now." Or, after many months, she would call and say she was coming home for a visit, only never to show up. "It was a big roller coaster for all of us," Alta recalls. "We were never sure she was okay. When we did see her, a lot of times she would show up with black eyes and bruises and things like that."[2]

Alta talked and talked, but it never did any good. She thinks back on the time they had just buried Tanya, their younger sister. The official cause of death was an overdose of methadone and valium. Tanya's young son, who was present at the death, told Alta that Tanya's partner had physically attacked her before injecting her. Alta is certain that domestic violence played a part in her sister's death. When Olivia ran out and got high right after Tanya's funeral, she and Alta had one of the worst fights they ever had. "I was so hurt about Tanya," says Alta. "Seeing Olivia, immediately after we had buried Tanya, it was shocking for me. That was one time that I could have really hurt her, and I am glad it didn't go that far. It was a struggle for the entire family."[3]

Olivia doesn't know anything more about how Tanya lost her life. She was fairly numb on drugs at the time. But during recovery after she left prostitution, Tanya's death was a great personal loss with which Olivia needed to deal, and, on one level, may never come to terms with.

> She was very special to me. When I think about it now, a week
> before her twenty-second birthday, what a loss. And the two
> children. Alta was their caretaker for many, many years. The
> youngest, Tanya's daughter, now twenty-one, has been my baby
> and is very close to me. Unfortunately, Tanya's son has been in
> and out of jail since my mother died. Interestingly, his charges
> have all involved sexual assault and sexual violence.

༄

More than twenty research studies, most of them in North America
within the last fifteen years, have documented an almost unimaginable
level of violence in street prostitution.[4] The two largest samples come
from San Francisco and Chicago.

In 1998 Farley and Barkan reported on their interviews with 130
women in prostitution on the streets of San Francisco. Eighty-two percent had experienced physical assaults in prostitution, with 55 percent
of them at the hands of customers. Sixty-eight percent stated they had
been rape victims since entering prostitution; 46 percent of these rapes
were at the hands of customers, and 48 percent of these respondents
had been raped more than five times.[5]

Posttraumatic stress disorder (PTSD) is a diagnosis describing psychological symptoms and adverse effects on mental health that can
result from violence; symptoms include difficulty concentrating, hypervigilance, flashbacks or the reliving of the trauma, and disassociation or emotional numbness. Sixty-eight percent of Farley and Barkan's
sample met the criteria for a diagnosis of PTSD.[6] PTSD severity in the
study was found to be related to the occurrence of sexual assault in
adult prostitution and the frequency of rape. Not surprisingly, the
more types of violence reported, the greater the severity of PTSD symptoms and the higher the likelihood of meeting criteria for a PTSD diagnosis.[7] The sample's overall mean PCL score (an index of PTSD
severity) of 54.9 was compared to a few other samples: 50.6 for an
equal number (123) of PTSD treatment–seeking Vietnam veterans;
34.8 for 1,006 Persian Gulf War veterans; and in a random HMO sample of women, 30.6 for twenty-five women who reported physical
abuse in childhood and 36.8 for twenty-seven women who reported a
history of physical and sexual abuse as children.[8]

Psychologist Melissa Farley explains these high levels of posttraumatic stress disorder:

> First of all, in order to continue in prostitution, you either have to be psychologically or chemically dissociated. You cannot do 15 blow jobs a night or get fucked by 10 men and stay in your body—the human mind protects us from experiences like that. And if you can't dissociate, then you've got to have drugs.[9]

Other researchers have recently corroborated Farley and Barkan's PTSD findings. Forty-two percent of a sample of 100 women on the streets of Washington, D.C., met the criteria for PTSD in a recent survey.[10] More than a third of a sample of 103 women on the streets in Florida had been diagnosed with a mental health disorder, the majority depression or bipolar disease. Almost 36 percent had been previously hospitalized for a mental health problem.[11] A study of 346 drug-using women in New York City's East and Central Harlem in the early 1990s found that those women (176) who were involved in prostitution had higher mean scores of psychological distress measured by two mental health indexes. Indeed, women in prostitution in the sample had higher distress scores than did samples of psychiatric in- and outpatients.[12]

Many women in street prostitution attempt suicide or have suicidal ideation. Sixty-three percent of the women in a U.S. sample said they had tried to hurt or kill themselves at some point,[13] and 80 percent of the long-term participants at a prostitution support group reported that they had seriously attempted suicide.[14]

PTSD and other mental health problems can have serious effects on women's abilities to make life choices. One prostitution researcher has concluded that "the presence of PTSD can limit an individual's ability to function effectively, decreasing the likelihood that he or she can take advantage of available resources and possibly minimizing any likelihood of leaving prostitution."[15]

Parriott's comments about her research illustrate the severity of the violence and its effects on the women:

> Anecdotally, there was often a marked difference in the demeanor of the women during the physical assault section

of the interview. The survey covered many extremely personal and potentially painful subject areas, yet by maintaining a private and respectful interview environment, the women were generally quite forthcoming and unhesitant in their answers. During the physical assault questions, however, women would become more quiet and distant, often lowering their voice and averting their eyes. It was the only section of the interview which would incite tears in the respondents.[16]

Having measured the frequency of violence from customers, the Center for Impact Research's sample of 113 women on the Chicago streets can provide more detailed information about the severity of the abuse that women face. Almost 20 percent stated that customers had threatened them with a weapon, 22 percent had sex forced on them, 24 percent had something thrown at them, and 32 percent had their clothing ripped, all more than ten times. About 39 percent reported being slapped, 33 percent punched, and 34 percent having their hair pulled more than ten times. With a few exceptions, women in drug houses, venues in which sex is exchanged for drugs, reported similar levels of violence.[17]

Eighty-five percent of a recent sample of women from the streets jailed in a large northeastern city reported that the most likely location for their sexual encounters was the customer's car in a secluded spot—where women are most vulnerable to violence. One prostitution researcher describes stories of assault similar to Olivia's:

> One woman respondent mentioned that the car door handle of a customer's car had been removed so that she was unable to escape being assaulted. Another was stabbed while performing oral sex. One prostitute continued to work despite a knife wound from a deranged street person. Her next customer was concerned, not with the fact that she was injured, but with the possibility that her bleeding would damage his upholstery.[18]

Women incarcerated for prostitution in a Midwestern jail told Miller and Schwartz that it was not uncommon for customers to refuse to pay, to rape them, and then to turn around and give them the money afterward. Because the men paid the women, they believed they were entitled to rape: "He ended up giving me ten dollars and taking me back to where he picked me up and telling me, 'That's how I get my kicks, baby.' You know, 'I pick the girl up, I threaten her, and I end up paying her for something.'"[19]

Sterk found that all of the 180 women she interviewed who were involved in street prostitution in the Atlanta and New York area in the 1990s had experienced physical abuse at the hands of customers. Injuries included bruises, stiff necks, or strained muscles owing to arm or leg twisting during sex in the car. Some rough and uncaring customers burned women with cigarettes, beat them up, or left them naked and stranded. The women agreed almost unanimously that customers assumed that their payment gave them the right to psychologically and physically abuse them.[20]

Maher, who interviewed forty-five women on the streets in Brooklyn, New York, also found that customers regularly robbed and beat them, routinely pushed or forced them to jump from moving vehicles, and, less frequently, shot at them. One customer stabbed a woman repeatedly and cut off her breasts. A respondent reported:

> They [two dates] wanted their money back after we finished—threw me off the van naked—then he hit me with a blackjack caus [sic] I jumped back into the van because I wanted to get my clothes. It was freezing outside so I jumped back on the van to try and get my clothes and he smacked me with a blackjack on my eye.[21]

In a widely cited study of 361 women on the streets of Glasgow, Scotland, in the 1990s, McKeganey and Barnard found that the potential for violence in every encounter created extremely stressful conditions:

> Emma recounted an attack by a client. "He was a body builder, massive. He was having sex with me for about 20 minutes, that's a long time and nothin' was happening. I asked him to get off me and he got off and I started to get my sel ready. He pulled the Durex off and started to tuck in his trousers, but then he pulled a gun from the door

compartment and said that if I didn't make him come he was gonnae blow ma brains out. I looked at the gun and kept saying to myself, That's a gun, that's a gun, and I actually peed myself. I knew that if I didn't do exactly what he said he was gonnae shoot me. I thought, Just play along with him. He raped me, took ages to come and made me do all different things doggie position."

Such incidents as these represented the backdrop to the women's work. They were recounted by women not in a tone designed to shock or elicit sympathy but with an almost matter-of-fact acceptance—if you worked the streets, sooner or later something similar was going to happen. You could do various things to reduce the likelihood of such incidents occurring but this was unlikely to prevent something happening at some point. As frightening as such violence clearly was, what in a way compounded things was not knowing why some men suddenly took it upon themselves to attack the women. [The authors' use of Scottish dialect has been left intact.][22]

According to Bourgois and Dunlap, who interviewed in Harlem, women on the street endure violence on a daily basis. "Rape is banal. . . . The frequency of these extreme forms of violence leads these women to interpret their abuse as 'nothing' or 'no big thing.'" The researchers concluded that the "low-budget street prostitute scene" undoubtedly attracts violent and sexually perverted clients like this one:[23]

So when I told him I wasn't goin' for it, he pulled out a razor and told me to take off all my clothes. I told me I wasn't doin' nothin' and he cut me in the face, then he started cuttin' my clothes off me, then he put on a condom, then he got what he wanted and he ran, and I called the police.

He had took all my clothes and put them in an incinerator, and I had to walk outside butt naked.[24]

Although we do not know if the men who write comments on the Internet about their experiences with women in prostitution are representative of all the males who patronize women on the streets, among them must surely be some of the hostile men Olivia and others often encountered. Hughes and Raymond quote one man's deliberate humiliation of a woman that is indeed a typical example of Internet statements:

> Once I picked up a lady and we proceeded to an abandoned shell of a house . . . Shortly I asked her to get between her tits w/o the rubber (I had my plans) . . . At just the right moment I leaned way forward and shot my load on her face! Good amount on her lips, cheeks and an eye shot as well! She was suprised [sic] and shocked, this got me more excited than the act. I left her there with nothing to wipe the cum off and her exclaiming to get something. Yeah right![25]

More often than not in these men's writings one encounters such contempt for the women on the street that it is a wonder they continue to flag them down for sex. Obviously their feelings of power, control, and superiority in such encounters are part of the attraction.[26]

Certainly Internet statements suggest a process of dehumanization that might in men's eyes facilitate or justify women's brutalization. Typical examples from the World Sex Guide's archive of comments demonstrate the contempt and cruelty of some of these men:

> Blowjobs should never exceed $20, unless the woman has huge tits, a tiny waist, a reasonable face and a throat you could shove your forearm down. Then $30 could be considered a bargain.[27]

Or:

> Huge tits. not very pretty but makes up for it in talent. Does bbbj to comp, anal and lots of other kinky stuff [water sports etc.] had her on the bed on her back with her head hanging over the side and fucked her mouth and throat . . . was great!![28]

"Chester" says he travels for his job and often for leisure, which puts him in a position to "check out the sex scene in many different cities" and to offer advice for other men in what he calls "Chester's Sex Guide," compiled in 1997. Among other suggestions, he admonishes the men to be extremely cautious with African-American women on the streets of Chicago.

> First, understand that most street prostitutes are in some type of dire straight. It's probably drugs and other problems. . . . Some of these girls have had the shit beat out of them for years, and are so hard and callous that not even Mother Teresa could get through to these girls. . . . I have to tell you that I never pickup black street hookers. I'm not racist, and I've tried. I can tell you that the vast majority of black people are honest, of good character and hard workers. However, the black hookers are not. They tend to always have pimps, who beat the shit out of them if they don't bring in enough money. These girls have had the shit beat out of them most of their lives; and believe me, they could probably kick your ass if it came down to it. [The pimps] manipulate, abuse, and beat these girls so much, they are afraid to leave. . . . They'll get them addicted to crack and/or heroin and these girls will work all night turning tricks . . . just for 20 dollars worth of crack.[29]

Now and then the mask slips, and we get a rare glimpse of the motivations of men who are entrepreneurs in the prostitution industry. In 1999 an American named Sandler added a live bondage sex show to his Web site, operated out of Cambodia, called "Rape Camp," which featured "Asian sex slaves" used for "bondage, discipline and humiliation." The men blindfolded, gagged, and/or bound Vietnamese women with ropes while they were being used in sex acts. Some had clothespins clipped to their breasts. A new feature involved live Internet transmission of the shows with pay-per-view access whereby customers could relay requests for torture that would be fulfilled in seconds.

Sandler explained that no one in Cambodia would see the shows because few there had Internet access. The target audience was the

United States. In an interview with a German newspaper, Sandler stated, "It might promote violence against women in the United States, but I say, 'Good.' I hate those bitches. They're out of line and that's one of the reasons I want to do this. . . . I'm going through a divorce right now. . . . I hate American women."[30]

Such overt hostility raises questions about the men who pay for sex and the reasons for the violence in prostitution. Martin Monto, a leading expert on the customers in prostitution, is certain that the number of men frequenting women and girls in prostitution has been declining over the years. In 1948 Alfred Kinsey estimated that 69 percent of American men had visited women in prostitution at some time in their lives, a figure seen as flawed because it was based on a convenience sample rather than a random or representative one. Benjamin and Masters followed suit with an 80 percent prevalence rate, which experts have found equally questionable. Both reports have helped create the impression, however, that prostitution is an inevitable aspect of modern life.[31]

By contrast, the National Health and Social Life Survey of 1992 (3,432 adults, aged eighteen to fifty-nine, selected from a stratified random sample of households) found that 16 percent of men in the United States had ever visited a woman in the sex trade, and only 0.6 percent claimed to have paid for sex each year. Interestingly, the study determined that men who came of age in the 1990s paid for sex far less frequently than those who came of age in the 1950s (1.5 percent compared with 7 percent).[32]

Information from the First Offender Prostitution Program in San Francisco, which serves arrested customers, suggests that habitual buyers may account for a large share of the demand. More than one-third of the participating men had had five or more encounters with women in prostitution, while more than 10 percent had had between four and fifteen visits within the previous year.[33]

Gauging the extent of prostitution demand by arrest data or by interviewing men picked up for sex trade activities is unlikely to provide an accurate method for determining a representative sample of men buying sex, because so few customers are ever subject to apprehension, and these may be primarily first-time offenders whose inexperience makes them more easily noticeable to the police. In Grand Rapids, Michigan, for example, the number of men arrested in a recent two-year period was 222; yet in a one-day sting operation, seventy men were netted, which may be a more accurate indicator of the number of men seeking to buy sex in a known prostitution area on any given day in that city.[34] Another undercover exercise between the months of January and March 2000 in fifty locations in Detroit resulted in police rounding up 1,400 customers and collecting $1.3 million in fines.[35]

Monto has completed the only major large-scale study of the clients of women in prostitution, interviewing 1,636 of them between 1995 and 1999 in court-sanctioned voluntary diversionary programs. Nearly all had propositioned female police officers posing as women in prostitution in the streets in three cities. In the sample, first-time offenders were mixed with men more frequently involved; 23 percent claimed that the unconsummated sexual proposal for which they were arrested was their only prostitution experience, and another 19 percent stated that they had not visited a woman in the sex trade during the past twelve months.[36] Monto then compared the arrested customers' answers with those from men in two national surveys, finding some interesting results.

In all three samples, customers were evenly distributed across income brackets.[37] Concentrating on the characteristics of nonclients in the national samples and repeat users in his own offender sample, Monto found that marital status emerged as an important discriminator, with repeat offenders less likely to be married, even though they were not younger. Repeat offenders purchased sexually explicit magazines or videos more often than first-time offenders. They were also significantly more likely to have been involved in other parts of the sex trade industry than either group (clients or nonclients) in the national sample, and they were more than twice as apt to have visited nude establishments. Monto concludes that these frequent offenders are individuals "prone to see sexuality as a commodity, something that can be bought and sold," and they may represent those clients who are responsible for most of the violence against girls and women in prostitution.[38]

When Monto asked the offenders a series of questions about their sexual preferences, more than half indicated that they liked to be in control when having sex, they enjoyed being with a woman who likes to get nasty, they were excited by the idea of approaching a woman in the sex trade, and they saw prostitution as positive for women. The frequency of prostitution encounters was strongly associated with these factors.[39]

In a further analysis, Monto and his colleagues explored issues related to power and control over women. Fourteen of the participants (1 percent) reported threatening force in order to get sex, and eleven said they had used force to obtain sex, with eight answering "yes" to both items. Variables that predicted these responses included having more sexual partners and more prostitution contacts over the past year, greater use of pornographic videos, not subscribing to sexually liberal views (sex before marriage, same-sex encounters, etc.), being sexually touched or physically hurt by an adult during childhood, breakup or separation from a partner during the last year, having served in the military, and having levels of sexual desire dissimilar from those of their regular partner.[40]

In addition to the small size of the sample, this research is limited by the fact that many men may be unwilling to admit to violence or may not view their activities as falling within the rubric of "using force to obtain sex." Nevertheless, the small number of violent men in the sample may account for most of the violence against women, as these men buy sex frequently. Prostitution expert Jody Miller agrees. She postulates that the proportion of men overall who seek to sexually assault or degrade women in prostitution because they are viable targets is a constant. If, however, the number of men introduced to sex via prostitution as a social rite of passage has declined, then what we have is a decrease in the proportion of customers with more benign motives for participating in prostitution and a proportionate increase in the number of violent customers.[41] Dennis Altman asks whether the prostitution industry facilitates violence against women because "sex occurs because of a lust for power or revenge or cruelty as often as it is an expression of desire."[42]

In the alternative, most of the men may not subscribe to violent and abusive attitudes. But the very existence of a set of women and girls willing and available to trade sex for money may contribute to violence; males who are not abusive in other venues may be encouraged to behave in these ways because they believe they are paying for the service and the women are agreeing to be victims. The fact that the women are stigmatized "others" whose feelings do not need to be considered may also contribute to the belief that force may be used. Monto wonders whether customers, believing that the women are sexual liberals since they are involved in prostitution, may assume that their partners are open to everything and anything.[43]

One important behavioral theory, the routine activities theory, postulates three prerequisites of crime: the presence of likely offenders motivated to commit the crimes; the absence of effective guardians to prevent the crime; and the availability of suitable targets.[44] When Schwartz and his colleagues tested the theory by studying date rapes on college campuses, they found a correlation between date rape and alcohol, concluding that motivated male offenders view women who drink or consume drugs as suitable targets. Peer social exchanges served then to motivate the men to act in aggressive ways, and the lack of punishment on campuses for this behavior enabled the crimes to occur.[45]

This analysis may usefully be extended to the violence and abuse in prostitution. To be sure, men have been socialized to view women in the sex trade as suitable targets of sexual aggression. Also provocative is the issue of drug and alcohol use; as in campus rape, many women in prostitution are under the influence of drugs or alcohol at the time of the assault. Society's contempt and lack of concern for the women in the sex trade not only encourage likely offenders to make the women their targets, but also means that no one intervenes to support the women or punish the men. All the preconditions for crime have been met.

This inquiry takes us in a different direction, giving us new tools with which to evaluate the sex trade as an industry. Now we see clearly that the sex trade industry creates a permanent supply of suitable targets and even encourages exploitation of them through "anything goes" advertising and the raunchy, misogynist atmosphere deliberately created in today's stripclubs.

The author's earlier question about what kind of men would be attracted to Katrinka—drug-addicted, pregnant, and ill with pneumonia—has surely been answered. Not surprisingly, the most vulnerable girls and women will attract those men who want someone they can control and dominate. Poor, drug-addicted women on the street can meet this need, and, like Olivia, owing to their substance abuse, lack the ability to resist the violence. One male customer caught in a police

sting in Washington, D.C., remarked that, looking back, he should
have known that the woman offering her services for $40 was a cop
because she was too healthy looking.[46] This segment of the prostitution
industry, peopled with so many young, needy women of color, undoubtedly serves as a magnet for male abusers and facilitates the perpe-
tration of violence against women.

CHAPTER SIX

Doped Up

We exclude from our consciousness all sorts of knowledge
that we have acquired because it might distract us from the
problems we must solve if we are to go on living, and it
might even make us doubt whether it is prudent to live. But
sometimes it is necessary for us to know where we are in
eternity as well as in time, and we must lift this ban. Then
we must let our full knowledge invade our minds, and let
our memories of birth crawl like serpents from their core
and our foreknowledge of death spread its wide shadow.

— REBECCA WEST, *Black Lamb and Grey Falcon*

During her years on the streets, Olivia gave birth to three boys. She
never thought much about birth control. Olivia had been sexually active for so many years without getting pregnant that until her first
conception she didn't think that she could. By the time she did, she
was deep into her addiction, which resulted in a kind of adolescent
stage of development that militated against using contraception: pregnancy won't happen to me, she believed.

The two eldest children were heroin babies, who had to be de-
toxed for sixteen days. One was born with pneumonia as a result of
the addiction. Olivia does not know who the fathers of the first two
boys were. Happily, the father of her third son convinced her not to
use heroin during her last pregnancy, but she abused alcohol throughout the nine months. Strych was out of the picture then, serving time

for an armed robbery, but he would be back in Olivia's life soon enough. The new man in her life tried to help her, but she was too far gone by that time. "In his own way he tried to shield me from a whole lot of things," Olivia remembers. "He wasn't abusive. But I took total advantage of his kindness. I would constantly go off and turn my tricks, and then come back."

Although the boys were delivered in major area hospitals, and Olivia's drug tracks were visible, the medical staff there never offered her an opportunity for drug treatment. Olivia hopes this neglect would not be the case today.

Olivia's sister Alta vividly remembers the birth of Olivia's first child. Both their parents were ill—their mother had cancer, and their father was dying. Once Olivia contracted pneumonia, she was not allowed to care for the baby. So Alta ran between three hospitals during those weeks. As soon as she could, Olivia's mother took custody of the oldest child, but Olivia eventually won him back.

Three days after the birth of her second child, Olivia was back on the streets and her mother came to the hospital to feed and care for the baby, who was still undergoing detox. Tanya, their youngest sister, had just died. Alta describes the situation:

> When she had the second one, Olivia was well into her addiction. When I first saw him, he was at the drug pusher's house. He was two months old, had a bottle of sour milk in his mouth, and his diaper was soaked. I saw the condition he was in, lying on the couch by himself, with the bottle propped up with a pillow, with the sour milk smell. I made him a bottle, I changed his diaper, and I looked at him and said, "I'll be back for you." And I did, I went back home to Florida, I worked for two months, made the money to come home, and when I did I asked Olivia if I could take both of the boys, and she said okay.[1]

Alta kept the boys for six months, but then Olivia came and got the kids. She told Alta she had met a man and wanted to take her children to meet his parents. Alta was cooking Christmas dinner for the kids, but Olivia insisted on taking them out. She did not come back with them until about three weeks later. When she returned with the boys, she asked her mother if she could take the children. Her mother said she couldn't—she already had Tanya's two children, four and eight years old at the time. Alta then agreed to take the boys again, but this time she wanted to do it legally. She had no problem obtaining temporary custody when Olivia became pregnant with her third child.

But the following years saw a continual pull and tug over the children. At some point Olivia told the child welfare workers that she did not want the children with Alta, so Alta agreed to release them. A six-month stay in foster care for the boys was the result of this episode, because Olivia was not deemed responsible enough to care for them. Then Olivia's mother agreed to take the children. By this time there were three.

Alta and her mother were always trying to instill in Olivia a sense of responsibility, and so at several times Olivia had the boys, while her mother lied to child welfare and said that Olivia and her children were doing fine. But they weren't fine. The hotel they were staying in caught fire, but they never moved. Alta and her mother found them living in the burned-out shell with ashes underfoot and no electricity. Olivia's mother later became ill again, and Olivia took the boys for another year. Alta looks back on that time:

> I have no idea what all three of those boys witnessed. I do know that they have talked about being hungry and their mom going out to steal food at the local grocery store. I remember her trying to leave them at a railroad track one time and calling me to come and get them.[2]

Finally, Alta decided to move to Wisconsin, and her mother went with her. When Olivia agreed to let the boys stay with them again, they received public assistance for all five children. During this time Olivia continued to disappear for months from the children's lives.

> *I could manage a long weekend, four to five days at most. I would run out there whenever I was beat up really bad, maybe eight times a year, when I was in crisis. It wasn't like I showed up for birthdays or holidays or anything like that. I would be in pretty bad shape. My mother would literally nurse me back to health, and I would be off and running.*

Olivia's mother tried to keep her in Wisconsin. She got her daughter Valium and gave her alcohol to try to overcome her heroin addiction, and she begged and she cried. But after two days, the alcohol and pills could not overcome the urge for dope. Olivia had to have it, but she was ashamed. She would tell her children she was going to the store, and then she would get on the train back to Chicago. And before Olivia rejoined Strych, she would make sure to have some money for his dope, so his violence would not be as bad. That meant turning a few tricks immediately upon her return.

Many times Strych appeared in Wisconsin to drag Olivia back. His violent threats would always persuade her to return: "After a couple of days, I would get pretty scared that Strych was on his way, and I didn't want him to start anything. He used violence to control me."

Alta says that she could not think of any way to help Olivia, now in the throes of deep addiction, with visible, serious marks and injuries. She was tired of the constant fighting with Olivia, who didn't want to listen to anybody or anything, and whose jealousy would not enable her to leave the children with Alta for any length of time.

"My concerns drifted from her to the kids," Alta says. "I sort of gave up on her, and said to her when I saw her, 'I love you, and you deserve better than this.' And that is all I could think to tell her at that point. 'I love you, and you deserve better than this.'"[3]

With Olivia's consent, Alta sued for custody of all three boys. On the day of the court date Olivia changed her mind, but Alta proceeded anyway. Olivia was very angry.

> She said, "What did you say to them to make them give you my kids?" And I told her, I said, you know, "All I said was that you loved them, but you weren't able to take care of them right now. Olivia, it doesn't have to be you or me, it's you *and* me. They have two mothers." And then she seemed to be okay with it. It wasn't long after that that she actually went into treatment. But when she dropped the kids off in mid-December, she took off with the welfare check, leaving me with no money for the children during the month. I really scrambled trying to get Christmas presents, winter coats, and school clothes and supplies for them.[4]

Nothing upsets Olivia more today than the realization of how she put her children at risk through drug addiction and then their abandonment.

> I have a lot of guilt and remorse about some of the choices I made. Some of the things my mother had to witness, some of the neglect of my children, my two children being born drug-addicted. Some of these things that I look at, that I shudder about, that are horrible. I realize that my addiction played a big part in a lot of the worst things that happened. Through recovery I found out that although I can't undo what happened, I am responsible for the person that I choose to be today. I am trying to be the best person I can be, and that means giving back a lot.

Alta says that the boys still get furious today about what they went through.

> They do get angry. They still have memories. I don't think a lot of times that Olivia understands they're angry, because they don't talk about it. They don't want to hurt her. There was a bond, there always has been a bond. They love her. Oh my god, they love her. No matter how a child is treated, if there is a bond, they want their parent, and they wanted her, and they want her today. They love her so much. And I'm glad that they do.[5]

❧

Significant numbers of women in street prostitution, like Olivia, become addicted to drugs and alcohol. Percentages of 92, 95, and 100 are typical.[6] Some women may turn to prostitution to support a preexisting drug habit. Olivia's story illustrates a different scenario in which women and girls already in prostitution turn to or step up drug or alcohol use to help them cope or disassociate while in the sex trade. Once addicted to drugs, they must stay in prostitution in order to support their habit.

Do we know how many women fall within each category? Research studies have found equal numbers for both scenarios, cautioning against a single conclusion. In one sample of 212 female detainees in Manhattan in the mid-1980s, marijuana tended to predate the onset of prostitution, while the use of heroin and cocaine was as likely to precede prostitution as to follow it, and a little less than one-fifth of the respondents said they had started prostitution and heroin or cocaine use at the same time.[7] Researchers with a large sample of female jail detainees in Chicago between 1991 and 1993 concluded that drug abuse was as likely to follow the onset of prostitution as it was to precede it.[8] Sterk identified the same complexities in her sample of 180 women on the streets of Atlanta and New York in the 1990s: 20 percent of the women did not use drugs at all, another 20 percent began using drugs an average of three years after they started work in prostitution, another 20 percent used drugs an average of five years before they began in the sex trade, and another 20 percent began smoking crack and engaging in prostitution simultaneously.[9]

Half of Miller's sample of street women in Columbus, Ohio, began using drugs while in prostitution, while the rest said their drug addiction led them to the sex trade. She cautions, however, that "In some cases, the distinction was difficult to discern; entering 'street life,' especially as a teenager, usually meant participation in both."[10] Indeed, unless researchers ask about the amount and frequency of drugs and alcohol used, they cannot address the issue with any accuracy. Studies that make distinctions between recreational use and regular or addictive drug usage generally find that the majority of the regular or addictive use occurs after prostitution activities have begun.

Pariott, in her study of women active in a broad range of prostitution activities in the Twin Cities area of Minnesota, found, for example, that 38 percent of the sample used heroin, and of these, 69 percent began the use during the time of prostitution, as in Olivia's case. Likewise, 96 percent of the women used crack cocaine, and 78 percent of these began its use during the time of prostitution. When alcohol and marijuana use were measured, almost all the sample used these substances, but only 19 percent had begun alcohol use during sex trade activities and 15 percent had begun smoking marijuana, confirming that for the majority of this sample, use of the heavy drugs began during prostitution, not before.[11]

In a sample of forty-three women in prostitution on the streets in a midsized Midwestern city, 95 percent of whom were addicted to drugs, 53 percent reported recreational drug taking before prostitution entry, but 76 percent said they became regular users following prostitution entry. Thirty-seven percent reported that they had turned to prostitution to support an established drug habit.[12]

Norton-Hawk interviewed a total of 106 women, some serving jail time for a prostitution-related offense and others awaiting trial in a large northeastern city in 1998 and 1999. As teens, the women all had experimented with drugs, with a median age of alcohol and marijuana use at fourteen and cocaine at seventeen. The median age for first paid sex was eighteen, but the median age for heroin use was eighteen and a half, and twenty for cocaine, indicating that serious drug addiction occurred after involvement in prostitution. Norton-Hawk reports that the women addicted to crack cocaine did not enter prostitution to support their drug habit, but rather began drug use once on the streets. Because a crack-induced high lasts only ten to twenty minutes, many customers are necessary to assure a constant supply of the drug. Norton-Hawk found that few of these crack-addicted women ever were involved in stripping or other forms of indoor prostitution.[13] This study corroborates the findings of one study of crack-addicted women, in which they were involved with both other drugs and prostitution before their use of crack. Researchers found that the women turned to crack to increase their confidence and sense of control and to decrease their feelings of guilt and distress. Women in the sample who were involved in the sex trade had more severe levels of addiction to the drugs that helped them cope with the experiences of prostitution.[14]

However, Norton-Hawk discovered that the heroin-addicted women in her sample were more likely to have engaged in an indoor venue of the sex industry, such as stripping or escort services. As their addiction progressed, they, like Olivia, moved to the streets. Norton-Hawk also found that the heroin users in her study were more likely to report coming from seriously dysfunctional families in which they had been physically and sexually abused as teenagers. Heroin-addicted women generally said that the reason they first sold sex was to finance their drug addiction. However, Norton-Hawk found a difference between the heroin abusers who were mostly White and the African-Americans who turned to drugs only after being involved in prostitution.[15]

Women involved in street-level prostitution activities in Chicago stated in a recent survey that they significantly increased their drug and alcohol usage during street prostitution. Almost 59 percent took more kinds of drugs more frequently, and 26 percent used the same drug more often. Only 1 percent used fewer kinds of drugs, and 4 percent reported no change. Of those in prostitution in hotels, almost 10 percent used the same drug less frequently, and 14 percent experienced no change. Women in drug houses reported only increases or stable drug and alcohol use rather than decreases.[16]

One largely unexplored issue is the role that male, drug-addicted partners play in women's entry into the sex trade and drug taking. Thirteen percent of women in prostitution in the Netherlands had been active in the sex trade at some point to finance the addiction of their male partner, to prevent him from committing criminal acts, "for love," or because of varying degrees of pressure. Later they themselves became addicted to hard drugs. In this mixed sample of indoor and outdoor Dutch women in prostitution, those addicted to heroin said street prostitution was the only venue in which heroin addiction was tolerated.[17] Many of the women in prostitution who were intravenous drug users in a Glasgow sample said they were financially supporting their partners' habits through prostitution.[18]

Also unelucidated is the relationship between serious drug addiction and male violence against the women users. El-Bassel and colleagues found that women on the streets in New York were likely to experience more physical abuse from customers if the women used cocaine or injected heroin.[19] Women seriously addicted to drugs may be less able to protect themselves from violent customers or, alternatively, might be targets for violent men who know they will be less likely to resist. Further research on this topic might help us better understand the reasons for the high levels of violence against women in the streets.

The issue of drug addiction in prostitution is also complicated by the fact that women do move from one prostitution activity to another, experiencing different levels of abuse and addiction. For example, Sterk found that one-fourth of the women in her Atlanta and New York samples experienced mobility during prostitution activities, with most having moved from escort services or clubs to the streets. In an e-mail exchange, Sterk explained:

I tend to think that the issue of downward mobility receives little attention because it is somehow easier for society to deal with women whom they see as already "low"—it fits with the paradigm of blaming women. Often the downward mobility happened slowly and very often the women did not realize this was happening to them until it was too late. It is also a world in which once you start sliding down, there is no way up. A true slippery slope.[20]

Similar trajectories surfaced in a recent Chicago study. The majority of the women in the sample had participated in more than one prostitution activity, and the total number of activities in which each respondent had been involved ranged from one to fourteen, with a mean of 2.69.[21] Of the twenty women who began with exotic dancing, 75 percent progressed to other sex trade venues, and close to half of these involved outdoor prostitution—mostly streets, survival sex, drug houses, and hotels. In the small group of women who began in escort services, 39 percent began solely there, with the remainder combining escort services with streets, exotic dancing, and others. Thirty-eight percent of these escort service women moved to other activities, 63 percent of which were outside—streets, drug houses, and truck stops.[22]

Of the seventy-seven women in the sample whose first activity included street prostitution, only 39 percent were involved solely on the streets. The remainder of the women in this group participated in the full range of sex trade venues about which researchers inquired, and 14 percent engaged in them simultaneously with street prostitution. Where did the women who progressed end up? Less than one-third were to be found outside, mostly in drug houses. The other 69 percent graduated to indoor sectors, primarily escort services, exotic dancing, pornography, and parties.[23]

Two hundred and fifty women in Los Angeles were involved in 470 prostitution activities, while even higher numbers of women in the Los Angeles jail indicated they had participated in more than one; since women in the jail sample had been, on average, involved in the sex trade for a higher number of years, they might have, like Olivia, started in other prostitution venues before hitting the streets.[24] A majority of the women in a Victoria, B.C., study had been involved in more than one venue, sometimes moving from outdoors to indoors and other times the reverse, leading the researchers to conclude, "The fluidity of movement across venues reported by our respondents suggests that the distinction between indoor and outdoor sex work is not as clear-cut as previous research suggests."[25] In another British Columbia sample, 38 percent of those currently active in prostitution had participated in two different venues, while 35 percent had been active in three or more. Involvement in two different activities concurrently was not unusual.[26]

These trajectories caution against simplistic analyses of prostitution patterns. Considerable movement from one prostitution venue to another, as well as many simultaneous activities, appear to be typical. Women may not experience violence or drug addiction in the sex trade sector in which they began, but may be subjected to violence in the second or third sector. Characterizations of violence or addiction in the sex trade industry are difficult to make unless women's movements across venues are taken into account.

Our perceptions of drug addiction among women in prostitution in the streets also affect our views of the extent of pimp involvement in prostitution. Frequently the assertion is made that pimps no longer control the business to the extent that they did previously, insofar as the crack pipe or crack dealer has replaced the pimp. Drug-addicted women, this argument goes, are less reliable sources of income for pimps, intent as they are to take the money to purchase crack, or content to trade sex for it.[27] This observation and the many published research studies on which it is based relate to an earlier drug scene dominated by crack cocaine, when now crack is no longer as large a factor as it once was on our urban streets.[28] Current research with women in the sex trade reveals a much more complex picture, indicating that the industry still relies substantially on pimps, and that adolescent girls are most likely to have entered prostitution through the offices of a male serving the pimp function.

Estes and Weiner recently determined that 52 percent of juveniles involved in prostitution on the street had a pimp, most of whom managed one to three girls at a time. At least 50 percent operated strictly at the local level and were not part of larger criminal organizations. Approximately 25 percent of the pimps were part of citywide crime rings, about 15 percent were part of regional or nationwide networks, and approximately 10 percent were said to be involved in international sex crime associations. Youth older than twelve years of age were said to be prime targets for same-sex peers, who recruit them with money and drugs for organized crime.[29]

According to law enforcement agents in New York City, the average age of pimps of juvenile girls is eighteen to twenty years, said to represent a decrease in age, as young men purportedly view pimping as being more lucrative and less risky than selling drugs. Over the last few years, special task forces in Brooklyn and Queens have arrested as many as thirty-two suspected pimps. Girls in youth shelters and group homes are special targets of the pimps, who use their own girls to recruit others, rewarding them with luxury incentives.[30] Sterk found that all 180 women in her street sample had been involved with male partners of some kind or other, most of whom were unwilling to relinquish them or the money they earned. Many of the women failed to realize the difficulty of leaving the relationship until they tried to do so.[31]

Norton-Hawk reported that 40 percent of her sample of fifty women in street prostitution had been controlled by a pimp, the same figure cited in a sample of street women in a midsize Midwestern city. Of these, 80 percent turned over all the money they made on the streets to these men.[32] She found that women whose parents were divorced, separated, or addicted to drugs, or who themselves had run away from home, were significantly more likely to have a pimp, "suggesting that psychological wounds from childhood made living in a 'family' run by a pimp attractive." In her research sample, women controlled by pimps were significantly more likely to have exchanged sex for money on a regular basis by the age of eighteen than women who had never had a pimp.[33]

Twenty-seven percent of the women in the Los Angeles jail survey reported they had had a relationship with a pimp.[34] Miller states that the women's relationships with drug dealers and/or hustling partners in her Midwestern research "revealed many of the patterns that have been found to exist in prostitute/pimp relationships."[35] And only 16 percent of Raymond and Hughes's sample of U.S. women said they had no pimp; 28 percent of these women explained that their husbands or boyfriends acted as pimps.[36]

Persons serving the pimp function were an important factor in many women's lives, regardless of the prostitution venue, in the Chicago survey. The questionnaire asked whether the women, when involved in a specific prostitution activity, gave a percentage of the money they made to someone else. Using this definition, 41 percent of all women involved in street prostitution said they had a pimp, corroborating other studies. Of these, 75 percent stated they would have been subject to physical harm if they were to stop giving money to this person. Fifty percent of the women involved in escort services said they were involved with a pimp, and 77 percent of these stated that they would face harm or threats if they ceased to cooperate.[37]

Pimp involvement in exotic dancing was lower, but surprisingly high: 24 percent, with 75 percent of these women saying they risked harm if they broke off the relationship. One-quarter of those women operating out of their own private residence were involved with a pimp, and of these, 83 percent stated they would face harm or threats if they ended the relationship. Forty-four percent of women in drug houses stated they had a pimp, and 80 percent of these feared harm. Thirty-three percent of women in hotels reported having pimps, and 57 percent of these faced harm or threats.[38]

Women in the streets, in hotels, escort services, exotic dancing, and drug houses in Chicago all reported violence from pimps in significant numbers. Those in escort services and hotels reported the highest percentages of pimp-related violence; women in escort services identified pimps as perpetrating up to half the violence against them, as did women in hotels. Many of the women on the streets and in drug houses also reported experiencing violence from pimps.[39]

In a sample of 800 participants from the Portland, Oregon, Council for Prostitution Alternatives, 85 percent had experienced rapes, 95 percent assaults, and 77 percent kidnappings at the hands of a pimp. The average number of beatings at the hands of pimps was a staggering fifty-eight.[40] Over half of the U.S. women in the Hughes and Raymond study described frequent, sometimes daily, physical assaults from pimps.[41]

A significant percentage of North American prostitution may well remain pimp-controlled, regardless of how the women may want to characterize the relationship. Celia Williamson believes that the involvement of pimps in the sex trade is grossly understated in research because of methodology limitations. She suggests that those under the control of pimps are unable to stop and speak safely with researchers, with the result that the more independent women are more likely to be accessible for study purposes. Crack cocaine–addicted women, argues Williamson, usually among those not controlled by a pimp, are also more visible to researchers because they need to be back out on the streets more frequently to fuel their drug habit. "By disproportionately finding and interviewing women who are drug dependent and not involved with a pimp, researchers imply that street level prostitution is made up of women who are independent workers and addicted to crack cocaine."[42]

Interviewing one pimp and six women who were involved in pimp-controlled prostitution, Williamson confirms a reeling-in process that involves love, money, and flattery. Pimps told the women they were beautiful, that many men wanted them, and that they would pay money for them:

> Although pimps never guaranteed emotional or financial security, the potential for success inspired women to test the waters in this new life. There was a sense of belonging that women longed for, a sense of exciting hope for the future, an adventure that would take them from their meager existence into a life with a man that told them they had special skills, intelligence and beauty. In return for his attention, protection, and love, she would be required to work to bring their dream into reality.[43]

The many instances of violence pimps perpetrate against women demonstrate methods of control that can only be described as brutal. As in domestic violence, the situation is marked by a mixture of love and fear. Physical abuse often results from violations of pimp-imposed rules, but often it is unpredictable, intended to remind a woman of the pimp's capacity for violence to ensure that she would follow his rules:

> One day he came to my motel room to beat my ass. And made it clear that he came over to beat on me. He said he had some extra time on his hands, that he didn't have anything to do, so he wanted me to know that he knew I was thinking about doing something stupid. And I was too. I was thinking about leaving him again. The last time I left

him, I ended up in Cleveland. . . . He beat me until I blacked
out. . . .[44]

Pimps themselves are only too happy to confirm their successful techniques. Eskimo, a San Francisco–based operator, explained how he
does it: "A 14-year-old that's hopelessly in love with you. There's
nothing she won't do for you. It's brainwashing, really."[45]

And consider the chilling words of a pimp interviewed in the 1998
HBO documentary *Pimps Up, Ho's Down*:

> You tell a chick that you are going to kill her, she's going
> to try to see if you going to kill her, she gonna bring some-
> thing up, she gonna do something to get your attention in
> that area. And when you whup her, you got to whup her
> like you're trying to kill her to convince her that she should
> be dead when she beg you, "Daddy, please don't kill me
> like you said you were going to do, I won't do it no more."
> Because they going to test you, man, and whatever you said
> out your mouth, they going to make sure you stand by that,
> otherwise you ain't gonna be a good pimp.[46]

As in domestic violence, this deliberate pattern of random violence
makes escape difficult. Stories of flight can be dramatic. One woman
told Williamson that after working four tricks, she jumped into a taxi
to the train station and confided in an Amtrak police officer there. She
was anxious, knowing that her pimp would be looking for her. Luckily
the Amtrak officer responded positively and allowed her to sit in his
office. Eventually, he gave her some money and paid the cab driver to
take her to the airport, from where she was able to fly home.[47]

Of special interest is Alexa Albert's research in the legal Mustang
Ranch brothel in Nevada. Although historically all women in licensed
brothels in Nevada were required to have pimps, Albert learned this is
no longer the case. To her astonishment she found that all the women
at Mustang Ranch had pimps. The brothel took half the women's earnings, with the rest given to their pimps, whom most called their "boyfriend" or "friend." Since the women, being off the unsafe streets, did
not appear to require protection, Albert wondered why they needed

these men. At first she blamed the women for emotional dependence on them:

> The brothels functioned as stand-in pimps. Most of the women had portrayed themselves as tough and independent-minded women who viewed prostitution simply as a job, a way to earn a living. I hadn't detected any signs of coercion. And I had never heard any of the women talking about pimps.
>
> Brittany [a woman in prostitution at the ranch whom she was interviewing] wasn't surprised to learn this. None of the women would've wanted to admit aloud to being exploited, to giving up their hard-earned money to a man when the brothel already extracted half the earnings. Moreover, Brittany said, most of these women denied that their pimps *were* pimps, considering them 'boyfriends" and "friends."[48]

Ultimately, however, Albert came to understand that only by means of pimps could the Nevada brothel industry assure itself of a steady supply of women. She also found that law enforcement officials in Oregon estimated that pimps in the Eugene–Springfield area had more than forty women in Nevada's brothels, regularly sending thousands of dollars back home.[49]

One expert who assists women in prostitution also believes that brothel arrangements are completely pimp-controlled: "Brothels do not run employment ads. The brothel owners require that any new 'employee' be referred by someone ready to supply whatever force is necessary to control the woman."[50]

Taken altogether, the data suggest that girls in the United States are most prone to enter the sex trade through deception, blandishment, or coercion—important because the majority of U.S. women in prostitution begin during their teen years. Since vulnerable teens are frequently the desired partners of men buying sex, they become the targets of pimps. Certainly, the girls' age and neediness make them less able to resist violence and easier for pimps and customers to control.

Although Olivia did not begin in prostitution because of a pimp, her involvement with Strych, a dangerous abuser living off her earnings, severely restricted her ability to leave prostitution.

CHAPTER SEVEN

Trapped

The working woman, whom childbearing and continual
drudgery have made a bruised and withered thing at forty-
five, feels herself an offence against beauty and life. She is
too weak, too tired to shift the blame to those who ought
to bear it, and feels humiliated.

— REBECCA WEST, "Battle-Ax and Scalping Knife"

To survive street prostitution, Olivia had to maintain a sense of power
and control within the situation.

> I didn't like what I did with these men, but now I know it is
> what they did to me. I did not like what these men did to me,
> but I had to internalize it that way, because that gave me that
> false sense of power and control. I allowed them to do this to
> me so I could get their money. Otherwise I would be crazy, I
> would have killed myself out of disgust and self-hatred. But
> having that false sense that I was in control of this, and I let
> them do that to me because they paid me for it, gave me some
> sense of power.

Because of her need to assert some sense of control, Olivia attempted
to seize power in ways that made her life even more dangerous than it
already was. She began, for example, to try to take advantage of cus-

tomers by robbing them or by agreeing to physically abuse them but
doing it with a vengeance.

> *I had gotten so tired and angry that I found myself taking*
> *advantage of every opportunity that I could to take out my*
> *hatred of what had been done to me, if not by him, then by*
> *some other guy. The longer I did it, the worse my hatred and*
> *contempt became. I was able to steal from them because they*
> *weren't people, they were animals. It was like a retaliation. I*
> *wonder how I survived it, I really do.*

Olivia's life on the streets was made more difficult by the actions of
the police. They could randomly stop her, even when she was just on
the way to the store. Others would pick her up, drive over to the beach
and demand oral sex in exchange for not arresting her. Two officers on
the North Side were known to take women, push them out of cars,
and leave them at the lake. That happened to Olivia once when, to
avoid arrest, she gave a blow job and the police officer then laughed
and threw her out of the car, saying "Get back the best way you can,
slut."

"You are scared to death," Olivia remembers. "You don't know
which cop is going to pick you up, you don't know whether you will
be taken straight to jail, or whether you will be propositioned to do
something else, or whether you'll be beaten."

Olivia was submissive because she never had the energy to resist
arrest. In the lockup she could hear officers making derogatory comments about the arrested women in the sex trade, some to their faces
and others loudly enough to be heard. Police always treated the women
in prostitution worse than other women in the lockup. At that time,
female officers often forced the women to squat and subjected them to
total strip searches that were intrusive and horrific.

Nor would Olivia ever think about going to the police if she had
been raped or badly beaten by a customer: "The response would have
been: 'you got what you had coming.' You would never report anything. You would get laughed at, and you'd be revictimized."

In November 2001 Olivia visited the headquarters of the Chicago
Police Department and paid $16 to obtain a printout of her arrest rec-

ord. The six-page document listed sixty-six arrests in a seventeen-year period between 1973 and 1990. As Olivia had remembered, her first arrest had occurred when she was eighteen years old and at the Rush Street club. Police took in six or eight of the girls, but the club owner came and got them released without being charged. In later years, no one came to bail her out after arrest, not even Strych. "Strych was always in the background," Olivia says. "As soon as I came back from a date, he had the money, but he wasn't going to spend good money to get me out of jail. They lure women to think they'll protect you if something happens. He would let me sit in jail."

With the exception of four arrests for retail theft, Olivia's arrests were strictly for prostitution-related offenses. According to the arrest record, judges usually released her for time served after about two days, a short period of time and one that does not provide much opportunity for social service intervention. A few longer terms from five to seventeen days occurred, with one stretch of four-and-a-half months. If Olivia served time for more than a week, during the first ten days she would be sick to the point that she could hardly move. Nothing was done for her medically. Nor were there any interventions during any of the arrests. No one ever said, "Aren't you tired of this? Here are some options for you." Olivia doesn't recall anyone telling her that she should change her life.

> I would come out of jail, and most of the time I would try to
> catch a trick right there on 26th Street. The whole cycle starts
> over again. It is a hopeless life, you don't see anything else,
> going to jail becomes just a part of it, it is just about how long
> you are going to wind up there. It would cross my mind in jail:
> my god, I should go up to Wisconsin, I should go up there this
> time when I get out and really try to do something different and
> that thought just goes out the window when you know you are
> headed out the door.

Olivia's arrest record mirrors the trajectory of her history in the sex trade. Toward the end, when she was exclusively on the streets in prostitution and more visible, the number of yearly arrests increased. In 1990, for example, her last year on the streets, there were ten arrests in eight months. Interestingly enough, the record also reveals that Olivia often interacted with the same judges, who made no attempt to intervene in her life. Between 1978 and 1981, she appeared nine times before one judge, and in 1990, five times before another.

After one of these judges told Olivia he did not want to see her before him again, she asked for a change of venue on the occasion of her next arrest. But her request backfired. Olivia's case was assigned to the northern suburbs, where ultimately the judge exercised his discretion and upgraded her charge to a felony with four-and-a-half months of jail time.

During all this time only two policemen really tried to help Olivia:

> I can say that most of the time when I was picked up I was also beaten up, and it wasn't by a trick. They knew it, because they knew the pimp I was with. A couple of them did try. They picked me up, put me in a squad car, and acted like they were arresting me for prostitution. They would just drive around and talk to me. Aren't you tired of being here? That guy's going to kill you. Then they would drop me off. It made no impact. I was too strung out—the fear of not being able to get drugs, or not having the money. It fell on deaf ears. I look back on it now, and I wonder if they would really have tried to help me if I had picked up on it.

While on the street Olivia was in a constant state of hyperarousal that has left lasting physical damage. She agrees wholeheartedly with researcher Melissa Farley's statement that many women in prostitution are "on accelerator" all the time, with the foot on the gas pedal pressed to the car floor.[1]

Several times Olivia just couldn't take it any more. One time she was on the street with Strych and for some reason was having difficulty picking up tricks. Strych began yelling at her and hit her several times. Olivia started pretending to be mentally ill. She went to a nearby hospital emergency room and screamed nonstop. The staff ended up keeping her in the psych unit overnight, but no one talked to her about drug treatment or provided her with a referral.

> There were a couple of other times. I would just be so tired. I remember walking into a hospital and saying that if they didn't

keep me, I was going to kill myself. *Again, they let me see a*
psychiatrist who kept me for stabilization for something like
three days, and that was it. Between the Librium or Valium and
whatever else they gave me, I didn't get drug sick right away. I
was so tired. I slept. And after I rested up a couple of days, I
was right back out on the street. It just shows you how hospitals
fail. Either they didn't care because I didn't have insurance, or
they weren't real sure of what to do with me. You are talking
about people that nobody wants anything to do with. And people
still believe that these people could stop if they wanted to. It's
probably a lack of training and overwork.

Olivia had reached "ground zero," the end stage.

Such a subhuman way to live. I was so tired. I was so totally
abused. I was in such bad shape. I felt nothing. I cared about
nothing. I was a walking zombie.
    I have to believe that God had a greater purpose for me,
that my life's purpose was to go through to where I am today.
It is a miracle to be delivered safely through it. I should be
dead, and I know it.

∽

Olivia's enormous number of prostitution arrests is not unusual. When
fifty women incarcerated for prostitution were interviewed in a large
northeastern American city, almost two-thirds (64 percent) said they
had been arrested five or more times. Quite a few reported as many as
eighty to one hundred arrests. Forty-three percent had been eighteen
years or younger at the time of their first arrest. Almost all had been
involved in prostitution for more than a decade.[2]
    Researcher Norton-Hawk firmly believes that trying to avoid jail
forces women on the streets to stay out of the public eye, increasing
their chances of customers victimizing them. Nor does jail provide
women with new insights, but instead confirms them in their chosen
way. For example, while in jail one woman Norton-Hawk observed
actively solicited new employees for her pimp by approaching fellow
inmates, including those not serving time for prostitution-related offenses. "Jail is not a path away from their deviant lifestyle, but a place

where the techniques of prostitution and the rationalizations for remaining in that life are reinforced," Norton-Hawk concludes.[3]

Seventy-four percent of the 212 women answering in a Chicago survey had been arrested, and almost 37 percent of the women had first been brought to the police station on prostitution-related charges. Significantly, 48 percent had arrived for the first time between the ages of eleven and eighteen years of age; the mean age of the first arrest was 18.5.[4] As almost a majority had been arrested on prostitution-related offenses as minors, would some of the women have been able to avoid further years of prostitution and substance abuse activity if the criminal justice system had responded with a helpful social service intervention?

Women in prostitution surveyed in the Cook County Jail had higher rates of detention that those in the larger sample who were not regularly involved in the sex trade. Although 13 percent of the sample as a whole had been detained more than six times, 42 percent of the women in prostitution had.[5] In a Los Angeles jail sample of seventy-nine women, there were 408 total arrests, an average of almost six per woman.[6] And in a sample of fifty-three women in a county work release center in Florida serving time on prostitution-related charges, the mean number of episodes of prostitution was 487 in the past year, while the mean number of arrests was 1.59.[7]

In 2000, two thousand women served time for prostitution-related offenses in the Cook County (Chicago) Jail, or about 9 percent of the total female jail population. County officials caution, however, that more women in prostitution may be in the jail but charged with other offenses such as drug possession.[8]

These numbers are high enough to occasion fairly large municipal costs. In a 1985 study of the sixteen largest U.S. cities, after estimating the number of hours officials (police, judicial, and corrections) spent for each prostitution arrest, researchers calculated that the average cost of enforcing prostitution laws was $7.5 million per city, with a total expenditure of $120 million. Of this figure, $53 million was spent on direct police costs, $35 million on judicial personnel, and $31 million on correctional expenses. Half the cities spent more on control of the sex trade than on either education or public welfare.[9] A San Francisco report calculated police, incarceration, and jail costs at $7.6 million annually for approximately 5,000 prostitution-related arrests.[10] And the Mary Magdalene Project estimates annual jail costs for prostitution-related arrests in Los Angeles County at $7,210,680.[11]

Research also corroborates women's stories of police harassment. Fifty-two percent of Norton-Hawk's jail sample said they had provided sexual services to a police officer. Some stated that they had police personnel as regular customers, but other police officers threatened arrest if the women did not provide free sex. On the other hand, some officers looked the other way or even tried to provide assistance to the women. This unpredictable police response contributes to the oppressive atmosphere in which the women operate.[12]

Of those women on the street in the Chicago study who were called abusive names, almost 53 percent indicated that police officers were the perpetrators; 27 percent of those forced to masturbate a man recalled that he was a police officer; 18 percent of those who had had a man expose his penis and 19 percent of those who had had men rub their penises on them said that the men were police officials. Significant percentages of exotic dancers and women in escort services also reported forced sexual acts from police officers.[13]

Women who traded sex for survival items such as housing or food (not for money) appear to be the group in the sample most often victims of police abuse. Thirty-three percent of those forced to masturbate men reported that police officers were involved; thirty percent of those whose vaginas were grabbed said that police had perpetrated these acts; and 20 percent of those who were robbed claimed law enforcement personnel were the perpetrators.[14] The Canadian National Juvenile Prostitution Survey reported that 21 percent of males and 18.6 percent of female teens involved in the sex trade industry had suffered beatings and other forms of abuse at the hands of police.[15]

As she interviewed women on the streets, Claire Sterk observed frightening actions by police officers:

> Police sweeps are a frequently occurring event on prostitution strolls. Typically, a police bus pulls up, and the police arrest all the women whom they can snare. On one of my first nights on the streets, I barely escaped an arrest because nobody warned me, nor did I realize that the police were coming. I believe that my university ID and my nervous, quick chatter allowed me to go free. This event, however,

helped me understand the harassment encountered by the women I interviewed. The women are booked and usually charged with time served. Moreover, the booking process also includes demeaning body searches during which a woman has to undress completely, squat ten times in a row, and bend over for an anal examination, all the while listening to derogatory comments.[16]

A woman employed by an escort service described what had happened during an undercover raid in Chicago. At the police station, one officer remarked, "I can get what you give for ten bucks down on North Avenue." Another commented, "Brutality is the fun part of this job." The young woman claimed she was not fed for twenty-four hours.[17]

Most women and girls in prostitution do not report customer violence to the police because they know the officers will not take them seriously. Women in the sex trade on the streets told researcher Jody Miller that, although they did not expect the police to follow through on an individual complaint, they would report an especially menacing man in the hope that law enforcement would run the man off so that further violence could be avoided.[18]

Linda Fairstein, a former Manhattan sex crimes prosecutor, has written that in a southern California community in 1991, police dealt with all rape reports from women in prostitution by placing them in a closed case file marked "NHI–No Human Involved."[19] Undoubtedly, wrote Fairstein, the lack of police and prosecutor response encourages violent men to believe that they may do with women in prostitution what they will, since the women "live outside the law." The cases that Fairstein has prosecuted involving women in the sex trade led her to comment that:

> prostitutes are victims of rapists whose motives are degradation and humiliation, control and possession, anger and hatred, intimidation and terrorization. These women desperately need the protection of the law and yet are too frequently denied access to the system of justice.[20]

◈

The hardest question to answer is this: why do Olivia and other women like her stay in street prostitution? Since she had hit rock bottom, why didn't Olivia just get out? Part of what traps women in prostitution is their own rationalization of their activities. As in domestic violence, the survival or coping mechanism ends up becoming a trapping mechanism. Today, Olivia struggles to describe her state of mind in the late 1980s:

> When you are in it, that is your only sanity; your only lifeline to reality is to accept it and say that it is not as bad as people think. I said it too many times for too many years, and I glamorized that, such an easy way to make a living, people were crazy for working eight hours a day. It wasn't just the chemicals. I thoroughly convinced myself to avoid committing suicide.

Rabinovitch and Strega, who work with the PEERS group in Victoria, B.C., directly acknowledge the contradiction:

> Sex trade workers are also reluctant to share accurate information about their experiences with service providers because they manage to stay in "the life" in part by dissociating from and denying their negative experiences and thus distancing themselves from the stigma associated with sex trade work. The ability to simultaneously acknowledge the danger and degradation of the work, and see it as a source of power and self-esteem, is difficult for service providers to comprehend.[21]

Olivia admits that she found some self-esteem in succeeding within the narrow and dangerous milieu in which she found herself. In her own world, she was a success.

> I would turn the dates, get the money, buy my own drugs, not be sick. It gave me a false sense of power. Being on the streets, I was part of that culture. I wanted to be the best at what I was doing. I was trapped. I became part of the environment, and I made the most of it at the time.

Researcher Sterk has also observed this phenomenon: "They became serious about recruiting customers, avoiding arrest by the police, seeking protection from the dangers of the street, and determining the prices of sexual services."[22] As one young woman in prostitution touchingly told researcher Leon Pettiway: "I wish I hadn't prostituted, you know. It's degrading. I can't go back. I did it. I have to live with it. Simple as that. So I'm not happy about doing prostitution, but like anything I do, I do my best."[23]

Since many women in prostitution, like Olivia, simply have never done anything else, the notion of escape from one thing to something else is meaningless. When this author asked Brenda Myers, a Chicago survivor of twenty-five years of prostitution, why she had not quit earlier, she faced her questioner with disbelief: "Leave for what? When we leave, where do we go to start over? I wanted to stop, but how do I?"[24] For many of us it is fundamentally inconceivable to imagine that level of existence.

Pimps, like batterers, it is important to remember, intentionally keep girls and women in the sex trade isolated from the rest of the world, which reinforces the idea that there is no going back. One prostitution survivor has described a two-year period when she lived in a medium-sized city and had no contact at all with anyone outside the sex trade.[25]

For another thing, the stress of Olivia's daily life, with Strych's batterings violence from customers and the police, and her heroin addiction, gradually caused her mind to cease to work.

> You get so caught up in the cycle of surviving—get the money,
> get the drugs, pay for a room—that it doesn't dawn on you to
> look for a way out. My world had become so small. I didn't
> even know that a place for detox existed. If it wasn't part of
> those few little blocks that I traveled in, it simply didn't exist.
> Your mind shuts down, day in, day out, if this is all you have
> done, that is all you think about doing.

Auschwitz survivor Primo Levi describes how, when the body is under severe stress, its thinking mechanism shuts down. He writes: "In the lager [concentration camp] it is useless to think, because events happen for the most part in an unforeseeable manner; and it is harmful, because it keeps alive a sensitivity which is a source of pain, and which some providential natural law dulls when suffering passes a certain limit."[26] As liberation approached, Levi's former sensibilities had not yet returned: "I had no longer felt any pain, joy or fear, except in that detached and distant manner characteristic of the lager, which might be described as conditional: if I still had my former sensitivity, I thought, this would be an extremely moving moment."[27]

In the end, the violence had its intended effect: Olivia had internalized all the messages and accepted them.

> I was content at being a prostitute and a whore. I thought I was just destined, that was it. I was a dope fiend, and that was how I was going to die. I had become okay with that.
>
> I thought there was no way out. I was so sick of it, but I didn't know any way out. It had gotten to the point that I was really sick and tired of living the way I was living. I prayed sometimes that when I injected drugs it would be the last time, or I would put myself in positions, either with tricks, trying to pick their pockets, or jumping into cars that other girls had said be careful of, that guy doesn't look right, or put myself in situations where someone else could kill me. I was just that tired of it, I didn't care. You lose all hope.

And that loss of hope further narrowed Olivia's world. Her shame served to isolate her even further from persons and institutions that could help her.

> I was a dope addict. I had no second guessing that that was what I had become. I lived to shoot dope, and I needed dope to live. I knew it, my body cried out for it if I didn't have it. I did feel that was the lowest you could be in life. I had a strong sense of that. Was I embarrassed about it? Yes. Was I ashamed of it? Yes. I know that is why I stayed away from my family. I know that is why I stayed away from any interaction with anybody other than people who were doing the same thing.

Writer Barbara Ehrenreich witnessed the same internalization of abuse when she temporarily became a blue-collar worker. She was astounded at the physical severity of the work and the degrading treatment employers meted out. Not only did motel housekeepers have to clean

guests' pubic hair out of bathtubs for minimum wage, but their supervisors also treated them with contempt as they did it. Why didn't they
fight back? Ehrenreich concludes:

> As much as any other social animal, and more so than
> many, we depend for our self-image on the humans imme-
> diately around us—to the point of altering our perceptions
> of the world so as to fit in with theirs. My guess is that the
> indignities imposed on so many low-wage workers—the
> drug tests, the constant surveillance, being "reamed out"
> by managers—are part of what keeps wages low. If you're
> made to feel unworthy enough, you may come to think
> that what you're paid is what you are actually worth.[28]

Olivia explains that her own view of herself as a woman in prostitution, and the shame of what she allowed others to do to her, effectively
maintained her in the sex trade under the most degrading circumstances. This is a kind of colonization that keeps people in their place
because they start believing what their oppressors say about them. Successfully colonized people "believe the dominant ideological myths
about their collective being, act accordingly, and often collaborate in
their own oppression."[29] In short, Olivia could not stand up for herself
when she was crippled by such shame and self-hatred.

One way to cope with a loss of power is to accede to the conditions
of enslavement and to seek to survive within these narrow confine-
ments. Describing the conditions in which women and children in the
sex trade existed in Cambodia, Physicians for Human Rights wrote in
a recent study:

> At some point in the process, the young woman becomes
> submissive in order to avoid further beatings and torment;
> her "spirit is broken." She surrenders, becomes resigned
> and accommodates to the circumstances of captivity. Au-
> tonomy, self-agency, control or influence over one's fate
> are no longer possible. . . . As people find the best way to
> survive, some of the behaviors may raise questions if
> viewed out of context. For example, the young women's
> flirtatiousness, seeking out clients, and getting clients to feel

pity or love for them represent strategies aimed at enhanc-
ing their survival. If they accept customers they will not be
beaten.[30]

Colonization is an apt construct, because Olivia believes that her race
and that of many of the women and girls in prostitution serves to trap
them in the prostitution lifestyle. Olivia says this is the case because as
a Black woman she has always been subjected to sexual stereotypes,
and it is difficult to avoid actually acting them out.

> The stereotypes destroy your self-esteem and self-image. It is
> difficult not to internalize the differences. And if you're acting
> in that manner, it kind of doubles the impact it has on you.
> You have to do esteemable things and recognize that no one on
> the outside has any real impact on your own self-esteem. Your
> self-esteem is simply the reputation you have with yourself.

The racial stereotype to which Olivia refers is the jezebel or bad Black
girl—the hypersexual Black female who yearns for sexual encounters.
Scholars believe that the jezebel image originated with slave owners
who were looking for an excuse to hide their interest in female slaves.
The masters, who privately coerced their female slaves, offering them
harsh alternatives if they were unwilling to submit to their sexual
whims, publicly attributed these liaisons to the hypersexuality of the
female slave, who was purported to be the aggressor or seducer.[31]

A jezebel is defined as a whore: sexually aggressive, promiscuous,
and easily aroused. In every way she is the reverse image of the mid–
nineteenth-century ideal of the White Victorian lady.[32] Biracial women
like Olivia can attract customers because their European features make
them attractive to White men, while their bronze skin marks them as
stereotypically hypersexual.[33] Adult entertainment advertisements feature multiple examples of the jezebel stereotype, such as one that describes a biracial woman as a "Black, kinky Panther," and another that
reads, "I am your bronze goddess. I am as exotic as my roots." A
message from another potential escort trades on the stereotype: "Hello,
I'm one of Chicago's most finest, famous, deep dark, chocolate, sexy
scorpios. I'm full of that hot ebony passion, fulfilling that desire that
you've only dreamed about."[34]

Although White men initially promoted the jezebel stereotype, it appears to have spread to and found acceptance in the Black community as well. Almost half of African-American men surveyed in a recent research study endorsed the jezebel typecasting, attributed in part to the fact that this image of African-American women has permeated to all sections of society through the popular media. Belief in the stereotype was, in the survey, related to the men's justification of domestic violence. The researchers surmise that men may feel more justified in using physical force to keep women from behaving in the sexually promiscuous ways of the label. Stereotypes, concluded the researchers, influence power dynamics in personal interactions, pointing up the need for self-reflection and education of members of the African-American community: "Men, women, and children need to be educated regarding the historical origins of these stereotypes, their manifestations in contemporary society, how the African-American community itself helps to perpetuate them, and how they negatively affect relationships between African-American men and women."[35]

Prostitution survivors Vednita Carter and Evelina Giobbe believe that African-American girls in poor neighborhoods are especially vulnerable to prostitution because of the power of this racial stereotype in these communities. The double bind of racism and poverty, they write, gives Black teens fewer and more constricted choices:

> Poor, Black communities have become de facto combat zones where street prostitution is highly visible and readily available. The implicit message to white men is that it is all right to solicit Black women and girls for sex, that we are all prostitutes. On almost any night, you can see them slowly cruising our neighborhoods, rolling down their windows, calling out to women and girls. The message to Black women is equally clear: this is who it is, this is who we are, this is what we're for. With all the negative images and labels ascribed to Black women, it is no surprise that many of us remain confused about who we really are and who we want to be.[36]

Patricia Hill Collins describes how the jezebel stereotype contributes to the perception that all Black women are interested in selling sex:

When the "white boys from Long Island" look at Black women and all they think about is sex, they believe that they can appropriate Black women's bodies. When they yell, "Bet you know where there's a good time tonight," they expect commodified sex with Black women as "animals" to be better than sex with White women as "objects." Both pornography and prostitution commodify sexuality and imply to the "white boys" that all African-American women can be bought.[37]

Nelson quotes an African-American prostitution survivor about the effects of racial stereotyping within Black communities:

> Young girls get their role models from somebody. In my family and in my neighborhood and around me was that kind of lifestyle, the fast lifestyle and that's where I got mine. . . . Pimps taught me, society taught me, my neighborhood taught me how, men in general taught me that the way to get over is to use my good looks and my body.[38]

To this problem about role models in Black neighborhoods, Nelson adds the lack of supportive response from poor communities when African-American women are killed or injured, which demonstrates to Black girls how their community views them. She compares the community outrage in Los Angeles, when four White officers received acquittals for the savage beating of Black man Rodney King, with the lack of response when eleven Black women in the sex trade were found strangled and dumped in abandoned buildings in Detroit. In the latter instance, there was every reason to believe that the killer would strike again.

> So, I had to ask myself, where was the outrage? One Black male is beaten up by four white police officers and every Black community activist in the country, including the Reverend Jesse Jackson, is crying out against racist violence and the culture of poverty that precipitated the L.A. riots. Eleven poor, Black women are murdered and mutilated, their bodies are thrown away like so much trash, and the only thing

we hear, besides the deafening silence, is a local Baptist minister mourning that these women "were already among the walking dead." Where do racism and sexism meet? If you ask me, they meet in a trash pile, in an abandoned building, in Detroit.[39]

As a result of the extreme poverty in these neighborhoods, the colonization often means that the poor themselves collaborate in subjugating others. Olivia reminds us that the friends who suggest prostitution are probably making money from their referrals or recruitment: "When you are exploited, it is so easy for you to do it, too. You don't realize it is happening. The exploited become the exploiters." Undoubtedly, this collaboration accounts for some of the indifference to women's plight in Black communities.

Antagonistic relations between the police and members of the Black community also contribute to officers' contempt or indifference to girls and women of color on the street and militate against the women seeking help from law enforcement officers. As a result, Black women in the sex trade become invisible persons in their communities.

They are not so invisible in U.S. jails and prisons. Out of fourteen million arrests nationwide in 2000 in the United States, 34,228 men and 53,403 women faced arrest for prostitution and commercialized vice. Given the broad definition of prostitution and commercialized vice used by the federal government, it is not possible to know how many of the arrested men were customers.[40] In an in-depth sample of 61,347 persons from about 9,000 jurisdictions, 39.5 percent of those arrested for prostitution were African-Americans, and 58 percent were Whites.[41]

Although Blacks represent only 36 percent of the population in Chicago, African-Americans made up 75 percent of the city's prostitution-related arrests of women in 1999.[42] In Minneapolis (Hennepin County), African-Americans constituted 52 percent of women arrested and convicted for prostitution in a six-month period in 1991, although Blacks (men and women) represent only 13 percent of the population.[43] Another Minneapolis study found that the average number of days served by African-American women was almost double that for Whites for sex trade offenses.[44] In Los Angeles County, Blacks accounted for more than 50 percent of all female prostitution arrests eight years out of ten between 1990 and 1999.[45]

Given the lack of resources for sting operations in indoor prostitution venues, we can assume that most of these arrests are made at the street level. Even if we factor in multiple arrests of the same women, a very large number of African-American women are involved in the criminal justice system for sex trade offenses, undoubtedly owing to their visibility on the streets. In Canada, it is Aboriginal youth who participate in prostitution in numbers well beyond their representation in the general population. In some Canadian communities, the visible sex trade is said to be 90 percent Aboriginal.[46]

Women of color appear to start in prostitution earlier and stay in longer than White women. In a sample of forty-five women in three western Canadian provinces, all of whom had been involved in street prostitution before age eighteen, the Aboriginal respondents were significantly more likely to still be on the streets (68 percent) than the White women (25 percent).[47] The median age of entry for females was eighteen in a sample in Victoria, B.C., but Aboriginal respondents were younger still: their median age of entry was seventeen.[48] Racial differences also emerged among subjects interviewed in the Cook County (Chicago) Jail between 1991 and 1993. The respondents reported to have had their first prostitution experience at a mean age of twenty years and nine months; African-Americans, however, began at significantly earlier ages than Whites or Hispanics.[49]

Carter and Giobbe point out that escape from the sex trade is more complicated for Black women because prostitution is so embedded within the culture of their communities:

> They must abandon their homes, flee from pimps, husbands or boyfriends who forced them to turn tricks, or at the very least benefited financially from exploiting them. Black women must receive emotional support and advocacy services in order to escape prostitution safely and establish new lives for themselves and their children.[50]

These women may need to relocate to different communities—a difficult feat because of lack of resources and the inability of poor persons of color to gain entry to White or mixed-race neighborhoods.

Considering street prostitution from the standpoints of race and class, the reasons for the violence and abuse come further into focus. Women whose race and poverty put them at the bottom of the societal ladder make them the most vulnerable to abuse and certainly more easily trapped and unable to resist. Melissa Farley agrees that by hiring the most helpless victims, the customers are able to exploit the women's lack of power:

> You cannot understand prostitution unless you understand how sex, class, and race all come together and hurt a person at the same time. . . . People are chosen in prostitution because of the extreme imbalance of power. The poorest, the most vulnerable women are basically made available for constant sexual access.[51]

Laurie Shrage points out that a large percentage of customers, whether men or women, seek paid sex from those whose racial, ethnic, or class identities are different from their own. In most countries the women and girls in the sex trade represent lower economic classes and social castes. Large percentages of women in the sex trade in the Netherlands, for example, are natives of South America, Southeast Asia, and Africa.[52]

We can trace the reasons back into history. In medieval Italy women in prostitution came from Flanders, the Rhine Valley, or northern France. Using foreign women and girls meant that the men would not subject their own local girls to participation in the sex trade. If the Italian men viewed the women as already impure, then they as customers were not really corrupting them; hence prostitution was viewed as less sinful for the men.[53] In the United States, before Black prostitution began to proliferate, the majority of the girls and women in the sex trade around 1900 were native-born daughters of immigrant parents.[54]

These lessons of history demonstrate that racial, ethnic, and class differences between girls and women and their customers are part and parcel of what makes buying sex acceptable to some males. As Schrage writes, "Every black woman was, by definition, a slut according to this racist mythology; therefore, to assault her and exploit her sexually was not reprehensible and carried with it none of the normal communal sanctions against such behavior."[55]

Primo Levi has described what he calls the "useless violence" perpetrated against those who are already exploited. He wrote: "Considering that you were going to kill them all . . . What was the point of the humiliation, the cruelties?" The answer:

> To make it possible for them to do what they were doing.
> In other words: before dying the victim must be degraded,
> so that the murderer will be less burdened by guilt. This is
> an explanation not devoid of logic but it shouts to heaven:
> it is the sole usefulness of useless violence.[56]

This is surely the reason for some of the otherwise inexplicable violence and abuse experienced by women on the streets, most of whom are women of color. Degrading the women makes them humiliated, ashamed, and less human, thus justifying the treatment meted out to them. These racial, ethnic, and class imbalances are an intrinsic part of a significant segment of the prostitution industry in the United States.

∽

On October 11, 1990, the five-foot, four-and-a-half-inch Olivia was down to ninety-three pounds. The thirty-five-year-old's teeth were mostly gone, eroded by heroin, and her hair was thin and unhealthy looking. She had two black eyes, ribs that had been broken for the twelfth or thirteenth time, and visible stab wounds. Olivia didn't know it, but her rescue was about to begin.

CHAPTER EIGHT

Escape

> Above the plain were the soft white castles of the clouds
> and a blank blue wall behind them. Into this world I had
> been born, and I must resign myself to it. I could not move
> myself to a fortunate planet, where any rare tear was in-
> stantly dried by a benediction. This is my glass, I must drink
> out of it. In my anxiety to know what was in the glass, I
> wondered, "The world is tragic, but just how tragic? I won-
> der if it is finally so, if we can ever counter the catastrophes
> to which we are liable and give ourselves a workshop of
> serenity in which we can experiment with that other way
> of life which is not tragedy, but which is not comedy."
>
> — REBECCA WEST, *Black Lamb and Grey Falcon*

October 11, 1990—an unusually cold fall day for Chicago, thirty-five degrees in the morning, and foggy. An outreach worker approached Olivia on the street. A research project was offering $30 if she would answer some questions. All she had to do was show up the next day at the Board of Health's office at Clark and Diversey. Thirty dollars just to answer some questions seemed like a wonderful deal, so Olivia went to the Board of Health the next day.

The researcher asked Olivia how many tricks she turned a day, how many a week, for how many weeks. She multiplied it.

> I remember the tears just coming. I was very vulnerable and
> emotional, and it all of a sudden hit me. I sat there realizing
> how sick I was at this moment. I wished this guy would hurry
> up so I could go get my drugs. I just started crying, and I
> couldn't stop. He left for a while, and then he put his arm
> around me and he said, "You know, those outreach workers that
> gave you this card to come here, they have a place."

Olivia told him she had no home. What's more, there was a guy on the street looking for her. The researcher arranged for a worker, herself a survivor of prostitution, to come over from Genesis House, a prostitution recovery program founded by Edwina Gateley. Because Olivia was on heroin, she couldn't stay at the recovery home until she went through detox. An appointment was made for drug detox the next day.

Olivia returned to the streets for what would be her last night there. Using the $30, she bought heroin, turned four or five more dates, purchased some more drugs, and went to a senior citizen who always let her stay at his place in exchange for sex. She shot half the dope and saved the other half for the morning. To her amazement, Olivia actually followed through on the drug treatment referral the next morning.

For Olivia drug treatment really was the end station. She simply had no physical or spiritual energy left to keep going anymore.

> I didn't have an ounce of hope. I never thought in a thousand
> years that it would work. I was just tired, tired, and vulnerable
> enough to be willing to stay. That is all that I wanted for that
> moment, never knowing, because I didn't know there was any-
> thing better. I thought that was it. I was going to die that way,
> either from a shot of dope, a trick killing me, or a pimp killing
> me. I wasn't looking for a better way or wanting to change. I
> didn't know change would be possible, or that you could change.
> I thought that after you became something, that is what you
> were.

With a patch consisting of Librium and drugs to reduce the craving, Olivia went through detox. She experienced some diarrhea and chills, but surprisingly found it wasn't unbearable. She never felt that she was going to jump out of her skin. Olivia was supposed to wear the patch for nine days, but because she feared what would happen when the patch was removed, she started taking it off at night and putting it back on the next morning. Olivia wanted to be prepared when they took the patch away. Three days before the end of treatment, she threw it in the garbage and never put it back on again.

Once the patch was off, Olivia experienced some psychological cravings from time to time, but nothing she couldn't overcome.

> I was so happy not to wake up sick, I was so grateful to have a clean place to stay. I used to pray to God, don't let me mess this up. I would wake up so sick when on drugs. I would be throwing up, having to use the bathroom all at the same time, your skin feels like bugs are crawling over you, your body is lifeless, you feel like you can't pick up one leg to step in front of the other. You have dry heaves because you have no food in you to come up. You really feel like you are going to die.

Olivia's health problems necessitated a longer stay in detox. She had to have several teeth pulled, abscesses lanced, and antibiotics administered at an off-site dental clinic. As a result, she missed some of her drug groups and had to extend her stay in the program for a total of twenty-one days.

On the day of her discharge, the recovery home transported Olivia to its premises. Niki Surico, the house's residential coordinator, opened the door. Niki vividly remembers Olivia on that doorstep:

> I remember Olivia as this frightened, scared little girl. She was very thin and frail. She talked tough, but underneath I could see that she was mistrustful, scared to death of her own shadow. She was pretty frail. Just wiped out. She had been beaten up, had broken ribs. She was in bad shape.[1]

Niki explained the program, telling Olivia that the staff was a mixture of prostitution survivors and professional therapists. She took Olivia upstairs to show her where she would be sleeping. Edwina Gateley,

the program's founder, was taking the group on a weekend retreat.
Olivia was welcome to go, too.

> The next day came Edwina. She says, "You must be Olivia,"
> and she gives me this great big hug, and she says, "Get your
> stuff, sweetie, we're off for the weekend." In the car I remember
> that I was so quiet, and I was so scared. Edwina would look
> back as we were driving, and ask, "Are you okay?" My mind
> was racing. Is this real? Can I do this? Can I be like them, so
> carefree and happy?

After they arrived, Edwina gave Olivia a journal, suggesting that she
might want to write down what she was feeling.

> That night, she just held me and cried with me. It was some-
> thing she said that made me believe that I could do it. To this
> day, anything that I wanted to do, she has made me feel like I
> can do it. That weekend, the cottage, the walks around it, and
> the laughter. It was brisk and cold. It was such a life-trans-
> forming event for me. Periodically, after coming back, Edwina
> would come in and spend the weekend or the night with us, and
> this was an integral part of my recovery. I look back at how
> the little gifts were placed early on to let me know that that
> wasn't the only life there was. It helped me really make a
> decision. I was going to stay on track.

Edwina emphasizes Olivia's fragility at this time:

> She was dazed and beat. She was like an animal that had
> been beaten down, with a tail between its legs. She was in
> another world. When I saw Olivia, I sensed there was a fear,
> and a kind of hesitance about her, but it never occurred to
> me not to involve her in the vacation.[2]

Olivia recalls that she continued to be rebellious and distrustful. "They
were too huggy-kissy for me, even after that weekend. Was this a cult?
What was going on here?"

Like many women suffering from posttraumatic stress disorder,

Olivia continued to run on adrenaline. Used to living in crisis, to being alert to danger, she was not yet ready or rewired for peace and calm. And she had yet to learn to manage pain and depression without self-medication.

Kim, a prostitution survivor who was a house resident at the time, recalls Olivia's tendency to manufacture crises and to create the tension to which she was accustomed. But mostly she remembers Olivia's withdrawn character when she first came to the house:

> She was a very hurt and sad and lonely person. She wouldn't let people get close to her, and she did things to keep people away. Those were her defense mechanisms coming out, and you can't blame her for that. She was taught that that was how you act, and she was conditioned to behave that way so she could survive.
>
> When they come to the house, the women all have a suit of armor on because that is the only thing that we know. Once you get inside, into a place where you feel like you have some commonality and you can take that off and be yourself, that is where the true healing begins. Knowing there is a place and that you belong is important as well.[3]

Niki agrees that Olivia had to drop her guard in order to begin the healing.

> You are not going to allow anyone in. If I am going to open to you, and I am going to be vulnerable and allow myself to be vulnerable, I have to feel safe enough to be vulnerable. You still have that fear lingering in the background, and it is a very real fear. The broken ribs are still there. That was still vivid. The women on the streets on a daily basis are definitely going through posttraumatic stress disorder all the time.[4]

The fear was very real because Strych had found Olivia. Olivia had left behind her bond slips with various court dates, and a menacing Strych was waiting outside the courtroom for her. Repeatedly he denigrated the recovery home, mumbling that the house was "a bunch of lesbians," and he also made threats of physical harm. He was going to kill Olivia if she didn't come back to him. Both approaches are classic techniques of batterers.

The next time he was there, Olivia called Niki from the courtroom. Until Niki arrived, the court workers let Olivia wait in the judge's chambers. Niki arranged with the judge that if Olivia stayed off the streets, she would not have to come back to court on the various outstanding cases and charges. Niki came armed with a cup of hot coffee.

> I remember crying. I was shaking like a leaf, and I was so happy when Niki walked through the door. I remember my fear helped me make that phone call. I didn't for the first time try to just handle it on my own. I think I was thoroughly convinced that these people had my best interests at heart and they would be there to help me some kind of way. And sure enough, they made some phone calls, and before I knew it, someone came out and got me and took me back and let me stay in the judge's chambers until Niki got there. Niki was very angry. She said, "He's not going to mess with you," and she took the lid off the cup of coffee, and she said to Strych, "If you come one step closer, I'm going to scald you." It was a very long time since we saw or heard from him after that.
>
> I think Strych knew he had total control over me, and I think that part of his ego didn't want to admit that maybe he had lost that control, so that it became a challenge. I remember it being such a warm feeling to know that he couldn't get to me.

Niki remembers the episode well:

> Olivia was looking back all the time, traumatized. She was definitely in a heightened state of arousal, absolutely. We drove back to the house, through a complete maze of routes so he couldn't follow us. Once we got there, there was a major wind-down. This was a terrorizing time in her life, major.[5]

At this point Olivia turned a corner. For the first time she felt that Strych wouldn't kill her.

I knew I had a way out. How do you describe a divine intervention? At some point I began to believe in people again, and I believed enough to know that this guy wasn't going to hurt me unless I chose to go back again. His mentality hadn't changed, but mine had, and my safety had finally become important enough to me that at all costs I was going to use what resources I had been given. I started to believe that nothing was going to stop me from making it.

Indeed, Olivia had to learn to nurture herself and to protect herself from harm.

One of the counselors told me to think back to a time when you really tried to take care of yourself, you cared about what was going on with you. The only thing I could think of was when I was a little kid going to school, and I ran from awning to awning because I didn't want to get wet. "Stop right there," Carol says. "That was the part of you that wanted to protect Olivia. Now think of the times when you were out in the snow, you're standing on street corners. You moved away from that, but it was always inside of you." At one time I pinpointed a time when I cared enough to keep myself dry going back and forth to school, and she taught me that I need to try to begin nurturing that. "Think of the times that you are doing something for you, and stop and write it down." That is how basic I had to go back to. I had gotten so far from that.

Niki used a similar technique with Olivia.

The tracks on my arms were so bad. I felt so nothing, so empty. Niki said, just find one spot on your arm and begin to pamper it, wash it, put some perfume on it, put some lotion on it, and every week that spot was supposed to get bigger until I could learn to touch myself and nurture myself. It was just that simple task of finding one little area and begin to tell yourself that you care enough so that you are putting some lotion on, it was just that basic. I had to start to care about me.

I guess I had really felt that my life was torture for what

I had done. Kind of deserved. I had to go inside and find the
good in me.

Olivia fondly remembers a woman Edwina brought in for the day.
During the activity, called "Color Me Beautiful," she helped all the
women with makeup advice. When Olivia had been in stripping, she
had applied layers of showgirl makeup that was part of her costume,
her mask, the transition from Olivia to stripper. Later, when she was
out on the street, she had lost all desire to present herself as attractive
to the public because she no longer cared how she looked. In recovery,
applying makeup represented a big step, a communication to the
world that she was attractive. But Olivia needed to know now what
was appropriate and what was not in terms of makeup.

> *Makeup represents care for the body. The body has been violated.*
> *For this reason, women need to see the outside of themselves as*
> *attractive. The biggest milestone for me was being able to get*
> *my teeth fixed. Edwina knew that was one of the most devastat-*
> *ing reminders, other than the tracks on my arms, of how bad*
> *my life had gotten. If I was ever going to feel employable, I*
> *needed to be comfortable in my own skin.*

Developing a sense of self-protection was another key developmental
task that Olivia had missed during adolescence and now needed to
learn. As Niki says:

> She had to go through the whole cycle of being reparented
> almost. It's almost like they are going through all the devel-
> opmental stages over again.
>   Every life task you can think of has to be relearned:
> work tasks, the social tasks, the relationship/sex tasks. The
> women get overwhelmed in these new life situations and
> need to retrieve critical thinking skills. It's not a question of
> intelligence, it's just being able to organize these functions
> in the brain.[6]

One struggle was over clothing. Olivia still wanted to wear her little
spandex dresses. "She was using it to get attention, to define herself by

her sexuality," Niki recalls.[7] Olivia thought that as long as she wasn't turning tricks, she could dress as she liked. Niki told her that if she wasn't looking to be picked up, she shouldn't dress, walk, and carry herself as if she was. Olivia explains today that it would have been detrimental for her in this instance to make her own mistakes and learn from them.

> One [reason] was the reputation of the house. Edwina fought
> for years to be accepted by the community. Secondly, they
> weren't going to put me in a position where I would be picked
> up for prostitution for no reason because of my past or because
> I was dressed in the same manner. The police around there knew
> me. I was recovering in the same area that I had prostituted in.
> These are life-threatening decisions that I didn't perceive at the
> time as that.

Olivia thought she was being infantilized by being told what to wear, and she reacted like a "bratty child." Now that she has worked for years with women recovering from addiction and prostitution, Olivia knows that in the beginning this kind of strong advice is helpful. One error can send a woman into a dangerous and life-threatening relapse. Because of this risk, as well as fear of change, women, Olivia realizes, need in the beginning to enjoy some successes and to build on them— the key to empowerment when dealing with prostitution and addiction.

Olivia remembers being told many times that she couldn't leave the house dressed as she was, and she was quite angry with Niki over this. Kim recalls the struggle:

> Olivia slowly but surely started to dress differently. She
> started to wear her hair differently. She started not to wear
> as much makeup. When she came in, she had big red circles
> on her cheeks and a lot of eye makeup; slowly but surely
> her true beauty came out. She had been doing this for so
> long that she didn't know anything else.[8]

Kim saw these changes as part of Olivia's starting to take some responsibility for what was going on in her life. "Yes, she may have been victimized, but you know what, now she is doing it to herself, and she has to be able to move from that place. Wearing certain clothes, looking at cars when they honk, treating men as if they are tricks."[9]

Another area of contention involved manipulation. Niki says Olivia had difficulties with self-honesty, as well as with veracity toward others. To survive on the street, manipulation and dishonesty are important attributes and key avenues to power. Niki cured Olivia of manipulative and slick behavior by denying her weekend passes. The issues might have been petty, but both women believe that if Olivia's manipulative behavior had continued uninterrupted, it would have compromised her safety and ultimate recovery.

> The purpose of being in a recovery home is to be given modeling and mentoring. You are used to living by your own rules. All of a sudden now you want to mainstream back. In the beginning you need structure and guidance to give you some parameters. There are addictive behaviors that have to be unlearned. If you get away with something once, you are going to do something bigger. You are cutting the addictive behavior that can lead you back to addiction, whatever the addiction may be.

Even after the drugs were gone, Olivia still had the urge to go back to prostitution. Olivia still hadn't lost her dreams of big money, and prostitution was all she knew about obtaining money.

> You begin to feel that you have lost so much of your life to drugs that now, if you just solely prostitute, how much money you would make and save. You would do it by yourself, you wouldn't have a pimp, you aren't going to spend it on the dope man. You still have that street mentality that validates who you are by what you have, and that encourages the thought that you could make the money and not spend it on drugs. It didn't dawn on me that I wouldn't be able to do it again without getting sick or throwing up. I hadn't gone that far in addressing the prostitution issue. I have to laugh about it now, because after the first date I would have had to get high, and I know that now.

In recovery Olivia began to realize for the first time that having a lot of money is not even minimally important.

> That is not the important thing in life. Just waking up every day and being able to live and give something back, you feel worthwhile again. But until that happens, you are stuck in there. That is why there is a whole psychic change that has to happen in the recovery process, not just the stopping of alcohol and drugs. That is why it is an ongoing process and why you need your support systems in place.

Olivia's life now consisted of going to groups—drug treatment outpatient groups on a daily basis for the first four to six months, down to four days a week after that, and prostitution recovery groups, later supplemented with one-on-one counseling from a therapist at the house.

Without the drugs, however, Olivia found it more and more difficult to face herself.

> There was so much shame and guilt. I couldn't face myself or my children. When the drugs are removed, you have to face it. That is when I would find myself running to the bathroom, gagging. There is so much shame and guilt to it, I felt like I was going crazy. It would have been much easier to wind up in a mental hospital. After removing the drugs and alcohol and realizing everything I had been through, I didn't see any worthwhile reason to continue my recovery.

Olivia also started vividly remembering the sexual abuse and assaults she had suffered during prostitution.

> I had flashbacks of being gang-raped, being in a car with a trick with a gun at my head, or a knife pulled on me. I saw thousands of penises. I was so fragile during that time. I think that one of the things that kept me going was just the whole concept that physically I was feeling somewhat better not waking up in the morning needing drugs. Okay, I can do this. If I could stop that, I can do this.

What was Olivia ashamed of?

> It was degrading. I was abused, I was raped, I was beaten, I
> was talked to like no human should be treated or talked about.
> Degrading is the word I am using. The shame of the children
> who don't know who their fathers are. The babies I had and
> dropped. Situations I put my children in. That is not the kind
> of person that I want to be. That is not the kind of mom I
> wanted the children to know or ever see. That they had to see
> me high or drunk, or find a needle on the floor in the bathroom.

Olivia still struggles to overcome the shame and replace it with guilt
instead, because guilt is easier on the body. But at times even now the
shame engulfs her.

> The shame of the medical problems I have now as a result. Every
> time I get joint aches or severe cramps, reminding me of my life
> in prostitution, I feel ashamed again. I have to call the people
> who are supportive in my life, to not step back and feel totally
> shamed again. And as far as I think I have come, all it takes is
> a flashback and all of a sudden I feel worthless again, and I am
> reminded again of what I went through. And it happens every
> time, and it takes me a couple of days to come to terms with it.

Coming to understand the extent of the prostitution in her own family
helped Olivia frame a lot of things that she had never fully compre-
hended before. There was anger, and there was sadness, but ultimately
the realization was liberating for her.

> I saw a lot of external reasons that put me in situations in
> which I made some choices that had subconsciously been planted
> early on. It was very empowering to see that my environment
> and circumstances led me to make some choices, or how limited
> the choices were at the time. Before that, I thought I was just
> crazy. I didn't think that my drugs had driven me crazy. I just
> knew I was different, I knew it wasn't normal what I was
> doing, but I couldn't articulate it, I couldn't make sense of it
> in my head. Recovery helped me put some pieces together.

During recovery Olivia was surrounded by other women who had walked the same path and made the same journey out of drugs and prostitution.

> They were there when I needed to cry. They were there when I was scared. They were so different from people I knew on the street. I didn't really trust them at first, but as I watched not what they said but what they did, and how they treated me, as bad as I looked and as horrible as I was walking through the door, I began to slowly believe in people—in women. Men, it took much longer.

Edwina Gateley well remembers Olivia's progress:

> The recovery process is not just recovering from drugs or prostitution, it is recovering who one is. The further one gets along on the path of recovery, the scarier it becomes. The further you go along, the more honest you get and therefore the more frightened you get. You see more. The chances of relapse occur much later on in the process. It never surprises me that there are relapses, because of the self-knowledge that comes with the recovery. Recovery is a process of transformation, and it comes about through walking on a journey together with equality, mutuality, trust, and compassion. No phoniness. These women can see right through phoniness. There are a heck of a lot of phonies out there.[10]

Kim, who was in the house with Olivia, agrees: "When the drugs are gone, that is when the growth starts. That is why you need to be in a safe place to deal with these issues."[11]

Olivia's mother succumbed to cancer eleven months into her daughter's recovery. This event initiated another difficult period.

> I was grieving. I was grieving the drugs, I was grieving everything that happened before the drugs, and I was grieving the void that was my mother. I was so confused. God put angels in my path that kind of guided me through the process. You can't

do it yourself. You'd give up, either winding up back at the
drugs or committing suicide.

Edwina Gateley had evolved an approach based on her earlier work
with women on the streets of Chicago. She views prostitution recovery
as a dying and a rebirth.

> The recovery process is a death, it is a dying. It is the dying
> of everything these women have ever known, it is a dying
> to the way you dress, it is a dying to the social group they
> have spent their lives with, it is a dying to the sexual activ-
> ity, it is a dying to the drugs, it is a dying to the alcohol, it
> is a dying to the geographical location where the women
> have walked. It is like being born again. They have to let go
> of everything they have ever known.[12]

Gateley understood that love and genuine care would be needed if
Olivia was going to be able to complete the journey.

> Basically the brokenness that has gone on in their lives has
> somehow to be healed, and the glue that heals is a glue that
> says, I am a human being. How do you know you are a
> human being? You only know you are a human being who
> is lovable when people actually love you, when you actually
> recognize that somebody does care. I think that what we
> did at that time was that we surrounded Olivia and the oth-
> ers with a real genuine care. We love you, we care for you,
> we'll walk with you, no matter how long it takes. We will
> never leave you, we will continue the journey. I think that
> when women realize that they are lovable and they deserve
> to be respected, no matter what they have done or where
> they have been, then there is a transformation.[13]

The person who was Olivia had to be recovered. Through group work,
keeping a journal, making collages, and visualization, she was helped
to put the pieces back together.

> *I had to learn that I had made some bad choices along the way,*
> *but it didn't make me a bad person. I learned to trust my*

*instincts, to listen to these voices inside that I damped down. I
learned to look back and say, okay, whatever I have survived,
thank God I did, I'm not going to be bound by it anymore, I
refuse to let it hold me down.*

Olivia makes it clear that neither Gateley nor the recovery home emphasized religion, and her own recovery did not depend upon a reli-
gious-type conversion. It was not religion, but spirituality. What does
spirituality mean to Olivia?

*Spirituality embraces you as to who you are, whatever you have
done, it is just your experience. You are not judged by it. You
are loved for being who you are. We weren't forced to believe in
anything in that house, but we were overpowered with a lot of
caring and giving. Their spiritual sense of self helped me to
identify the spirituality within me, which is caring, giving, and
loving.*

*It wasn't heavy therapy or that I felt this enormous break-
through, it was someone just taking your hand and walking you
through it, instead of being judgmental. It was safety, love, and
care.*

Louise, a prostitution survivor, now a college student, was in a position
to observe Olivia's transformation. She first met Olivia in a Chicago
homeless shelter. Louise had a newborn, and Olivia had her three boys
in tow, but was in the process of shipping them back to Wisconsin. At
that first meeting, Louise says she was transfixed by Olivia. She was so
vivacious, so vibrant, so authoritative and street smart. Years later Louise made her way to the prostitution recovery home, where she met
Olivia again. Louise came and went from the home, but everyone always welcomed her back with love and affection. Had Edwina Gateley
shut the door in her face because of her recidivism, she believes she
would have been dead by now. Gateley agrees. "She would have been.
She was at the gates of hell and back."[14]

Louise will never forget the sight of Olivia's physical deterioration
and frailty at that second meeting at the home. But Louise also sensed
something totally different:

When I saw her again at the house, I was still into my
madness. I walked through the door. There was something
totally different about this house. I looked at Olivia and the
other two ladies there. Olivia wasn't on any type of mission
of the street life anymore, and it kind of scared me. It was
like they are not playing around. This is the change, there
was a feeling of respect in the house. We are here for you,
and they were looking at me, like, see, this really can be
done. They were showing that this could really be done.[15]

What kept Olivia from relapse? She says right away it was a gift: "The
gift was opening the door, opening your eyes to see that it is there.
The miracle was being able to stay there."

Olivia recognizes some of her own attributes that enabled her to
stay the course. In recovery there is such a fear of the unknown. But
Olivia was always a risk taker, and here was another challenge to meet.
Then, too, she had lived and worked independently before Strych.
Based on her subsequent work with many drug-addicted women in
prostitution, Olivia believes that issues of power and control in relationships contribute to relapse. Many women, who simply do not believe they can survive without that pimp or partner, remain extremely
dependent on men and the role they play in their lives, and are drawn
back to the life of prostitution.

Probably even more important was the fact that Olivia had no-
where else to go: "I was pretty beat down. I was desperate. There was
nothing short of death that I had not experienced. It was either something was going to work, or I knew I would kill myself. I was that
desperate. This had to work for me."

Niki agrees: "When the fear of staying the same is greater than the
fear of change, then you will change. You have to tap into the fear."[16]

Olivia stayed at the recovery house for twenty-two months. Niki
describes Olivia as she departed:

When she left, her hard exterior turned into strength of
character. The vulnerability or the fearfulness was like a
healthy vulnerability. She could leave herself open and feel
safe enough. Her posture was one of strength and character,
and it didn't have to be tough or mean, or scaring off. It
was the strength . . . of a woman.[17]

Women who are the victims of an act of rape experience feelings of shame and guilt. Trauma expert Judith Lewis Herman explains that violence survivors universally experience feelings of inferiority; after all, the perpetrator uses sexual violence to express contempt for the victim and wants her to feel dirty and second-class, as though she "deserved it." Herman believes that shame and guilt may help the victim draw useful lessons from the event; her failure to protect herself is easier to bear than the reality of utter helplessness.[18]

We are indebted to Holocaust survivor Primo Levi for one of the most complete and moving explorations of the shame and guilt experienced by trauma victims as a result of the humiliation they have experienced. The Auschwitz jailers had continually humiliated their prisoners, who were powerless to retaliate. Levi identifies the loss of dignity as the source of the humiliation: "Dignity is necessary for life. Whoever loses one loses the other, dies spiritually: without defenses he is therefore exposed also to physical death."[19] And this feeling of shame is impossible to totally eradicate: "That many (including me) experienced 'shame,' that is, a feeling of guilt during the imprisonment and afterward, is an ascertained fact confirmed by numerous testimonies. It may seem absurd, but it is a fact."[20]

Feelings of shame and loss of dignity and self-respect were blunted during captivity, but after liberation, the sense of humiliation and guilt rushed back in, never to be cast away. Part of the soul has been crushed, never to be repaired, writes Levi. One must live and find a means to come to terms with the fact that one has been the subject of such humiliation and loss of dignity in the past.

> Coming out of the darkness, one suffered because of the reacquired consciousness of having been diminished. Not by our will, cowardice, or fault, yet nevertheless we had lived for months and years at an animal level: our days had been encumbered from dawn to dusk by hunger, fatigue, cold, and fear, and any space for reflection, reasoning, experiencing emotions was wiped out . . . in the Lager there were few opportunities to choose: people lived precisely like enslaved animals that sometimes let themselves die but do not kill themselves.[21]

There can be no better description of the shame and its causes that engulfed Olivia during her recovery process and that can still paralyze her today. To cite Primo Levi is not to equate the sex trade industry with the Holocaust and the deliberate slaughter of six million Jews in Europe. But Levi himself, and no more poignantly than in his last published work, recognized that the concentration camp tactics to which he bore personal witness can be and are used in other venues. Their employment may be sporadic, and they may occur in private episodes or through government lawlessness, both in the western world and in the Third World: "It can happen, and it can happen everywhere."[22]

For victims of domestic violence and for prostitution survivors, who have experienced multiple violent attacks and at the same time have continued in the relationship with the abusers, the feelings of shame can be overwhelming. In an interview, Jenny Horsman, who has worked for many years with violence victims as a literacy educator, explains:

> Shame is a really big key piece. The women are incredibly firmly committed to the idea that there had to be something about them that caused the violence to happen. Another piece of the shame is the fact that they participated in the relationship and obtained favors as a result.[23]

As one prostitution researcher has stated: "She acts so that she betrays her own principles and betrays her own integrity. Due to virulent self-hatred, it is very hard to erase that sense of contamination and the differences with other people."[24]

A major factor is the women's shame and hatred of their own bodies, to which they must now reconnect. Victims like Olivia begin to believe that their bodies have undergone severe pollution. Actress Anne Heche has described the results of her father's persistent sexual assaults during her childhood, which she explored during later therapy:

> I had learned that a lot of terrible things had happened to me. I had learned that my body was filled with disgusting and gross things that my father put into me, and although I had screamed and hollered and cried and fought, I didn't

know what to do with that information. I couldn't even look at myself naked, I hated myself so much. My body was ugly to me, so ugly I couldn't touch it. I couldn't respond with pleasure when someone else touched it. But I pretended that I enjoyed it.[25]

Jenny Horsman explains that violence destroys the body's boundaries. If your body does not present limits to other people, you begin to feel that you do not have a right to exist, to take up space.[26] David Scott, the Las Vegas stripclub observer, captures the essence of this loss of body:

> The omega point, anticipated by those strippers who, in their floor show, spread their labia for the spectators in the front-row seats—the Sushi Bar—is to give the men a view right inside. The unavoidable implication of this relentless visual slide into the vagina is that the stripper has no private self, that everything about her is open to inspection and invasion, that her very soul is up for grabs, that she can be turned inside out, and that she has no boundaries, no conditions, and no limits on whom she lets in. She is simply transparent, like a milk bottle.[27]

Because women's bodies have been the instruments used for torture through rape and sexual assault, care and attention to the survivor's body is at the forefront in trauma recovery centers throughout the world. Olivia remembers sessions devoted to manicure and the use of body lotion. That these are not frivolous pursuits is confirmed by Andrew Solomon's powerful description of a visit to Phaly Nuon, a violence survivor who has established an orphanage and a center for depressed women in Phnom Penh, Cambodia. After Phnom Penh fell to Pol Pot and the Khmer Rouge, Phaly Nuon had to work in the countryside as a field laborer with her twelve-year old daughter, her three-year-old son, and her newborn baby. During this time, a group of soldiers tied her to a tree and made her watch while they gang raped and then murdered her daughter. A few days later, her tormentors tied and suspended Phaly Nuon over a mucky field in such a way that her legs had to be tensed lest she lose her balance. If she had dropped of exhaustion, she would have drowned in the mud. Her infant was tied to her, while her three-year old son cried beside her.

Once Phaly Nuon was miraculously free from this torture, she set up a helping program for the many women she saw who had been physically violated and now appeared paralyzed by depression and posttraumatic stress disorder. There she helps the women reclaim their bodies.

> I built a sort of lean-to and made it a steam bath, and now in Phnom Penh I have a similar one that I use, a little better built. I take them there so that they can become clean, and I teach them how to give one another manicures and pedicures and how to take care of their fingernails, because doing that makes them feel beautiful, and they want so much to feel beautiful. It also puts them in contact with the bodies of other people and makes them give up their bodies to the care of others. It rescues them from physical isolation, which is a usual affliction for them, and that leads to the breakdown of the emotional isolation. While they are together washing and putting on nail polish, they begin to talk together, and bit by bit they learn to trust one another, and by the end of it all, they have learned how to make friends, so that they will never have to be so lonely and so alone again. Their stories, which they have told to no one but me—they begin to tell those stories to one another.[28]

Another issue that emerges in recovery is what Joseph Parker calls the "death imprint." This immersion in death—friends and acquaintances dying by murder, attempting suicide and undergoing quasi-accidental overdoses, pimps and customers threatening to kill them—causes women in prostitution to believe that their survival was a fluke and that they have "lived too long."[29]

A related problem is that, owing to the moral stigma of the sex trade, many women believe that once in the sex trade they will always be labeled a prostitute and there is nothing they can do to overcome that.[30] Two practical consequences result. Later on, even the slightest hint of disregard or disrespect can take a person straight back to the depths of feeling worthless.[31] And because of the stigma of prostitution, women's experiences are determined unimportant and are not given the attention that they deserve.

> Many of the clients' losses, such as loss of children, loss of friends, incarceration, and addiction, are not recognized as legitimate losses, worthy of grieving. The public views them as deserved punishments, and withholds its support. The client is expected to go on as if what happened to him or her was appropriate and not an occasion for grief.[32]

After she had worked individually with women on the streets for a while, Edwina Gateley realized that her own expressions of support and love were not going to be enough. In 1984 she realized that the women she worked with, including two named Laura and Teddy, needed more than what she herself could give:

> Now I am getting more involved with Laura and I wonder what she needs to do to save her life. Would offering her a house make a difference to the choices she needs to make? I wonder. More and more I believe that they need to belong to someone, to a place, to a dream. . . . Community is vital . . . a loving understanding community to nurture people who believe in themselves. I have been able to do much alone—but it is still not enough. Someone like Teddy needs others also to affirm her.[33]

The women needed approval from a community. These thoughts led to Gateley's establishing a house that could create a system of support for recovering prostitution survivors. As described by Gateley, the house would create a community, a team of people, who could affirm and care for one another as a kind of ministry.[34]

With its emphasis on hospitality and human dignity, the program, which still exists today in the same North Side location, is a direct descendant of Jane Addams's Hull House. Addams wrote of her intent to create "the warm welcome of an inn," a place for shared fellowship that she and Ellen Starr strove to make "as beautiful as we could."[35] Like Gateley's recovery home, Hull House was dedicated to valuing

and developing the uniqueness and dignity of each and every person.[36]
Gateley built on the fundamental principle of Hull House: "If Hull
House does not have its roots in human kindness, it is no good at all."[37]
In short, Hull House was not an institution but a shared community,
illustrating a fundamental human solidarity.[38]

A place. Jenny Horsman and her colleague Elizabeth Morrish go so
far as to call it a "sacred space": "The space is a place to heal where
you can really be accepted and be yourself, and yet offer to others as a
part of that recovery."[39] In an interview, Horsman described how these
spaces throughout the world themselves contribute to recovery:

> If you offer space, you are using the space to give every
> version of the message that you can give; that is, these peo-
> ple who are coming to this space are worth something. The
> messages can be given by how you decorate the space, that
> you put flowers in the space, that you think the space is
> worth being beautiful, that it is worth beautiful music.
> They are all part of the message that you have a right to
> take up space. One of the things the women took to over
> and over again was that I was telling them that they were
> worth something. I was telling them explicitly and implic-
> itly through all of these things. They said that was the most
> powerful thing. That began to give them the glimmer that
> they could get to a place that they could think they were
> worth something.[40]

A recovery space is a *safe* spot in which to rebuild the whole self, to
bring body and mind into balance, and to forgive oneself. Prostitution
survivor Brenda Myers describes being in Gateley's recovery house: "I
was broken spiritually and physically. I could lie down and close my
eyes without anyone hurting me."[41] Such a space always must be organized around affirmation. Gateley explains:

> One of the things I always felt was important at the house
> was to have fresh flowers—live flowers. I threw out those
> plastic things. The house that we had then was the house
> I wanted to live in. It had to be good enough for me.
> The environment reflects how we feel about ourselves. We

have to have fresh flowers to remind you of how beautiful
you are.

The whole piece that is missing is the nurturing, the
emotional and spiritual nurturing that we have taken for
granted, because it is just part of growing up and being
held by your mom, being kissed, being taken on vacation,
going to the beach, getting presents at Christmas. Many of
the women I have met, when we give them Christmas presents, wrapped up, it blows their minds. Nobody has ever
given them a present before. And especially nobody has
ever wrapped it up before. It is a terrifying experience to
be given, to be loved is terrifying. So this whole process
where people are nurtured is a very important piece of a
wholesome recovery process. When we make it only intellectual or we make it only a process of going from one step
to another—meetings, interviews, the serious stuff—then
we neglect the very important piece of self-esteem that
comes from really believing, hey, you are beautiful, you
can dance, you can play, you can write, you can be creative,
and you can recognize beauty around you in the environment.[42]

Not only does this recovery process require space and affirmation, but
it also requires love. Edwina Gateley writes that one woman in the sex
trade stated that Edwina's love for her made her feel like a completely
different woman when she was with her. Gateley asks: "Am I one of
the few people who has loved her and seen beyond what she does to
who she is?"

Human beings deserve more. I doubt these women have
ever known real love. . . . Prostitution is a hard and violent
life. Except, perhaps occasionally, for a high-class call-girl.
For most it is a life of utter desperation and self-destruction.
The humanness, the warmth, the gentleness, the tender-
ness, the caring that makes us women is diminished, destroyed or distorted.[43]

Love. It is a hard prescription to fill. As Andrew Solomon writes:

> I think of my father, or the friends who came to stay with
> me through my third depression. Would it be possible to
> go into a doctor's office and have treatments and emerge
> capable of such generosity and love? Generosity and love
> demand great expenditure of energy and effort and will.[44]

Responding with love also benefits the caregiver:

> If we are to participate in movements of grace produced by
> healing, we must be willing to create the places for such
> healing to happen, whether through physical spaces or rela-
> tionships. Being with another, creating a safe space for heal-
> ing, is not easy, but being with the process gives courage
> and it gives hope. It opens the heart to compassion and life
> to grace.[45]

∽

After about a year at the recovery home, Olivia began to believe that
she could do something out in the world. She took courses at Truman
Community College, prerequisites she needed for a training program
in drug and alcohol addiction. She loved the classes and was doing
well. Unfortunately, Truman College was located in the neighborhood
where she and Strych had spent most of their time. As luck would have
it, Olivia bumped into him one day on her way to class. And she
became terrified all over again.

Olivia dropped out. One of her professors even telephoned her at
the house, urging her to return.

> *I quit school because I feared being killed. I had learned what*
> *peace was. To have a sense of peace and safety for the first time*
> *in many years, and he upset that. But I really believed again in*
> *God, that nothing was going to stop me from making it. But it*
> *upset me horribly.*

Olivia did not let this incident deter her. That fall she switched to a
downtown community college campus and eventually completed a

two-year course there to become an accredited drug and alcohol counselor.

> School was a good distraction. While at school I didn't have to
> think about the healing process I was going through. The mate-
> rial I was reading excited me. It gave me something, it began to
> fill a void. I'm really grateful my brain cells weren't destroyed
> as much as I have seen in some other women who have come
> from drug and alcohol addiction.

At the same time, Olivia began to volunteer at her drug treatment
program. The three boys remained in Wisconsin with her sister Alta.
But Olivia's recovery created new problems with the children, as Alta
remembers:

> When Olivia came out of treatment, she started working,
> she started going to school, she started doing things that
> she wanted to do for herself, and they didn't understand
> that. Before, they understood, she had this problem, and
> couldn't care for them. But then they saw her, and she
> looked good, she felt good, she was doing all this other
> stuff. So then it was really confusing, because she wasn't
> sick any more. So why are we still here? So the acting out
> became worse.[46]

Olivia's volunteering at her drug treatment program led to her first
full-time job when the program hired her as a drug prevention special-
ist. She had been active in her outpatient drug groups, asking questions
and exploring her experiences. The staff saw her potential and encouraged Olivia to volunteer and later to apply for a job. A difficult two-
stage interview process, which included a group interview with the
entire program staff, then ensued.

> It took quite a while to hear back about the job. I called back
> to the house from a Dunkin' Donuts near Harold Washington
> College, and they told me there was a message from Gateway
> and to call this number at a certain time. I remember shaking
> like a leaf. She wanted to offer me the job. She was going to pay

*me $19,500 and, oh my God, I was so excited. But I was also
scared to death.*

Olivia's supervisor didn't just throw her into the job, but mentored her
as she undertook more. In fact Olivia had had considerable experience
speaking in front of groups. It came from talking in Alcoholics Anonymous (AA) meetings. What could be more exposed than standing up
in front of a group and telling your story? But in AA you could be
nervous, and you could even cry while speaking. AA was Olivia's basic
training for her new job responsibilities. And Richard Booze provided
her with on-the-job support and mentoring. "The first paycheck was
very exciting—what a sense of soaring," Olivia remembers. "The reality of being independent."

The job enabled her to move out of the recovery home into an
apartment with other prostitution survivors. She didn't move far,
though, just a few blocks down the street. About this time she met the
man who later became her husband. He was a recovering addict in a
group attended by another house resident, who introduced him to
Olivia. They developed a strong friendship.

> *I wasn't looking for a sexual relationship. I felt like I had had
> enough sex for my whole life. My attitude has caused problems,
> but he is very compassionate. Thank goodness our friendship has
> been stronger than anything else, because I didn't want a rela-
> tionship.*

Olivia's sister Alta was experiencing increased difficulty dealing with
the boys' anger, and finally Olivia was ready to take them back.

> I told Olivia, they're not mad at me, they're mad at *you*, you
> need to deal with this anger. I know that the boys were
> happy when they went back. She was not happy that she
> had to take them back. She didn't feel ready, I know. It's
> not that she didn't love them, she just didn't feel ready.[47]

One year after Olivia left the recovery house, she married and brought
her oldest son to live with them in Chicago. After one school semester

and the summer, the fourteen-year-old got his wish, and Olivia moved his two brothers, then twelve and ten, in as well.

Olivia has often thought that the children's problems would have been less severe if she had reunited with them before getting married. It was a huge and difficult transition for everyone. Olivia says she had no concept about being a mother, much less about how to have a healthy relationship with someone of the opposite sex. For what Olivia's new friend was offering frightened her.

> How can I make a commitment to someone when I was so used
> to being so noncommittal and so used to splitting myself during
> a sexual act? I was also used to somebody wanting something.
> It was new to me, and I wasn't used to it, it didn't make sense.
> I figured that eventually I was going to have to do the same
> thing, that it was all a deceitful game luring me in. It was
> scary. A healthy relationship has to be built on trust, and I
> wasn't able to trust men, and I wasn't sure if I could trust
> myself to give, either.

Meanwhile, Olivia learned how to drive a car. First her husband tried to teach her, but that didn't work well. A friend at work then took her to a parking lot near the lake and helped her practice, and later took her to get the license.

> I learned I didn't have to feel ashamed to say that I didn't
> know. It also taught me that it is okay to ask for help and to
> know that I don't have to act like I know everything, like you
> do when you are out there on the streets trying to survive. On
> the street, you would be used and taken advantage of if you
> acted as if you didn't know. You don't want a lot of help out
> there, you want people to think you can do it on your own. I
> was able to let that ego down and get some humility. If I asked
> for help, people really were willing to teach you.

Because of her guilt and shame about not having been an active parent in their lives, Olivia worked hard to make up for lost time with the children. At first she did this through buying things, because she still tended to value everything by how much it cost. She did not really know her children that well and was trying to be both friend and parent to them. Eventually, parenting classes showed her the way. "I was so guilty about everything I had done," she explains. "I think I tried to buy them. I had a difficult time setting boundaries. I didn't need to say yes to everything they wanted. It was very difficult. It was so draining for me. I had no boundaries for them at first."

The boys were also very angry and tended to manipulate the situation. They quickly recognized Olivia's sore spots.

> In the beginning I cried a lot. If they got in trouble in school, they would say, had you been here, I wouldn't be having this problem.
>
> The children have to recover also. All of a sudden, someone who has not been in their life is thrust in there. It throws off their whole sense of who they are and what they thought was family. It is very confusing. There is also the problem that the kids think you left because of something about them you didn't like or want. There is so much to work on with the children.

Olivia's oldest son became introverted and his grades began to fail. She made the decision to share her drug past with the school social worker.

> I was so scared when the school called me in. I couldn't hide what I did if it is going to help this child. I've done enough to these kids. I said, forget your pride, be honest with these people, let them know what is going on. It was humbling. I took a big risk. This child was born addicted, I was a drug user, I haven't been there all his life, I just got these kids back. I need some help here.

The social worker proved to be caring and supportive, and Olivia's oldest son obtained an assessment and the counseling he needed. The three boys had a great deal of anger, and each child handled it differently. With one it was a speech problem; another was unable to sit still; and one had outbursts of tears or anger or became quiet and withdrawn.

At the same time the boys regained their mother, they were confronted with the presence of a man in Olivia's life who had no children of his own and who very much wanted to be involved with them. The boys had to struggle to accept the new man in their lives. When the oldest entered his teen years, he became upset that he did not know who his father was.

> He told me, "It sucks." I said, "You're right, it does, but you can either stay angry about that or be open. There is someone here who really wants to love you who is not trying to be your dad." Between the ages of twelve and fifteen, he struggled a lot with that. They have become the best of friends through struggling times.
>
> Everything was trial and error. I was a kid trying to raise them. It was hard. During the struggles with them, I was so fearful they would take the wrong path. The one thing I could never financially or otherwise repay my sister for is that they all have really good character. They do stuff I hate, but it is nothing like what I used to do. They turned out okay. It's worked out.

CHAPTER NINE

Other Voices, Other Rooms

But if we do not keep before us the necessity for uniting
care for security with determination to preserve our liberties, we may lose our cause because we have fought too
hard. Our task is equivalent to walking on a tightrope over
an abyss, but the continued survival of our species through
the ages shows that, if we human beings have a talent, it is
for tightrope-walking.

— REBECCA WEST, *The New Meaning of Treason*

A unifying theme of Olivia's story is her laudable and continual quest
for personal power, control, and independence, a struggle fought exclusively within the realm of the sexual arena. Olivia ultimately lost the
battle because she could not sustain the activity without recourse to
drugs and alcohol.

A number of published voices of women active in stripping and
other indoor prostitution venues depict altogether more successful experiences. As the women's motivations for engaging in the sex trade
emphasize power and control, their writings promote prostitution as a
method for women to achieve this sense of efficacy. Yet their own
struggles to maintain power within the industry shed light on the difficulties involved in the process, casting doubt on the ability of many
women and girls in the sex trade to succeed in the same endeavor.

The contrast with incest constitutes an important theme:

You've got to learn how to be the boss, and that is not like incest. The part about it being a sexual arena with older men is similar, but you're coming at it from a whole different angle. The power dynamics have shifted toward the woman who's offering the service and men are coming because they want this. You can take power. The sex is up front and negotiated. It's not like incest, where someone is sneaking around and trapping you and you're putting up with it because you're afraid of the hell that's gonna break loose if you blow the whistle, or because they've threatened to kill your mother, or kill you.

It wouldn't have been good if I couldn't handle it. If I couldn't keep control of the situation and was getting pushed around by these guys. . . . There were some people who worked at the parlor who would just do it for the money, but it was really intimidating for them, and they shouldn't have been there.[1]

In an interview one stripper explains that the feeling of power kept her in the sex trade:

I think I'll continue because I like the power that I have with men. I like making them do whatever I want them to do. But it gets stressful too. You have to be on your toes. But there's so much money in it. And there's a power thing in making them pay for it and on deciding whether or not I'm going to date them.[2]

For other women the attraction lies in the challenge to conventional and confining notions of proper womanhood and sexuality, fueled by a vision of sexual freedom and diversity. Here are two examples:

My inspirations were the Quadeshet, the "Sacred Prostitute" of our ancestors' temples. This seven-year experiment has paid off magnificently. By using prepatriarchal models of female sexuality as a noble, even divine power, I have constructed a life that is extraordinarily sweet, to say noth-

ing of confounding most of the culture's preconceptions
around female and male sexuality.[3]

> I advocate protection for consensual sexual expressions of
> all kinds. For all genders. I advocate amnesty for all mani-
> festations of sexual rapture. I willingly offer myself as an
> instrument for the dissolution of systems of shame.[4]

In the sex trade, women deny men unlimited access to their sexuality—the men have to negotiate and pay for it, which some women
identify as the heart of prostitution's attraction for them. One professional dominatrix has written that "In retrospect I think I resisted identifying as a woman as long as being a woman was associated in my
mind with powerlessness and victimhood. As a pro dom I can combine
womanliness and power in a seamless whole."[5]

Former stripper Nicole Grasse has described this reasoning:

> Today's strippers justify dancing topless as a validation of
> their bodies and their sexuality, a way to turn the tables on
> a sexist society and get paid handsomely for it. Spin wrote
> that, by "turning men into human ATM machines," strip-
> ping had become the ultimate act of feminism.[6]

Many of these voices are those of well-educated White woman whose
lesbianism makes sexual liberation and sexual nonconformity key centers of their identities. Ann D'Lorenzo is a woman from San Francisco
who worked for a few weeks in a legal brothel in Nevada. She was
surprised at the differences she found between the women in the
brothel and those she knew in San Francisco. Poverty or drug addiction
did not force the California women into prostitution. They were there
because they were sexual radicals "who frequently transgress many
constraints on sexual freedom." And many of these sexual radicals in
prostitution in San Francisco, she alleges, are bisexual or lesbian, which
was not the case in Nevada. "I had somehow acquired an irrational
faith that all middle-class sex workers would be radical queer activists,
committed to fighting for sexual freedom everywhere. I'd imagined
that whores automatically flouted the bourgeois expectations of privacy and sex."[7]

D'Lorenzo had difficulty discerning a motivation for the Nevada

178   women's prostitution activities. They appeared to be women with middle-class backgrounds and did not seem to be on drugs: "Many of them chose whoring over straight work precisely because they found that prostitution was less exploitative than straight jobs."[8] But as we have noted earlier, Alexa Albert's research at Mustang Ranch found that 100 percent of the women had pimps who were relying on their earnings. For women like D'Lorenzo, the sex trade challenges stereotypical feminine images such as nurturing, passivity, gentleness, and fragility. These women in the sex trade, flouting decorous and conventional images of femininity, believe they are working to reduce the power of patriarchy to divide women into madonnas and whores, a practice that gives men power over women.[9]

Researcher Julia O'Connell Davidson recognizes that women and girls in prostitution have varying abilities to negotiate power and control based on their age, experience, and personal biographies. Her detailed description of one British woman in prostitution, a financially successful, self-employed, thirty-four-year-old woman, "Desiree," well illustrates the difficulties involved, even in prostitution "at its best." Desiree earns £2,000 a week, has saved more than £150,000, and owns three renovated properties after only five years in prostitution. She works long hours out of her home, six days a week. The author describes in some detail the ways in which Desiree imposes and enforces limits on the clients to protect herself from harm and monetary rip-off. Davidson nevertheless believes that Desiree is still vulnerable to premeditated assaults from misogynist clients, and concludes that the psychological and physical toll she pays is immense, with few opportunities to deflect the stress.

The author asks why Desiree does not quit prostitution:

> Now, given that Desiree takes no personal pleasure in her work, has nothing but contempt for the men who exploit her, and has enough money to invest in an alternative business, it is reasonable to ask why she does not simply stop prostituting herself and do something else instead.[10]

Part of the reason, writes Davidson, is that Desiree never wanted to end up economically dependent on a man. Desiree is also an incest survivor: "There is a sense in which, for Desiree, as for many prostitutes, prostitution is also about returning to the site of abuse and sexual victimization."[11] Given Desiree's contempt for her customers, she achieves her sense of power and wealth from mastering those she despises.

One feminist theorist has taken this even further, writing that prostitution is a necessary institution because it represents an important healing process for incest victims. Pointing out that many women in the sex trade have suffered from childhood sexual abuse, Drucilla Cornell quotes prostitution survivor Ona Zee, who explains that "When you have sex for a living you split yourself off," the same dissociation that occurred when she was abused as a child. "So when I got into the sex business, splitting off was something I already knew how to do really, really, well."[12] Cornell states that life as a woman in the sex trade represents a persona that Ona Zee "had to live out," as a necessary therapeutic exercise of power over men:

> What does it mean for a feminist to argue that Ona Zee should not have been allowed to go through this journey, when she recognizes it may have been necessary for her, to make up her grandfather's abuse? We might regret that she had no other means to do this. . . . We have to fight back on every political level we can dream of to end the sexual abuse of children. For Ona Zee, the abuse necessitated her taking on the persona of the prostitute. . . . As difficult as it is to face, in a world of abuse some women will take on the life of a prostitute in order to work through their incestuous and violent pasts. . . . Thus a prostitute should be given the right to the self-representation of her sexuate being.[13]

Olivia can relate to these ideas of power and control and economic independence from men and, to a much lesser degree, to alternative expressions of gender and sexuality. But as a survivor of almost twenty years, she knows today that the sex trade provided her with only a false sense of efficacy.

> *Most of the time, women in prostitution have in the past been in some way violated or abused. You get this false sense—I can*

> say who, how much, when, where, what I will do and what I
> won't. Maybe they're a little rougher than I would like. I can
> say no. But you are exercising this power in a situation in
> which you really don't have any. You are being used by the
> system totally. Like the strings of a puppet being pulled. You
> don't see it when you are enmeshed in it.

Olivia remembers countless situations in which a man offered $200 for a certain act. She would bargain him up to $300, feeling in control—if he is going to do that, he is really going to have to pay. The woman feels in control: she's making him pay through the nose. "To him it is probably a joke," says Olivia, "He's got the money. He is here to do things he would never ask his wife to do, and would probably kill someone for asking his mother or sister to do. You don't see it, you don't want to see it that way."

Olivia describes another situation that she now also views radically differently:

> This is an example of one gentleman whom I had around for ten
> or fifteen years. I really thought he was my rescuer, one of these
> little angels who was always there for me, and when I started
> to really think about it, God, did he take advantage of the
> situation I was in. But I thought that he was this wonderful
> person who would love more me not to be in this lifestyle.

Davidson readily agrees that Olivia and others like her may experience prostitution differently from Desiree. Because women in the sex trade do not speak with one voice on the subject, Davidson writes that it is easy for theorists to "cherry pick" stories to support their own preconceptions about prostitution.[14] That some women may be able to exert more power and control than others does not relieve us, however, of the burden of determining how many women in prostitution are like Olivia and how many like Desiree. Olivia's story makes it incumbent upon us to establish, through research, where the numbers probably fall, to accept the results of these inquiries, and to hear from more women like Olivia who have heretofore not had the ability to express themselves in public arenas.

As prostitution survivors Vednita Carter and Evelina Giobbe have noted in an article published in a law journal, the law school forum automatically excludes voices like Olivia's from being heard in published writings about prostitution: "Having never read a law journal (feminist or otherwise) while waiting for the next trick to arrive or in between sets at a strip club, we question the intrinsic value of using scarce time and resources to prepare a submission."[15] Survivors working with women in prostitution view their audience quite differently and use their time to reach them rather than the broader public, with the result that their ideas are rarely included in books and articles on prostitution. This was not always the case. Survivors have wearied of participating in public symposia and media discussions in which all different points of views are invariably represented, such as lawyers representing pornographers, madams, and the like. These events, survivors say, become entertainment that further trivializes the issue.[16]

There is indeed a trend now to publish writings that glorify the stripclub as a venue in which women can empower themselves. British journalist Martin Vander Weyer mocks this current tendency to demonstrate one's liberal *bona fides* by celebrating exotic dancing.

> And so to lap-dancing. Over the decade, I have had a go at most forms of journalism except war reporting, but I have avoided this winter's most overworked assignment: the visit to a lap-dancing club plus interview with a dancer who's really a drama student and doesn't feel exploited. . . . I confess that I have already experienced this phenomenon—on a stag night for a British bridegroom at a place called the Gold Club in Atlanta, Georgia, a couple of years ago. Far from being the chic post modern art form described by devotees, lap-dancing turned out to be jaw-clenchingly dull and creepy, requiring a kind of tantric detachment on the part of both dancer and customer.[17]

In July 2001 the prestigious Sunday *New York Times* Arts and Leisure section provided Judith Lynne Hanna with forty-six column inches of space (beginning on the front page) to sing a paean of praise to nude dancing and to sound a warning about suppression of free speech and artistic expression:

Certainly, many people find dancers' nude bodies to be icons of idealized beauty and female empowerment. Circular, theater stages in erotic dance clubs allow patrons to move around and marvel at living sculpture, much as museumgoers observe a statue and just as countless faces look up at the promenading new Miss America. Erotic dance, female or male, celebrates the body beautiful. . . . Nude erotic dance communicates dangerous-seeming messages to those who believe in the subservience of women and the right of the husband to the sole view of the woman's body.[18]

Two recent books, marketed as scholarly research, attempt to provide ammunition for the thesis that stripping is synonymous with women's liberation. Katherine Liepe-Levinson is a former exotic dancer whose recent study is the product of three years' observation in seventy strip-clubs in eight North American locations. Early in the work she makes a categorical statement, one contradicted by other strippers, that undermines our trust in the reliability of her other conclusions: "Contrary to popular belief, most middle-class strip clubs and bars, from the late 1980s to the present, at least attempt to comply with the laws prohibiting prostitution."[19]

Liepe-Levinson presents a thorough analysis and defense of stripping as a positive activity for men and women, based on her observations of the design, layout, and dance activities in the clubs she observed. She acknowledges the "horror show" atmosphere of most stripclubs, with their "scream ambiance" and "excesses exceeding social norms," but considers it as a liberating atmosphere for the stripper and her customers, who can experiment with sexual seduction and surrender.[20] The dancers, for example, may play the parts of hunted beasts while the macho stomping and hooting patrons act out the role of sportsmen, zoo keepers, or animal tamers. Yet, according to Liepe-Levinson, the women are really the hunters, strutting their sexual stuff, stalking the customers, and taking them for all they have.[21] Women massage their nipples with a special lotion and set them on fire, while one dancer sweeps flaming torches over her naked body and sets her crotch on fire. Although the author admits that these actions can represent male eroticization of violence against women, she herself sees them as "reenactment of the physical risks that women must endure in their quest for pleasure and agency."[22]

In fact, she writes, all these routines represent "extreme emotional and physical sensations, the disequilibriums of the mind and the body that are produced by erotic arousal." They are good for women and men, because carnal desire has "the potential to disrupt the established pattern of our lives." Sexual images that feature extreme physical exertions by performers or violence directed toward their bodies "satisfy the spectator's desire to view seemingly raw (i.e. 'real') reactions wrung from actors." The acts in stripclubs, she argues, involve both the dancer and the customer in transgressing established social norms in a nonpassive way for each.[23]

Liepe-Levinson's research mainly occurred in venues in which touching opportunities were limited and strictly enforced, and where lap dancing was not the norm, representing a small minority of exotic dance establishments in the United States. Nor does she even remotely consider the effects on the women and girls who light their nipples on fire night after night or have one hundred men watching them shower onstage while they use sex toys on themselves day in and day out. Alcohol or drugs, used by some women to cope as they pursue this kind of empowerment, go unmentioned. Liepe-Levinson's theoretical analysis of the content of stripclub routines serves only to glorify stripping, without bringing in the inconvenient facts about the effects on women who enact these scenes in public. Presented as scholarly research by a prestigious academic publisher, works like this one encourage feminists to disregard the concerns raised by individuals and organizations working with women like Olivia.

Brian McNair's book, describing and analyzing what he calls our current "striptease culture," has the same prestigious academic publisher.[24] With its "anything goes" mentality, striptease culture, he writes, is progressive because it represents the dismantling of patriarchal capitalism. In striptease culture we can articulate our own sexuality while showing due respect for the tastes and desires of others. Once marginalized groups such as gays can have increased public visibility and acceptance.[25]

The abstract arguments employed by McNair hinge on the concept of the free agency of girls and women involved in the sex industry. He approvingly quotes the words of Cathy Macgregor, another woman who has combined her career as a college lecturer with performing in stripclubs: "Lapdancing is a logical step from my intellectual feminist work. You are empowered. You choose where you work. You leave if you don't like it."[26] But leaving is just what Olivia, trapped in drug addiction and suffering from posttraumatic stress disorder, simply was not able to do.

Only in passing does McNair recognize violence, the pernicious side to striptease culture, and he feels constrained to challenge and question well-established statistics about violence against women. He writes about the "ease with which these bleak (and widely contested) statistics are bandied about."[27] McNair's work is an example of yet another ideologically based book, ignoring inconvenient factual data, which ultimately helps create a climate of opinion bolstering the sex industry and understating its effects on women participants like Olivia.

With its promotions of the empowering aspects of stripping, the media continues to play its part. National Public Radio (NPR) saw fit to report on the new interest in burlesque through its segment on Tease-O-Rama, a burlesque convention held in San Francisco late in September 2002. Burlesque is here depicted as an occasion for both sexes to celebrate the beauties of women's bodies in all shapes and sizes. Even law students, breathlessly reported NPR's correspondent, are taking part as dancers, where "The tease outweighs the sleaze."[28] The report serves to glamorize exotic dancing, contributing to our belief that it is harmless—indeed, that it is empowering for all women.

Journalists also have noted that the fall 2002 European fashion shows featured "bordello chic" clothing featuring corsets and lingerie-inspired dresses. One commentator found that the fashions "call to mind images of 19th–century demimondaines, flouncing in laced undergarments and high button boots,"[29] again with the effect of glamorizing those participating in the sex industry.

Of greater authenticity and value are the stories of strippers themselves. Within recent years quite a few trade publishers have brought out dancers' memoirs, but the authors' limited stripping experience, conveniently ignored by the publishers' marketing, has also helped to reinforce the idea that stripping empowers the women who participate in it. One such book is Toni Bentley's paean to naked dancing. A former New York City Ballet dancer, Bentley became enamored of stripping as a mechanism for living out sexual independence, liberation, and feminist empowerment. Like Judith Hanna, Bentley discusses public strip tease as it was historically, when women were physically separated from the audience, a phenomenon that rarely occurs now. And she glorifies the experience based on her one-time experience of stripping in such a club that forbade customer contact.

> I'd never felt such attention in all my life. His eyes lowered to my breasts and belly and then returned to my eyes with a look of shyness, shame, and excitement. His desire burned into my own gaze, showing me with a clarity I had not experienced before the power of my own body. I then knew what triumph felt like. In that moment, that nameless man, who was every man, was entirely mine. . . . Transient power, perhaps, but overwhelming in its force, it fused into my conscious memory and resides there still as a moment of victory over my inhibitions and every man who wanted to possess me. I was now in full possession of myself.[30]

Bentley's book tells the stories of four women who bared their breasts in public: Canadian Maud Allan, Mata Hari from Denmark, Russia's Ida Rubinstein, and French novelist Colette. These women, explains Bentley, declared their sexual independence by their public striptease. "Bold, beautiful, and defiant, each found her own form of liberation in a culture far more stratified than our own, not by directly pursuing equality with men or by competing with them, but rather by searching and expanding her own unique spirit, fantasy, and physique."[31] To be women of fatal attraction and to show their bodies to the world were their goals, and they did become famous and relatively wealthy from this activity.

But as critic Leo Carey has written, "the trouble with notoriety, however, is that it doesn't last."[32] In reality, the dancers had no power that was not related to their youth and beauty, and when that waned their utility was over. Then, for most of the dancers, their established images trapped them, making it difficult to strike out successfully to other venues. In the end it is difficult to understand how these particular women can serve as feminist exemplars.

Lily Burana's Strip City is another example of the current publishing craze for books about stripping, a phenomenon that one cultural critic believes trades on the new "no shock zone in American culture," offering titillation as opposed to literary values.[33] Emphasizing the power rush she enjoyed as a stripper, Burana soft-pedals issues of substance abuse, disassociation, and prostitution, although, as we have discussed, she is well aware of these aspects of the industry. As with Alexa Albert in her book on a Nevada brothel,[34] Burana's intent is good, and by eliminating these issues she can more easily present a human, engaging, and sympathetic portrait of the women in stripping. Yet avoiding these problems results in a less-than-accurate presentation of today's sex industry that ultimately helps to promote its societal acceptance as benign for women—even though, at the end of her book, Burana concludes that stripping is not good for women and girls.

Another White stripper-turned-journalist, Elisabeth Eaves, has written a book that her publisher has also marketed as an unstintingly honest depiction of stripping. Reminiscent of Burana, the first two-thirds of her book—and all Eaves's experiences save for three nights—occur in a peep show in which the women are separated from their customers by glass and where there is no possibility of physical contact, a situation that she later admits is not the norm in the exotic dancing industry. In a newspaper interview, Eaves explained that "I really found the Lusty Lady pretty easy. I am pretty OK, with dancing around and being looked at, if I feel safe and they can't get at me. So I did not find it that difficult."[35]

Eaves worked there only a year, although most of her dance mates were still in the industry well after she quit the stage. With a heavy heart, the reader realizes that Eaves is yet another in the parade of atypical women in exotic dancing who did not stay long, did not get trapped, and were able to come out and tell the story. Although Eaves too concludes that stripping is not healthy for men or women, her description of her experiences in a peep show, an unusual sex trade venue, further the public perception that stripping is benign, when the facts demonstrate that the opposite is often the case.

A precursor of these two stripping memoirs was Heidi Mattson's *Ivy League Stripper*, which appeared in 1995. After experiencing a near rape from a potential employer referred by the university, and a campus-related injury for which the university refused to be held responsible, Mattson began to dance in the nude at the Foxy Lady, a Providence, Rhode Island, club featuring one hundred dancers with all the up-to-date attractions such as lap dancing and shower stages. Unlike Burana and Eaves, Mattson, another blue-eyed blonde, actually worked for many years at the club. Because she experienced strong feelings of power and control in making the men pay for viewing her naked body, she says, she was able through stripping to overcome her earlier sense of powerlessness and victimhood at the university.[36]

But of lap dancing, harassment from customers, alcohol and drug abuse, or prostitution, Mattson herself experienced nothing. This is because she was such a strong feminist from the very beginning: "I allowed that my body, my exterior, was a sexual object, but my mind was mine. I was beyond being degraded or made powerless by a gaze."[37] All the customers, she admits, wanted more and were willing and able to spend more. It was her choice, and she drew the line at nude dancing.[38] Most of the other women in the club did not have this ability to control the men or their environment, or to maintain their self-esteem. Mattson describes dancers weeping in the dressing room and stoned on drugs, or making dates with the customers on the outside.[39] A careful reading of the book will indicate that Mattson was the only woman in the stripclub without mental health or substance abuse problems, and many readers may grasp what really went on at the Foxy Lady. This memoir, however, may also convince the reader that many women will, like the author, be able to withstand and survive the experience, when the opposite conclusion may well be true.

Do these books influence young girls to seek similar experiences in the industry? An ominous note was struck by a review of Mattson's book posted at amazon.com. A family counselor wrote that a nineteen-year-old brought the book to her attention. As a result of the book, the young woman had decided to try stripping instead of working two jobs while attending medical school. Only after the counselor insisted that the young woman visit a few stripclubs did she realize the reality of what goes on in these milieus. Yet another reviewer said she tried stripping after reading Mattson's book.[40]

Researcher Norton-Hawk summarizes the differential treatment that the media bestow on White prostitution survivors:

> On the rare occasions that heads of elite prostitution ser-
> vices are arrested, they tend to become celebrities, writing
> provocative books and dispensing sex tips on television talk
> shows. These madams are articulate, attractive, well-
> dressed, and engaging, in sharp contrast to the lower-class,

minority, school (and societal) dropouts who play their
trade on urban streets. . . . In short, cultural capital, material
resources, and social connections all combine to make one
group of prostitutes a fixture in urban courts and jails while
allowing their elite sisters to be largely invisible to the legal
system.[41]

Bernadette Barton's recent research over a three-year period with approximately 100 exotic dancers in nine stripclubs in a midsized south-
eastern U.S. city remedies the weaknesses of these stripper memoirs.
She found that a downward spiraling of satisfaction and self-esteem
occurred over time among most stripclub dancers. Her research provides a much-needed longitudinal perspective on stripping that most
of the published dancers lack because of the short time they were active
in the industry.

In the beginning, most of Barton's respondents felt exhilarated due
to the money, the attention from the men, and the power that they
perceived they had over them. They enjoyed the sexual abandon, the
ego gratification, and the experience of erotic power emphasized by
sex radical feminists.[42] Over time, however, the abusive encounters
multiplied, and Barton found that rather than becoming inured to the
abuse, the women's self-esteem became more fragile:

> She becomes more vulnerable to others' perceptions of her
> rather than hardened by the abuse. I think this is largely
> because the negative experiences women have working in
> strip clubs, along with the low social status of dancing and
> high consumption of alcohol and drugs, gradually erodes
> their self-esteem.[43]

Ultimately, Barton discovered, most of the women, like Olivia, found
the once largely affirming environment increasingly "degrading and
exhausting," and they moved from feeling empowered to feeling oppressed.[44]

Unfortunately, simplistic, stereotypical depictions of women in the
sex trade in recent popular works of fiction continue the trend of with-
holding the more complex facts of prostitution from the public. In the
best-selling *The Crimson Petal and the White*, Michel Faber tells the 834-

page tale of a young woman in the sex trade who ends up being in-
stalled in one client's home as his child's governess. Sugar, whose
mother introduced her to the sex trade as a child in nineteenth-century
London, is the woman with the proverbial heart of gold, a victim of
an evil mother who groomed her for prostitution. She is also well-
read, is writing a novel in her spare time, limits herself to no more
than three customers a night, and has managed not to become addicted
to substances or ever have been the victim of violence from her clients.

In a newspaper interview, the author revealed the autobiographical
underpinnings of his portrait of Sugar. As a child, several of his siblings
disappeared from the household; at five or six, he was hospitalized
because he stopped eating and drinking; and he has suffered from
crippling bouts of despair and depression ever since. Faber killed off
the heroine in his first version, but decided to end the book on a
hopeful note because of the happiness of his second marriage and his
wife's unfailing kindness and generosity to him.[45] Thus, the book is
less about prostitution and more about how life is a mixture of misery,
grief, and enormous sympathy and humor.

The motivation for Emma Donoghue's 2001 novel Slammerkin is less
clear. Intrigued by the true story of an English servant girl who murdered her mistress in 1763, Donoghue wanted to imagine how the
deed could have occurred. Fourteen-year-old Mary, the daughter of a
poor London seamstress whose husband died in jail, turns to the sex
industry after two rapes (like the Ivy League Stripper), which resulted
in a pregnancy that got her expelled from her mother's house. There's
no sugar coating of Mary's experiences in prostitution in London and
the country village of Monmouth, and the brutal psychological treatment meted out to her when she goes into service in her mother's
hometown after escaping a violent pimp in London. With references
to Mary's mistress, who obeys her husband's every command, and the
household's wet nurse, who also makes a living by renting part of her
body, the book somewhat heavy-handedly hammers on the theme that
all women are prostituted in one way or another.

Out of her longing for luxury and her rage against those who are
keeping her in her place, Mary bloodily murders her mistress. Ultimately, most readers will not experience much sympathy for this one-
dimensional character. The author agrees that her intent was not to
create a likable protagonist. "In a way it's the story of a girl who has

190   succumbed to one particular overwhelming idea which cuts her off
       from being fully human," she explained in a magazine interview.[46]
       Slammerkin thus contributes to a crowded portrait gallery of women in
       prostitution who are inhuman and bereft of morals. These two best-
       sellers perpetuate the two antithetical, polarized, and essentially sim-
       plistic views of women and girls in prostitution that have dominated
       the prostitution debate for over a hundred years: victims versus sinis-
       ter, immoral polluters.

       The public relations efforts of the COYOTE group ("Call Off Your
       Old Tired Ethics"), founded in 1973 in San Francisco to change the
       public perception of women in prostitution and to end their stigmati-
       zation, have combined with these paeans to stripping to help build a
       public acceptance of the sex industry as benign. COYOTE, a small
       group of prostitution survivors who support the right of women to
       participate in private, consensual sex, advocates for the decriminaliza-
       tion of prostitution.

       COYOTE believes that women in prostitution freely choose their
       participation in the sex trade, and those who say the women are brain-
       washed "totally belittle and take a super-patronizing attitude."[47] Al-
       though the group does admit to some violence in the sex trade, it
       attributes all of such abuse to the fact of its criminalization: the outlaw-
       ing of prostitution "enshrines into law the view that prostitutes are
       bad women, and thus legitimate targets for abuse." Violence by pimps
       is also a fact of life, but because of the illegality of prostitution, these
       women, who should be viewed as domestic violence victims, are un-
       able to obtain help from law enforcement officials or the legal system.
       And since most of the women in the sex trade who are arrested are
       those on the streets, the poorest bear the brunt of police enforcement
       efforts.[48]

       Priscilla Alexander, a COYOTE activist, agrees that the sex trade is
       a mixed bag: for some it is enjoyable, for others it is forced, and for
       some it is both. The major problem for women, she writes, is that it is
       illegal. Women in prostitution have no ability to pursue redress against
       either the violence or being cheated out of their money. Were the sex
       trade to be decriminalized, the law could prosecute the perpetrators of
       violence against women in prostitution on the same basis as it does
       other women.[49] On a 1980 Donahue Show, COYOTE founder Margo
       St. James explained that the illegality of the profession "heaps abuse

on the women that isn't inherent in the business itself. To stigmatize women sexually through the criminalization of prostitution affects every woman. It gives men the power to sexually intimidate them in the office, in public, and in the home."[50]

It is hard to understand, however, how decriminalization would bring about men's better treatment of the women in the sex trade. Their increased availability under legalization would not serve to remove their suitability as targets for aggression and, once prostitution was legitimized, violence against them would not magically cease, and might even increase.

However one might disagree with COYOTE's somewhat simplistic causation analysis, there is no denying that the opprobrium heaped upon women in the sex trade, especially those on the street, is great. A Chicago suburban social services agency, for example, fired one of its caseworkers when it found out she was a prostitution survivor.[51] When Kim Wrebeky was brutally assaulted and raped, prosecutors in British Columbia captured and charged the offender. But after they found out that Wrebeky had been involved in prostitution as a child, the case was dropped because she was, in the prosecutor's words, "not credible, a liar, and a tramp." Clifford Olson, the rapist, went on to commit eleven murders.[52]

In 2002 the National Organization for Women called attention to a new video game called Grand Theft Auto III, selling at $49.99, which reportedly had sold three million copies within a few months of its availability. Because the players pretend to work for the Mafia, they get to simulate killing police officers and innocent bystanders, stealing cars, and doing drugs. They can pick up a woman in prostitution in their cars, and if they want their money back, they can beat her to death and recover the cash. Those who have played the game claim that the bloody beating is done with a baseball bat that players can feel in their hands through the PlayStation controller.[53]

Prostitution survivor Brenda Myers provides one of many examples of how vindictively the authorities treat women in prostitution. Almost as soon as she was brought into a hospital emergency room with a gunshot wound, the police officer on duty advised her he was going to immediately run a computer check to see if she had any outstanding warrants.[54]

Despite its nod to the issue of violence in the sex trade, the centerpiece of the COYOTE position is the belief that prostitution per se does not represent a social problem. Although it has achieved no victory in terms of decriminalization in the United States, the group has contributed to a climate of opinion that in general has led to less societal concern about the plight of women in prostitution.

COYOTE's voice gained power from the perception that it spoke for and represented women in the sex trade. Later it came to light that only 3 percent of its members were women in prostitution.[55] And despite an overrepresentation of women of color in the U.S. sex trade, COYOTE is overwhelmingly a White organization. Gloria Lockett, an African-American prostitution survivor who works with COYOTE, admits that the organization has reflected the point of view of White women with perspectives radically different from those of Black women in prostitution:

> For the most part, white prostitutes work inside, and many of them get into prostitution because of power issues. Some were once in the professional world and felt like they were being treated like whores. . . . I knew that, for the most part, the people working on the streets were Black and other women of color. So I had a real problem with the fact that COYOTE was so white. . . . It was horrendous to me, the white women who would turn two tricks a month and call that prostitution, when Black women . . . were working six days a week in rain, cold, and snow. I felt it was important for me to be a part of COYOTE to let people know that Black women's issues were different from white women's issues.[56]

COYOTE believes that women have the basic right to occupational choice, sexual self-determination, and control over their own bodies, including the sale of sexual favors. Any regulation against these freedoms represents male control over women, perpetuating the divisions between those who sell and those who do not—whores and madonnas. Other sexual liberals advocate a similar position, but unlike COYOTE, they find it necessary to significantly downplay the abuse in prostitution.

Sexual liberalism is an important concept, representing rights and liberties that are a bedrock of a free society. Sexual liberals believe it is not the state's role to impose a particular morality on individuals or interfere with the sexual choices of others, as long as the parties involved are consenting adults.[57]

Freedom in the sexual sphere includes some of the most important guarantees for women, including the rights to use birth control, to have an abortion, to engage in cohabitation without marriage, and to form same-sex relationships. Sexual liberalism represents a movement against any public authority and repression that seeks to control women's choices. Central to most authoritarian regimes is sexual repression; historically, as now, witch hunts against sexual nonconformists have served reactionary political purposes.[58] So long as it is not coerced and occurs between two consenting adults, legalized prostitution has been a vital lynchpin of sexual liberalism's agenda for some time now. Drucilla Cornell's articulation of the tenets of sexual liberalism clearly illustrates the importance of prostitution for sexual liberals:

> To deny someone the right to the self-representation of her sexuate being would effectively mean excluding her from the moral community of persons. This would involve thrusting someone else's conception of the good or natural family upon a person who has chosen to organize her sexuality in a manner that is not in accord with that view. The sole justification for the violation of a person's imaginary domain can be only that the way in which she represents her sexuate being is so bad for her, or for others, the state then can warrant prohibiting it outright, or at least can try to discourage it. But I have argued that we should not do this even in the case of prostitution; history shows the dangers of allowing the state to be the source of meaning of acceptable "sex."[59]

This position on prostitution is also grounded in the lessons of history, as feminists remind us of the historical role that prostitution has played in nineteenth- and early-twentieth-century efforts to keep women within the control of patriarchy. Requirements of virginity before marriage and prohibitions against adultery kept a woman from engaging in any extramarital sex, and lack of access to birth control made sure that the unmarried woman could not engage in these actions without severe consequences. Prostitution constituted an important weapon in patriarchy's arsenal in this effort to control women's sexuality: "part of the system of control of a paterfamilias was prostitution. It provided a sexual outlet for all men that protected their own daughters and wives. Prostitution was, as their handbill stated, 'A necessary evil in all great cities, particularly in seaports.' "[60]

Moral crusaders in the nineteenth and early twentieth century wished to rescue women from prostitution and to reform the sexual conduct of their customers, whom they viewed as seducers and adulterers.[61] These activities played into the hands of those who desired to perpetuate the madonna/whore distinction as a means of restricting a woman's rights in the sexual sphere. As Nickie Roberts writes:

> Legislation against the sex trade historically goes hand in hand with intolerance of sexual freedom in general, and women's sexual freedom in particular. Whores have always been primary targets of this repression. The whore is seen as dangerously free: her financial and sexual autonomy strikes at the root of patriarchy, threatening the interests of male moralists and legislators—some of whom are among her best customers. And the whore is free in the sense that she does not bind her sexuality to any one man; on the contrary, she openly challenges the notion of female monogamy.[62]

Today, many feminist theorists who ascribe to sexual liberalism discuss the issue of prostitution only in the abstract: "Is sex without deep personal knowledge always immoral? It seems to me officious and presuming to use one's own experience to give an affirmative answer to this question, given that people have such varied experiences of sexuality."[63] And when the facts are referenced, such writers clearly have read only the most rosy-colored descriptions of the sex in prostitution. Martha Nussbaum has written, for example, that

> whatever position we take on this complicated question, we will almost certainly be led to conclude that prostitution lies well within the domain of the legally acceptable, for it

is certainly far less risky than boxing, another activity in which working-class people try to survive and flourish by subjecting their bodies to some risk of harm.[64]

In an attempt to downplay any abuse, others make an analogy with sweatshop labor:

> What is it that separates a Thai woman turning tricks in a cramped Toronto apartment from a Mexican immigrant toiling in a sweatshop in the suburbs of Los Angeles? Why does the former draw our scorn, the latter our sympathy? Clearly, many people react uncomfortably to the idea of sex as just another good that may be purchased in the open market. Yet for the women who make their living as strippers, escorts, prostitutes, and porn stars, sexual activity at the workplace is a job—a repetitive task that can be as unerotic and downright boring as cutting pork shoulders on an assembly line or sewing sneakers in a Nike Factory.[65]

Olivia's story, as corroborated by recent research with women in the sex trade, makes these analogies to boxing and sweatshop labor inappropriate. Boxing, after all, is an organized sport with defined rules and regulations occurring between trained athletes in a public setting, supervised by a referee. Nor is it accurate to say that it is the intent of one boxer to humiliate the other through the use of violence. Many women in prostitution must perform in isolated situations in which they are subject to physical and verbal abuse and in which they may resort to drugs or alcohol to better cope with the danger.

Olivia would not agree with the descriptions of sex in prostitution as banal and boring. For her, the sex in prostitution was a bit different from the work on a NIKE assembly line, however onerous the latter might be. Lap dancing—rocking in the nude on a man's lap until he ejaculates in full view of other guests—creates a particular atmosphere that Olivia thinks makes sexual harassment and violence impossible to eradicate. Consider the type of labor required in today's stripclub. Dawn Passar and Johanna Breyer, founders of the Exotic Dancers Alliance as a mechanism for ameliorating the sweatshop conditions endured in San Francisco stripclubs, have described the particular coercion the stripclub managers employ that extends beyond any requests routinely made by sweatshop supervisors to their female workers: "Sometimes you are forced to do a love act with a girl. You can't just do show, you really have to go down and do the real thing, and if you don't you're not scheduled to work next time."[66]

The sweatshop and boxing analogies ignore the special harm caused by *sexual* violence to women's bodies. Sexual assault is a form of torture that has uniquely grave effects. Physicians for Human Rights usefully reminds us of the difference: "Sexual trauma is unique from other forms of trauma. It is a violation of the most intimate and personal aspect of the self. One's own body becomes the setting in which the atrocities are perpetrated."[67] The analogies also miss a crucial point about some of the sex in prostitution, and that is its obvious intention to humiliate. It is not the sex per se, but sex-based humiliation and degradation that we are holding under the microscope:

> When a German customer of a Filipina prostitute demands to take a photograph to show his friends back home of the "two best things about the Philippines": a beer bottle in the woman's vagina, whose sexuality is being expressed? When a group of men pay a woman so they can simultaneously ejaculate on her, what sexuality is that? When Patpong offers . . . entertainment programs that tout "Pussy pingpong ball, pussy shoot banana, pussy smoke cigarette, big dildo show, fish push inside her, egg push into her cunt, long eggplant push into her cunt," . . . is this . . . sexual recreation, sexual liberation? In fact, it is true that freedom of expression is amply being exercised there, but whose sexuality is being expressed and what ideological statements are made about women? What is being demonstrated is a male will to dehumanize women.[68]

Indeed, because of the intent to dominate and humiliate, women subjected to persistent sexual abuse and violence respond in the ways intended by the abusers, which can have permanent consequences for the women's physical and mental health. As we have seen, the women internalize the abuse, adopt the batterers' worldview, and submit to them, collaborating in their own oppression.[69] The victim learns to switch on her disassociative state, but persistent disassociation causes a sense of complete disconnection from others and an eventual disintegration of the self.[70]

Those who use sex to torture and humble women employ a particularly humiliating strategy against women's bodies. Inger Agger, who has worked with traumatized women refugees, was struck by the power of shame that ensued from this practice and served to keep women silent and invisible.[71] Psychiatrist Judith Herman, one of the nation's leading experts on posttraumatic stress disorder in women, observes that the motivations of all persons perpetrating sexual abuse are the same:

> The methods of the torturer and the methods of the pimp or the pornographer are often similar. I think when we understand more about criminal gangs as an intermediary form of organization between, say, state-sponsored terrorism and one-family cells of domestic violence, we'll understand more about the transmission of methods of torture, methods of coercive control. But if you use the same methods in people, whether you're doing it in the name of the state, in the name of a criminal gang that's marketing your body, or whether you're doing it in the name of the authority of a father, or the name of some religious cult, the methods are the same and so the mental processes that they produce are likely to be the same. . . . So you're dealing with very profound questions of human evil, human cruelty, human sadism. The abuse of power and authority.[72]

As Christine Overall has extensively discussed, sweatshop work is not gendered, but rather undertaken by both men and women interchangeably.[73] Men, however, use sexual violence to control and shame women, and in prostitution, with poor women, women of color, and sexual abuse survivors, they find their special victims.

To the extent that sexual violence is involved in prostitution, the sex in the sex trade cannot be viewed as boring, banal, or benign. Why do so many feminists persist in this characterization? One academic explained it to this author:

> Feminists and academics generally who work on prostitu-
> tion feel very worried about being "anti-sex." . . . This has
> been complicated by the writings of women who claim the
> sex industry is their choice and empowerment. So there is
> a reluctance to appear critical of women's "choices." But
> mostly it is the dominance of sexual liberalism which makes
> it very hard and dangerous for people to be critical of any-
> thing to do with sex. They are likely to get attacked as puri-
> tans, anti-sex, anti-choice. Those of us who do criticize
> sexual exploitation do get attacked in these ways and it can
> be daunting.[74]

Lisa Brush believes that admitting to the many humiliations of prostitution makes women victims, and it is this label that some feminists
resist. For Brush, violence against women has become the "Achilles
heel of feminism": "This is the paradox of liberalism. Women cannot
be recognized as vulnerable lest we jeopardize our claims to equality.
But women cannot be equal without some redress of the vulnerabilities
that relegate us to second-class status."[75]

To deal with violence against women in all its forms, we must
recognize a less benign side of sex and be prepared to examine what
have been heretofore considered to be private acts. After all, violence
perpetrated against women by intimate partners is now subject to
criminal and civil penalties, and all states have removed the absolute
marital exemption to rape laws.[76]

> Intercourse can be rape; it can also be profoundly pleasur-
> able. Sexual experience with men or women can be abu-
> sive, objectifying, and degrading, but it can also be ecstatic,
> inspiring, illuminating. It can also be—and here the inade-
> quacy of a polarized discourse becomes clear—a peculiar
> mixture of all these things: objectifying and pleasurable,
> degrading and inspiring. We must bring together the com-
> plexities and contradictions; we must integrate what we
> know with what we do not want to know.[77]

Lastly, sexual liberals tend to focus solely on the issue of the right of
women to use their own bodies as they wish, without considering

how that activity fits within the greater economic order, much of which remains patriarchic. The global sex trade makes economic and profitable use of women's bodies, requiring new girls and women on a daily basis, and to meet this need, young girls are groomed, enticed, encouraged, and even coerced to participate. To center the discussion around a woman's right to choose is to ignore the role that the gendered sex trade industry plays in structuring these decisions.

As Lisa Maher notes in her discussion of drugs and prostitution in New York City, women have been viewed as passive victims of childhood abuse and sexual assault, or as volitional criminals, with little understanding of how these predictor variables move them into these roles:

> Our ignorance in relation to the contents of the black "box" (Daly, 1992) between women's experiences of victimization and subsequent lawbreaking means that not only is agency discounted, but that there is little room for the role that other kinds of structures and relationships may have in facilitating women's drug use.[78]

Maher's work describes how economic marginalization, coupled with labor market segregation, directs poor women into involvement in the sex trade. Two of Maher's respondents well understand the way the economy has dictated their activities as compared with men's:

> Lorraine: Guys have a hard time, they're limited. Girls got something that everybody wants. That's all they can do, but that's all they have to do.[79]

> And Candy: "Yeah, you know, you do what you do best, that's it. Two different systems."[80]

Maggie O'Neill has succinctly summarized the problem:

> However, they [the theorists] do not examine women's narratives to explore the specific problems women face within patriarchy, the socio-cultural and economic structures of domination that inform, support and give rise to

prostitution and the sex industry. The sex industry is instead taken as a given, a reified social structure, and unlike women's relationship to sex, sexuality, desire, and sex work it goes un-theorized.[81]

Because they have the unintended effect of convincing members of the public that prostitution is not harmful to most women most of the time, such well-intentioned attempts to downplay the violence and abuse in prostitution in the name of sexual liberalism result in the further marginalization of women like Olivia.

Another group of supporters of decriminalization of prostitution does not contest Olivia's story, but asserts that there is no one truth; women's experiences differ along a continuum, they experience prostitution differently, and one cannot characterize an entire industry on one woman's story. Melissa Farley's statistics receive praise and validity, but only for the 20 percent of women in prostitution active on the streets. Carol Leigh, for example, maintains that

> Melissa researches those who are in marginalized situations. She basically tries to define prostitution through statistics and descriptions of prostitution in the most marginalized circumstances, which of course represents prostitution from the perspective of her position.[82]

Leigh advocates a sampling of women in prostitution across the economic scale.[83]

Wendy McElroy also questions a great deal of prostitution research:

> This is because the sampling is almost always drawn from the streetwalking segment of the prostitute community, and usually from the further subcategory of streetwalkers who are in prison, who seek treatment for drug problems, or who otherwise enter programs to get off the street. In other words, these samples self-select for women who are most likely to have been victimized by prostitution and most likely to want out of the profession. Moreover, the women seeking treatment or leniency in prison are likely to

give an authority figure—the researcher—whatever answer they believe he or she wishes.[84]

Ronald Weitzer claims that since there is a great deal of variation in the sex industry, sweeping generalizations must be avoided. For example, he would vouchsafe the truth of Olivia's story, but would assert that her experience represents only a part of the prostitution story: "It is naive to assume that all sex work is essentially the same. There are *different kinds* of worker experiences and *varying degrees* of victimization, exploitation, agency, and choice."[85]

To support his position Weitzer makes several assertions. He claims that assault and rape are given as occupational hazards for women in the streets, but are "relatively rare for indoor workers,"[86] even though he later contradictorily writes that due to lack of research, "We know very little about the various types of indoor sex work; most studies examine street prostitution."[87] Hoigard and Finstad, the authors of an early and pioneering work on street prostitution in Norway that uncovered an almost unimaginable level of violence, are condemned for their "gratuitous moralizing,"[88] when, based on their field research, they call prostitution a form of brutal oppression. Weitzer concludes by calling for fresh research on indoor prostitution and evaluations of the sex trade based on concrete evidence.[89]

One of the alarming aspects of this approach is the surely unintended but cavalier treatment of the 20 percent of women on the streets. Their plight is apparently to be sacrificed to the need to support the larger number of women in the other parts of the sex trade industry who happen to be those less likely to be oppressed by race and class. These commentators also seem unaware of the new research studies with women in indoor prostitution venues that document violence, pimp control, alcohol and drug addiction, disassociation, and posttraumatic stress disorder, as well as considerable movement between indoor and outdoor prostitution.

In the end, the dominance of sexual liberalism has closed us off to, and limited our understanding of, today's sex trade industry. How can we reconcile sexual liberalism with concerns about violence, abuse, and degradation of women in prostitution? Can we support sexual liberalism at the same time that we condemn violence against

202   women in domestic violence and prostitution? Can we go down this road without it being a slippery slope toward repression?

The answer is not to choose one side or the other, but to learn to articulate and argue several points of view simultaneously and to move away from tidy, orderly systems of thought that serve to delegitimize some women's experiences. Ethicist Jean Bethke Elshtain has written of Jane Addams's conviction that "She wished mainly to highlight the negative dynamics of unforgiving dogmatism, and the needs for men and women of equable temperament to hold firm in their refusal to join one side or the other in such a way that their human sympathy freezes up and they cannot see things from another point of view."[90] Justice, wrote Addams, would come only through "broadened sympathies toward the individual man or woman who crosses our path; one item added to another is the only method by which to build up a conception lofty enough to be of use in the world."[91]

Women in the sex trade like Olivia have been caught in the crossfire of the battle against violence against women and the struggle toward sexual freedom for women. On the debate rages, and as Ann Russo has noted, "Meanwhile, a significant number of women working in prostitution continue to disappear. . . . This results in the systematic invisibility of women working in prostitution, who are relegated to the margins of discourse and practice."[92]

Jane Larson has written that narrative not only makes the experiences of others "real" to us, it also makes real our own "tendencies to cruelty." Such increased sensitivity makes it more difficult to marginalize people different from ourselves by thinking, "They do not feel it as we would," or "There must always be suffering, so why not let them suffer?" Larson believes that accepting the "stories of pain and suffering" has the effect of "substantiating the personhood of women and people of color."[93]

Olivia's experiences do not fit so neatly into our feminist theoretical boxes. Nonetheless, it is incumbent upon us not to disregard them. To ignore her story is, in the end, to discount Olivia's life and to drain her difficult recovery of any meaning.[94]

What Is to Be Done?

We could do away with all need for the intervention of the
law by giving every girl a full measure of knowledge and
economic freedom. But that is rank feminism and socialism.

— REBECCA WEST, "Battle-Ax and Scalping Knife"

Decriminalization of prostitution has long seemed to be a remedy that
everyone could support. Arrests and incarceration appear to have no
effect on preventing prostitution, the argument went, while the
involvement of the criminal justice system only makes matters worse
for women and girls, giving customers, managers, pimps, and police
officers a hold over them, stigmatizing them as "the other" or as law-
less criminals, subjecting them to harassment, and preventing them
from seeking help for the violence and abuse.

But, as we have seen with other issues in prostitution, new facts
continue to disrupt established lines of thought. The debate around
decriminalization has not kept up with the global expansion of the
multibillion-dollar sex trade industry as well as new evidence about
the experiences of women and girls in venues in which prostitution
has been legalized within the last decade. We now know that decriminalization has resulted in a startling expansion of local, legalized prostitution industries, an increase in illegal activities in these areas, and
stepped-up trafficking of women and children from other countries to
meet the new demand.

A 1999 investigative report found that the number of brothels more than doubled since they were legalized in the Australian state of Victoria, from forty to ninety-four. As there are said to now be 300 unlicensed brothels in Victoria, illegal businesses still largely outnumber legitimate and regulated sex businesses. In Sydney, which has similar legislation, the number of brothels—most of them illegal—has tripled since legalization.[1]

Once brothel prostitution was decriminalized in the Netherlands in 2000, the sex industry there is said to have expanded 25 percent, with most of the women involved coming from other countries.[2] And after several years of partial legalization of prostitution in Switzerland, a Zurich newspaper claims that the country now has the highest brothel density of any country in Europe, with encroachment into areas not zoned for sex trade activities.[3]

These expansions are noteworthy because a large majority of the women involved in prostitution in these newly legalized venues appear to be from somewhere else. In Germany, nine out of every ten women are said to be from eastern Europe and other former Soviet bloc countries. Eighty percent of the women in brothels in the Netherlands are from central and eastern European countries. The sheer volume of foreign women in the sex trade industry in these countries raises questions about the extent to which they have been brought there by middlemen, and the degree of coercion used for this purpose; outside help would certainly be necessary for so many poor women to arrange travel and to obtain the necessary documents.[4]

So great is the demand for women in the legalized sex trade in the Netherlands that the Dutch National Rapporteur on Trafficking has suggested that the nation offer voluntary legal immigration status to women from non–European Union countries, in the same way that guest labor laws encourage migration to meet specific labor market needs.[5] In Austria, where prostitution is legal but women are required to register, researchers also report surges in trafficking and in the involvement of criminal groups. A study in Vienna found the number of women registering declined to about 675 in 1995 when five years earlier it had been about 800, but the number of women and girls working illegally, most of whom were eastern European, was approximately 4,300, up from 2,800. The researchers found that the Vienna red-light scene was mainly controlled by Austrians, relying on recruiters in eastern Europe to meet their supply needs. Reported cases of coercion provided cause for concern that many of the women had been transported and kept involved in prostitution through violence and debt bondage.[6]

In Australia, Asian women are believed to be trafficked to meet the new demand. Melbourne has seen several cases involving large numbers of women crime syndicates have transported from Thailand and other countries. Girls as young as ten to fifteen were found at Sasha's International, one of Melbourne's legal brothels in the inner suburbs, in 2000. Chris Payne, who headed the federal police operation responsible for investigating sex trafficking in Sydney from 1992 to 1995, has stated that up to 500 trafficked women are working illegally in Sydney at any given time on false papers and are kept in servile conditions. Amnesty International in Australia has documented the cases of two trafficked women who died in Villawood Detention Centre. One, who expired in a pool of vomit at twenty years of age, was apparently trafficked to Australia at twelve years of age and continually used in prostitution thereafter.[7]

As in Australia, there are grounds to believe that child prostitution in the Netherlands has increased dramatically. ChildRight in Amsterdam estimates that the number of children in the sex trade has risen from 4,000 in 1996 to 15,000 in 2001, with at least 5,000 coming from other countries, including Nigeria.[8]

Some feminists in Australia have concluded that traffickers prefer to operate where there are venues to place their goods without fear of harassment; legalization, along with a lack of resources, has lessened municipalities' interest in rooting out illegal brothels. This strong linkage between domestic prostitution laws and international trafficking in girls and women for the local industry has meant that the new laws regulating, policing, or legalizing the sex trade do not clean up or make the industry safer for women.[9]

Brothel legalization and regulation do not appear to have lessened the stigmatization of women in the sex trade, who are still viewed as a class apart from others, used solely for sexual service, probably the result of their being confined to nonresidential "red-light" areas, out of sight of most city residents and subject to limited law enforcement protection. Although we need to learn more, the initial verdict, based as it is on solid evidence, is not favorable.

Janice Raymond understands that by calling for the legalization of prostitution, individuals believe they are destigmitizing women in the sex trade:

> But dignifying prostitution as work doesn't dignify the women, it simply dignifies the sex industry. People often don't realize that decriminalization, for example, means decriminalization of the whole sex industry not just the women. And they haven't thought through the consequences of legalizing pimps as legitimate sex entrepreneurs or third party businessmen.[10]

Given the reality of today's profitable global sex trade industry, decriminalization appears to have dramatically increased demand for girls and women in prostitution and, as a result, caused a growth in the number of middlemen recruiters. By legitimizing the sex trade industry, we accept the pimps, recruiters, middlemen, and club owners, who exploit needy girls and women for their own ends, as permanent parts of the landscape. If we are concerned about harm to women and girls in today's complex and profitable worldwide sex trade industry, decriminalization remedies fall far short.

For this reason, some groups, like the Victoria, B.C., PEERS organization, take great pains not to become involved in the legalization controversy because they believe that decriminalization does not offer women realistic and practical assistance. PEERS prefers to work for small-scale or local change that can improve the material conditions of the women, which could include more sensitive police response or an increased willingness of businesses to hire prostitution survivors.[11] Survivors Carter and Giobbe conclude, "Leading marginalized prostituted women to believe that decriminalization would materially change anything substantive in their lives as prostitutes is dangerous and irresponsible."[12]

Olivia and the other prostitution survivors in the Chicago Exodus group agree. They are dead set against decriminalization of prostitution. For Olivia, the fact that no one advocates the decriminalization of domestic violence is very telling: "Is it okay for someone to beat you, it's okay to be raped repeatedly, it's okay to be smashed against car windows? I have a real problem with that. We are humans. What is society saying, that we're not worth anything, that anything that happens to us is okay?"

Olivia believes that violence would snowball in legalized prostitution because the customers could do whatever they wanted without any fear whatsoever. For her, legalization is equivalent to a statement that prostitution is harmless, a signal to society that we need not be concerned about what happens to women and girls in the sex trade. Although legalization need not necessarily result in a lack of attention to women in prostitution, it would certainly confer legitimacy to the sex industry. Do we, asks Olivia, want to see prostitution part of a new totally legitimate sex and leisure industry, as it is in some areas of Europe?

Martha Nussbaum has written that, on balance, we need more studies of women's credit unions and fewer studies of prostitution,[13] meaning that eliminating the sex trade will require providing poor, marginalized women with more diverse economic options. Certainly, elimination of poverty and expansion of economic opportunity would lessen poor girls' enticement into prostitution. However, given the worldwide demand for young girls' sexual services, it is likely that teens will continue to flow into an industry in which they can make large amounts of money quickly at the same time that they receive attention from men. If we are concerned about the harm to women and girls in the sex trade, we must also address the demand side of prostitution.

What, then, can be done? Here is a proposed framework.

We must refuse to simplify or ignore facts in order to fit a political theory or particular outcome.

We must learn to hold different or even contradictory ideas at the same time. We must be able to support sexual liberalism and battle conservative groups advocating restrictions on women while at the same time calling attention to violence against women in all its manifestations and venues. Feminists, for example, have been able to raise issues about violence against women without holding positions against men, cohabitation, marriage, or sex.

We must eschew simplistic legal solutions in favor of multifaceted approaches. As in domestic violence, one single solution, such as decriminalization, likely will not have a chance of preventing violence against or exploitation of women.

We must be sure to embrace solutions that help the poorest and most marginalized women and girls in our society. Philosopher Simone Weil has written that we have an obligation to respect every human being, "for the sole reason that he or she is a human being, without any other condition requiring to be fulfilled . . . this . . . is the one and only one obligation in the areas of human affairs that is not subject to any conditions whatsoever."[14] In the debate, it is often easy to ignore women like Olivia, who defy our understanding of consent, choices, victimization, or agency.

As we consider options on prostitution, the human capabilities or human flourishing approach provides a good checklist for judging new approaches. Philosopher Martha Nussbaum has enunciated a set of human capabilities of central importance that make the life that includes them fully human. Because the dignity of the person constitutes the core of the idea of human worth, exploitation—treating the person as a mere object for the use of others—is the opposite of treating an individual as a bearer of value.[15] All social and political institutions, she writes, should have as their goal the promotion of at least a threshold level of these human capabilities, which include bodily health, being free from violence and assault, economic self-sufficiency, and being able to be treated as a dignified being whose worth is equal to that of others.[16] Once societal structures give women the full opportunity to develop themselves freely, the chance of their being exploited diminishes, writes Nussbaum:

> Nonetheless, for political purposes it is appropriate that we shoot for capabilities, and these alone. Citizens must be left free to determine their own course after that. . . . We set the stage and, as fellow citizens, present whatever arguments we have in favor of a given choice; then the choice is up to them.[17]

Jane Larson reminds us that "we have criteria from which to determine what human beings require in order to enjoy a flourishing life, and thus what amounts to an injustice when social arrangements violate these criteria."[18] Given the violence and abuse it metes out to large numbers of the vulnerable and the weak, the sex trade industry appears incompatible with the promotion of human flourishing and human capabilities. Larson believes that law exists to establish "the social basis for self-respect."[19] We will need some new laws and totally new approaches to deal with the prostitution issues that Olivia's story has raised. Some modest proposals follow.

Intervene with teen girls. Our attitude toward teen prostitution is simply astonishing. Why is there a well-organized and financed national campaign warning teens of the medical hazards of smoking and nicotine addiction, and no similar federal, state, local, or private efforts around prostitution? Researchers at the University of Michigan found that from 1996 to 2001 the percentage of eighth graders who were smoking fell from 21 percent to 12 percent, and that among tenth graders, smoking declined nine percentage points, and among twelfth graders seven points. The study's director attributed the decline to the aggressive national and state antismoking campaigns and the elimination of some tobacco advertising.[20] And as part of the World Health Organization's campaign to curb smoking worldwide, negotiators have drawn up a draft of an international treaty phasing in bans on cigarette advertising and sports sponsorships by tobacco companies.[21]

Chicago radio station WBBM-FM (B96), which caters to teens, ran a month-long series of public service announcements against teen smoking in May 2002. Funded in part by a grant from the American Lung Association of Metropolitan Chicago and the Cook County Department of Public Health, the campaign ran on the station at the same time as recruitment ads aimed at the station's female listeners for the Heavenly Bodies stripclub. Teens who pledged to quit smoking were eligible to win tickets to the station's June Summer Bash concert. Eleven different ads ran a total of 150 times. "I guess if we had one person quit smoking from the campaign, it'd be a success," said the sales manager for the station."[22]

All teen girls need information about the prostitution industry and its recruitment strategies, access to prostitution survivors for information and support, and basic sex education. Olivia states that as a teen she never had anyone tell her anything different. But would she have listened? "No, but is a seed possibly planted so that when things begin to go bad they may take a long look before I did? Had I known, maybe there would have been an intervention provided for me much earlier in life than thirty-five years of age."

Besides being warned, our youth need to observe the community holding grown men who buy sex with fourteen-year-olds accountable for their behavior. From the public advertisements for prostitution to the involvement of police officers in paying for sex, teens instead see a society tolerant of these activities, with unfortunate consequences for poor and needy girls in their developmental years.

Young girls also need a positive reaction when they tell someone they have been sexually abused. "If people only listened to me then, I wouldn't be here now," they say. Prostitution survivor Claudine O'Leary explains, "The youth are telling us a lot about the world through their actions. They need to see changes now in our response."[23]

The isolation of girls in prostitution cannot be overstated. Jannit Rabinovitch, who has interviewed many youth in prostitution in Canada, believes that this separateness prevents many young persons from seeking help from conventional social service agencies, mandating that peer-led services be available:

> They described their isolation, lack of connectedness and feelings of separation as the single most significant factor in making them vulnerable to prostitution to begin with. . . .
> In one discussion, a few described going for several years without talking to anybody who wasn't directly involved in the sex trade.[24]

Many of the youth Rabinovitch surveyed detailed the surprising lack of care and concern when they did intersect with the wider world. One teen told of being in a hospital and no one discussing her drug use or prostitution with her. Another had crossed international borders as a child, and no one had asked why he or she would be traveling alone. A young woman confided in a psychiatrist, who responded that prostitution was too difficult an issue for him to deal with and that he had no suggestions for someone else to whom to refer her.[25]

Graphic advertisements for illegal escort services in telephone book yellow pages and on the Internet often lead people to believe that these activities are now legal. The *Chicago Sun Times* runs ads for massage parlors in its sports pages. Law enforcement officials leave undisturbed *Chicago after Dark*, the free monthly available in news bins on downtown street corners. An inspection of the April 2002 issue found seventy-two separate advertisements for illegal escort services (most of which featured explicit photographs), sixteen massage parlor ads, and three stripclub ads, along with an exotic dance club directory. Most of the ads were explicit about opportunities for bodily contact, like the one for a club that promised "full nudity, full liquor, full friction."[26] Each issue the *Village Voice* publishes has several pages of ads for illegal escort and massage services, as does the *New York Observer* and *New York, Philadelphia,* and *Boston* magazines.[27] The publisher of the *New York Observer* commented, "I do not take a moral position one way or another. These ads are a component of real life in the city. They reflect the city. I hate the idea of sterilizing the paper and removing from it what is really a piece of the city."[28]

For the last twenty years, the *International Herald Tribune,* owned by the *New York Times,* has published advertisements for escort services. "In a perfect world, we would rather not run the ads, but they have been an important source of revenue for decades," said the paper's executive editor.[29] The New York City Police Department told a *Times* reporter that it did not believe it was its job to prevent or discourage publication of these advertisements for illegal services.[30] Sylvia Law points out the anomaly: some products that are legal, such as alcohol and liquor, are not advertised in mainstream media, but advertisements for commercial sex, which is illegal, are.[31]

These publications contribute to the glamorization of the sex industry as well as the sense that it is legal and acceptable. Because the prostitution industry wants and needs ever younger girls, law enforcement officials and communities need to make certain that the lines between child abuse and prostitution do not become blurred. Strong, unified responses are required. We will discuss these new approaches in some detail below.

Institute comprehensive programming for girls and women in prostitution, designed and delivered by prostitution survivors. Programming remains a challenge. We have seen that prostitution recovery is a long and involved process requiring a great deal of personal and emotional support, best delivered by prostitution survivors with recent experience in the industry. Survivors can more easily establish trust with women and girls who are disconnected from society and who do not trust professionalized services, where they believe (perhaps rightfully) they will be judged. Communities of prostitution survivors can create the necessary systems of connection and support that will feel safe. Survivor-led services also model the empowerment they are seeking to develop with peers still in the lifestyle of prostitution.

Rabinovitch and Strega observe that both youth and adults frequently experience the fear or reluctance of professional service providers to hear the nature and extent of their experiences of violence, degradation, and humiliation:

> Peer-led services reduce or remove the cultural and language barriers that most sex trade workers experience when trying to communicate with those whose education about the trade has been academic and professional. Talking with peers, or even talking to a non-peer in a predominantly peer-led setting, lessens sex trade workers' fears of confessing to a stigmatized identity and producing in service providers a range of reactions from horror to titillation.[32]

Sadly, many women and girls in prostitution have already sought help from social services programs but were not able to reach their goals. For example, 60 percent of a recent Chicago sample had participated in drug treatment programs, and the mean number of attempts at drug treatment was an astonishing 7.6. Almost 53 percent had tried drug treatment five or fewer times, while 47 percent attempted drug treatment six or more times.[33]

Norton-Hawk also found multiple tries at drug treatment in her jail-based sample of women in prostitution: 84 percent had been in treatment for addiction, with 57 percent in treatment at least once. She reported that the women told her a lack of money and employment led them, then drug-free, back into prostitution, making a relapse inevitable.[34] In the 2001 Los Angeles jail sample, 80 percent of the women in the sex trade said they had tried to leave prostitution, and 78 percent of a larger Los Angeles sample had made attempts to change their lives by quitting prostitution.[35] Almost 71 percent of the women in a recent Victoria, B.C., study had left the sex trade at least once over their careers, and more than half had done so three or more times. Prostitution survivors in the sample had attempted to exit an average 5.8 times before they were able to make a permanent break.[36] And in a Midwestern sample, the mean number of attempts to quit the sex trade was a startling thirty-three.[37]

Comprehensive programming, combining drug treatment with in-depth counseling around prostitution issues, as well as employment training and placement, are obviously required. These elements are currently lacking in many drug treatment programs, especially during detox, when counselors seek to interrupt drinking and substance use patterns but may make no effort to explore the important issues of childhood sexual assault or trauma from prostitution that may be the underlying cause of those addictions. It is also challenging to remain off drugs and away from prostitution without reliable and affordable housing.

Although many women in prostitution have children, like Olivia, they may have lost custody of them. This fact prevents them from being eligible for welfare (TANF) benefits in the United States to help support them while they are going through recovery. Lack of financial resources clearly serves as an inducement for women to return to prostitution after drug detox. Women trafficked into the United States are now eligible for monthly cash assistance for a period of eight months following certification, or for funds from the Matching Grant Program that can provide, in lieu of cash assistance, upfront funds for rental support and transportation.[38] Unfortunately none of these benefits is available to American-born women who are exiting prostitution.

Olivia describes what is needed to prevent backsliding into prostitution: "Not social service agencies. It's a ministry that can provide the nurturing, the hospitality, the continued support. There is no end to what is needed. It is almost like an extended family."

In short, women and girls have to believe that full recovery is possible and that someone will be there to listen to them and support them through the process. Although specialized prostitution programs can play this role, only a handful of programs around the country have the organization and funding to provide these kinds of services at the moment.[39] Nor are there any established funding streams for these kinds of recovery programs. Using fines from arrested customers is one creative funding mechanism that has been implemented in San Francisco.[40] Another suggestion is a new use or sales tax, added to stripclubs' or bars' cover charges, which could fund services for women.

In research conducted in 2001, the Center for Impact Research found a minimum of 16,000 women and girls in prostitution in the

214   Chicago metropolitan area.[41] Given these numbers, existing social service providers will need to step up to the plate to meet the gap. Youth serving agencies, domestic violence shelters, homeless shelters, and drug treatment providers all need extensive training in prostitution issues. By incorporating sex trade issues and services in their own programming for girls and women, they can begin to make a difference. Through in-depth training, personnel can begin to learn how to speak with women and girls in prostitution and help them get access to the special services they will need.

From Olivia's story it is also clear that hospital emergency rooms could offer critical intervention points for women and girls in prostitution. On many occasions Olivia threw herself at the mercy of hospital personnel, not one of whom ever responded. Things do not appear to have changed much. Tiffany Mason, a teen in the sex trade who was found murdered in Sacramento in 2001, was a fourteen-year-old runaway when she passed through San Francisco General Hospital for rape and sodomy treatment. The hospital notified neither the police nor child protective services. Tiffany's mother, did, however, receive a bill in the mail weeks later.[42]

One idea for intervention would be to extend the rape victim advocacy and domestic violence counseling services that operate in or are affiliated with hospital emergency rooms to women and girls in the sex trade. This approach will require training emergency room personnel to radically reorient their thinking about women in prostitution.

Prostitution survivor Brenda Myers emphasizes that the two main places for intervention are the county jail and the county hospital: "I was always going to jail or to the hospital."[43] Joyce, another prostitution survivor, explains that it was when she was in the hospital for a drug overdose that she had a moment of clarity: "Is this the way you want to die? I had self-destructed, you couldn't go any lower. I decided I wanted to live before I died."[44]

As a matter of fact, it was during her last hospital stay that Brenda finally got some help. One night the police had been out arresting women in prostitution, and it was hard to get customers. So Brenda went with someone she would usually have passed up—a man in a Mercedes-Benz who assaulted her, took her money back, and dragged her for a half a block when Brenda tried to jump out of the car. He beat her so badly that she almost lost her eye.

The emergency room was in the process of summoning the domestic violence advocate, but when Brenda revealed she was involved
in prostitution, the police officer picked up his walkie-talkie and
walked away. Once again, she just missed getting some help: "People
were always closing doors on me once I said the word 'prostitute.'"[45]

Then two things happened. The beating was so bad that Brenda
could not turn any tricks for a long while, and a woman doctor in the
hospital required Brenda to visit the social services office before she
left the hospital. The hospital social services office referred her to the
recovery home where Edwina Gateley's unconditional love was able to
overcome the effects of what Brenda calls the "unconditional violence"
she had experienced.

Today Brenda describes the effects of the rejection she experienced
from individuals like the police officer in the emergency room: "You
rejected me, so I'll reject you. I'm going to go out there and work at
prostitution even better and harder than before."[46] It is for this reason,
explains Brenda, that women in prostitution need outside help and
support. "I just couldn't save myself." She continues: "I deserved to
live. Every other woman deserves to live. They don't know any other
way to live."[47]

Provider training initiatives being implemented by Chicago's Prostitution Alternatives Roundtable and the Grand Rapids, Michigan, Prostitution Roundtable can serve as models for broad-based training of
social service providers to bring women in prostitution out of this kind
of ostracized ghetto as the criminal "other."[48] The Atlanta Women's
Foundation has spearheaded the creation of a special fund to launch
innovative programming, outreach, and policy advocacy for girls in
prostitution.[49]

Create alternatives to incarceration. Too often, decriminalization is con-
fused with alternatives to incarceration. For as long as prostitution is
criminalized, the criminal justice system should provide alternatives to
incarceration for girls and women like Olivia who would be interested
in hearing about opportunities to leave the life of prostitution. Given
that 75 percent of the Center for Impact Research's sample of women
in prostitution had been arrested, the police station or lockup presents
a point at which information about prostitution alternatives and programming could be provided. Police officers in Chicago have indicated

an interest in seeing women in prostitution sentenced to alternative programs in lieu of jail.[50]

In most jurisdictions, sentences for selling sex are short. By the time many women in prostitution appear in court, they receive a sentence of time served. This state of affairs makes structuring alternatives to incarceration difficult, because the women have no incentive to participate. Were nonjudgmental programs available in police lockups (an expensive proposition), perhaps more women would be exposed to the availability of peer-led opportunities that could provide them with much practical help and support. Certainly programming on prostitution-related issues needs to be instituted in all facilities housing women and girls. As Olivia has pointed out, at the times of her incarceration no attempts to disrupt the pattern of her lifestyle or to offer any information about community supports occurred. Over the years, numerous intervention opportunities were missed while she spent time in jail.

Operation Help in Saskatoon, Canada, is one innovative program designed to disrupt the lives of teen girls in prostitution. When undercover police arrest the girls, they activate a team of social workers and a native elder that convenes immediately and offers support and information at the police station and continually thereafter. Since its inception, fifty-one interventions have been made over a two-year period, and ten girls are now permanently off the streets.[51]

The benefit of such programs is that women may seek further help from government agencies and social service groups if they know there will be no criminal consequences and that there will be a nonjudgmental and welcoming response. This kind of positive, proactive approach can also help counteract the sense of fatalism and apparent immutability of the women's circumstances that sets in.

Adopting a treatment approach may encourage a necessary sea change in police attitudes toward women and girls in the sex trade. Involving prostitution survivors in police operations in programs designed to offer new job opportunities to women in the sex trade can provide an important opportunity for police officers to interact positively with prostitution survivors and to revamp their thinking about these women and girls. As in domestic violence and sexual assault cases, extensive training of police officers in prostitution issues would be a necessary first step to change entrenched misogynistic attitudes.

And were women not incarcerated for prostitution offenses, would they be more likely to report violent customers and abusive police officers?

Arrest customers. Although the law penalizes both the customer and the seller of sex in the United States, most of the arrestees for prostitution are women, the sellers. For example, there were 3,777 arrests of women for prostitution-related offenses in 2001 in the city of Chicago, whereas only 1,258 men were arrested that year for soliciting or patronizing a woman in prostitution. Thus, Chicago women in the sex trade were arrested three times more often than their customers.[52] The practice of arresting greater numbers of sellers than buyers institutionalizes the idea that to use a woman in prostitution is "natural," even though the woman who provides the service is "wicked."[53]

The problem with decriminalization is that it alone does little to eat into the demand for women and girls. Since January 1999, Sweden's law, the only such legislation of its kind, has decriminalized prostitution for the sellers, whom it considers to be violence victims, but arrests the buyers, who may receive a fine or up to six months' imprisonment. By focusing on the demand side with its criminal law, the Swedish government believes that it accomplishes two things: it makes clear "that we regard prostitution as an undesirable phenomenon in a civilized modern society in which women and men are equal," and it enhances public awareness of the conditions affecting women and children in prostitution. The Swedes regard the criminal law as only supplementary to an extensive network of necessary services for women and girls.[54]

Since the law went into effect, police have observed a tenfold decrease in the number of women on the streets in Sweden's three largest cities. Nor do they believe that these women are now selling sex in indoor venues. Women on the streets, addicted to drugs and plagued with mental and physical problems, are not welcome in brothels or escort services, and owing to their poverty, are generally not able to advertise their availability to customers through the Internet. Sweden has also outlawed and eliminated all the kinds of public advertisements for prostitution services that U.S. residents see in their own newspapers and magazines.[55]

To some extent street prostitution activities may simply have been displaced in Sweden. The New York City experience may be instructive.

218   One scholar has conclusively demonstrated that after the Giuliani administration cracked down on Times Square and other midtown prostitution venues, the women engaged in a variety of adaptive behaviors that included donning more conservative dress, relying more on regular customers through use of beepers, working out of cars, moving indoors to brothels, or relocating to adjacent areas. If the policy makers' goal was to rid an area of prostitution, the researcher concluded that a localized strategy of arrest will work, but if the aim is to decrease the amount of prostitution, this kind of intervention is largely ineffective.[56]

According to Swedish officials, the law has also encouraged more women in prostitution to come forward to report violence from customers, which police pursue with charges of rape or sexual assault. Reportedly, the amount of trafficking of women and girls into Sweden has also slowed, because it is easier to bring women into other countries where prostitution is legal. The Swedish government remains convinced that it cannot combat trafficking of women and girls without strengthening its work against the local prostitution industry. An additional benefit has also surfaced: arrested customers are more readily cooperating with the police to identify indoor prostitution venues such as brothels, which then are subject to raids. A public education program that includes billboards, seminars, and programs in schools is also a part of the government's effort.[57]

Gunilla Ekberg, special adviser to Sweden's Division for Gender Equality and coordinator of the Nordic Baltic Campaign against Trafficking in Women, cautioned in an interview with this author that much more still needs to be accomplished. There are still insufficient funds for social services for women and girls in the sex trade, especially in the less populated areas, and some police forces, "male-dominated with male values," need training and consciousness raising before they will be willing to arrest male customers. Eckberg also points out that the number of women and girls in prostitution in Sweden has always been low (0.3 per 1,000 compared with the Netherlands' 1.6 per 1,000).[58]

Of course, customers need not be incarcerated if teens are not involved. Stiff fines could make needed social service interventions and prevention strategies for women and girls in prostitution available and might, in and of themselves, cause men to shy away from women in the sex trade. The San Francisco First Offender Program (or Johns' School) has been operating since 1995 and has served over 2,000 men. In lieu of prosecution, first-time offenders enroll in an eight-hour seminar during which they receive information from survivors of prostitution and educators who address the impact of prostitution on women's and girls' lives. Only eighteen men have been arrested for prostitution-related offenses after completing the program. The men pay up to a $500 fee that funds the program as well as services for women and girls. Since 1995, 1,850 girls and over 6,000 women have been assisted with these funds.[59]

Some prostitution experts challenge the effectiveness of such schools for those customers who are the most violent and abusive. Based on research with convicted rapists, they believe that the programs may dissuade the casual, nonviolent user from patronizing the sex trade, but will not persuade the dangerous abusers who need a more long-term intervention.[60]

Pursuing solutions within the framework of violence-against-women initiatives, however, may provide some new approaches that send consistent messages about acceptable social behavior. In the summer of 2002, four women in prostitution were found murdered in Chicago neighborhoods. The *Chicago Tribune* commented several times on the "high-risk lifestyles" of the dead women, and the chief of detectives issued a community alert warning women in the sex trade of the "dangers of their lifestyles."[61] A focus on the women and their choices, not on the violent offenders on the loose in our low-income communities, is the unintended result of this approach. Rather than accepting the inevitability of the violence in prostitution, we need to begin to hold the men accountable who are physically abusing and murdering women and girls. These men, who are deliberately inflicting pain on other human beings, should also be charged with more serious crimes than relatively minor prostitution-related offenses.

Men who buy sex from teens also need serious prosecution. Prostitution survivor Norma Hotaling reminds us that adults are the primary beneficiaries of the commercial exploitation of children, from the customers to the adults who run and profit from the bars, brothels, and escort services that use them. "Why is it," she asks, "that sex with a girl child who is getting paid for it doesn't get attention?"[62]

We have to remember that these prostitutes are children.
It's the same wherever you go in the world. People see a
girl with too much makeup, too little clothes, and they say
"That is a bad girl." . . . This has to stop. It's time we
figured out who the real perpetrators are—and they're not
children.[63]

Remarkably, the authorities almost seem afraid to act when they receive information about crimes that constitute child abuse if they involve paid sex. Tiffany Mason was found in a car performing oral sex on a forty-nine-year-old man in San Francisco. Although the police knew Tiffany wasn't eighteen, they wrote the customer a misdemeanor citation and sent him on his way. When Tiffany was in the police car, she confessed to being fifteen. Yet the officers took no further action. They didn't file a felony charge against the man or even alert their supervisors to the situation, and he never served any time for the offense. "Protecting johns like this is collusion," said Norma Hotaling.[64] Tiffany was dropped off at a youth center from which she fled to reunite herself with her twenty-six-year-old pimp, Damien "Pairadice" Posey, with whom she was romantically involved. Tiffany herself was found a few months later, in August 2001, naked, with a smashed head, floating in Lake Natoma outside Sacramento. She had been dead for about a week.

And in Detroit, a thirty-two-year-old pimp who had been operating a ring of girls as young as thirteen had been earlier brought to the attention of the authorities. Four years before, a girl jumped out of a car and told officers she had been raped, but the authorities filed no charges. Two years after that, police answering a disturbance call at a motel found the pimp with two fifteen-year-old girls, a seventeen-year-old, and an eighteen-year-old. The eighteen-year-old said she had been raped, but again the police did not charge him.[65] More responsive and aggressive action would have put this dangerous abuser behind bars much sooner.

Police, prosecutors, and judges must be trained to overcome their reluctance to prosecute or convict a man for statutory rape or child abuse even if the girl has received payment for her participation. After seventy children were found in the grip of violent, coercive pimps in the West Midlands in the United Kingdom, Detective Sergeant Whitehouse admitted they needed to stop treating children in prostitution as adults and view them as victims of serious crime.[66] Legislation proposed in the United Kingdom in 2003 would create a series of new laws designed to meet the realities of child prostitution and to provide the government with more flexible tools to respond with more specifically tailored punishments. These include severe penalties for those who exploit children for their own gain, as well as a new offense of adult sexual activity with a child. Buying the sexual services of a child would carry a life penalty when the youth is under thirteen years of age, fourteen years' imprisonment when the child is aged thirteen to fifteen, and seven years' imprisonment when he or she is sixteen to seventeen. With these new laws the government stated its intent to establish an unambiguous social standard that it is wrong for an adult to buy or deal in the sexual services of a child.[67]

A new ordinance in Tokyo also provides stiff fines and up to a year in prison for adults who pay for sex with youth under the age of eighteen. As in the United Kingdom, the intent of that ordinance is to shift the focus to the men who patronize teens. The city is aware that the ordinance is not likely to eliminate use of juveniles in prostitution, but it hopes to direct the "spotlight onto the men who are perpetrating this crime and, as a consequence, on society itself."[68]

Media and financial institutions need to do their part. Ads for illegal escort services should not appear in newspapers or in the yellow pages, and credit card companies should not accept purchases from child pornography sites. Determined action from credit card companies and Internet service providers could quickly shut down those sites depicting sexual acts perpetrated against children.

These strategies will require additional police officers, as well as an increased number of male and female officers working undercover. No other method is available to apprehend customers in indoor sex trade locations, and there is no other way to make certain that illegal prostitution is not occurring in the back rooms of otherwise legal strip-clubs or bars. Until localities understand the amount of violence in indoor prostitution, they will be unwilling to make this kind of resource commitment. At the same time that an arrest strategy against customers is pursued, it is important that women in prostitution be given real and practical assistance to leave the sex trade; to deprive the

222   women of money-generating opportunities without providing alternatives could cause more damage to them.

Prosecute pimps. The problem of local pimping is likely more extensive and serious in North America than that of the international trafficking that has claimed much more of the media's attention. In 2001 fifteen of the most notorious pimps in the Atlanta area were federally indicted under the Racketeering Influenced Corrupt Organizations Act (RICO). Prosecutors were said to have used the federal charges because, until recently, pimping was a misdemeanor in Georgia that brought penalties no more serious than for a traffic ticket. All but two of the men pled guilty, and those who went to trial were convicted of engaging in a racketeering conspiracy, enticing juveniles to engage in prostitution, extortion, involuntary servitude, and providing drugs to minors. They received long prison sentences.[69]

As with international trafficking, where federal laws needed modification to take into account previously unacknowledged practices of human trafficking, debt bondage, and slavery, we must take a closer look at the state laws that criminalize pimping to make certain that they give prosecutors and judges the tools to eliminate this kind of human exploitation. In the wake of Tiffany Mason's death, San Francisco authorities have created a "pimp enforcement team," as well as a special prosecutor to work on crimes against women in prostitution.[70] The political will to prosecute men who prey on and exploit vulnerable girls is also required. Law enforcement must learn to identify pimps, brokers, and middlemen, as distinguished from those intimates of the women who may be living off the earnings of their partners but who do not coerce them to participate in the sex trade.

New legal responses, such as those implemented in the human rights field, may be necessary. Analogies to international human rights law are not misplaced. A few years ago, human rights scholar and activist Rhonda Copelon described the close relationship between torture and domestic violence. One of the purposes of abuse of the body is humiliation, she wrote, and "the body is abused and controlled not only for obscene sadistic reasons but ultimately as a pathway to the mind and spirit":

> The purpose of obliterating the personality captures the ultimate horror of both torture and domestic violence as an

assault on human dignity. While severe pain is world-destroying, the person usually regains her "self" when the pain abates. Torture—both intimate and official—seeks more than temporary pain. It seeks to reduce a person to passivity and submission, to destroy self-esteem, confidence in life and capacity for resistance. It involves degradation, humiliation, terror, and shame, which outlast the physical pain and work on the personality, the sense of wholeness and self-worth.[71]

Given the horrifying parallels between torture and domestic violence, understanding the violence experienced by Olivia and other domestic violence victims as torture may help us envision new remedies, focusing us on the roots of this violence in gender inequality and subordination of women.

Broader efforts, beyond those in the legal realm, will also be necessary to combat pimping. For starters, we need to bring an end to our lackadaisical attitude toward pimps. Should it be acceptable to come to a Halloween party dressed as a pimp? A look at Internet costume purveyors' Web sites revealed nine different pimp costumes available on one, and a "Pimps and Hoes" category on another featuring both Black and White models.[72] Pimp costumes were also for sale in a major Chicago grocery store chain. We need to ask ourselves: do pimp costumes help trivialize the violence perpetrated against women and girls in prostitution?

Undertake more research on local prostitution industries. Until we better understand how local prostitution industries operate, we will continue to focus on the women and girls in prostitution, asking why they enter and do or do not leave prostitution, an inquiry that contributes to their being further pathologized and stigmatized. Our need for more information about the men who pay for sex from young teens or from women strung out on heroin is acute. Also essential is a better understanding of the organization of the sex trade industry and its recruitment strategies. Research of this kind, however, is difficult, time-consuming, expensive, and even dangerous. Although funds have been forthcoming for studies of international trafficking, they have generally been lacking for research into local prostitution industries, despite the close connection between international trafficking and local prostitution venues.

Create a community response. In many cases, women on the street attract the attention of neighborhood residents or police officers. Owing to lack of undercover resources, the results have been a de facto decriminalization of the indoor sex trade and a focus on street prostitution, which often leads to an overrepresentation of poor women of color in arrests.

A community's response can help guard against this result. In Chicago, the police department has told activists that, given limited resources, it can only respond to prostitution in those communities in which the residents vociferously complain. In the near north Chicago communities of Wicker Park and Bucktown, residents of this rapidly gentrifying area did begin to complain in 2001–2002, with the result that a high-priced prostitution area or "stroll" began to be broken up through a community policing strategy involving neighborhood residents alerting the police and stepped-up arrests of the women and girls in prostitution. Within months the stroll started moving west into a neighborhood that is poorer and located in a different police district, one that probably will not put similar pressure on its officers, at least for a while.

Interestingly enough, the impetus for the complaints that led to the crackdown was the fact that customers cruising the neighborhood were soliciting residents as they returned home from evening outings or walked their dogs in the early mornings. That neighbors organized to protest this harassment of the community's own women is a positive sign. Yet they also attacked the women in the sex trade as "bad," demonizing them as compared with the women of the neighborhood. A small number of community residents organized, however, to protest the arrest of the girls and women, demanding that the customers be arrested instead, as well as the pimps whom they regularly observed dropping off and watching the young girls. At a well-attended community meeting in March 2003, an approach was discussed centering around stepped-up arrests of the customers and provision of opportunities to women wanting to leave the sex trade, in lieu of prosecution.[73]

These proposed remedies eschew the current popular approach to the problem, a tendency to leap onto the legalization bandwagon because nothing else has been working. Scotland Yard's commissioner has stated, "You've got to be careful about legalizing things just because you don't think what you are doing is successful."[74] And certainly all the evidence should be enough to question a legalization approach that is non–fact-based, oblivious to its implications for the expansion of the global sex industry, and defined by a narrow vision of the role of government in protecting the basic human rights of women and girls, as evidenced by this glib editorial statement in a major international publication:

> In a liberal society, buying sex for money should be regarded as a legitimate commercial transaction, where it takes place between two consenting adults. It might be a transaction with peculiar psychological implications for both parties, but that sort of anxiety is beyond the law's remit.[75]

What can be done, however, to destigmatize women and girls in prostitution? Many of the well-intentioned efforts promoting decriminalization of prostitution are intended to change public perception of women and girls in the sex trade; unfortunately, those undertaking this task downplay the violence and abuse in the process of repositioning paid sex into a category of a legitimate employment or trade. This recharacterization is intended to permanently alter the profound disrespect society bestows on girls and women in prostitution. At first blush, stories of pain and suffering like Olivia's would appear to further stigmatize girls and women in the sex trade industry.

Philosopher Charles Taylor has stressed the importance to individuals of this kind of stigmatization or lack of recognition:

> Non-recognition or misrecognition . . . can be a form of oppression, imprisoning someone in a false, distorted, reduced mode of being. Beyond simple lack of respect, it can inflict a grievous wound, saddling people with crippling self-hatred. Due recognition is not just a courtesy but a vital human need.[76]

Writing that respect is essential for the dignity of men and women, sociologist Richard Sennett tries to build a case for mutual respect among unequal social classes in a new book. Recognizing that inequalities will always be present, owing to disparate natural endowments, luck, and life circumstances, Sennett makes a plea for greater respect from the stronger to the weak.[77] His ideas exemplify the limitations of the approach that many contemporary feminists have taken to prostitution. Respect involves accepting in others what one does not understand, he states; by bestowing respect on someone whom you do not understand, you grant them his or her dignity. And, in a nod to Hegel, by granting them dignity, you strengthen your own.[78]

The danger in this proposal is its acceptance of harmful societal inequalities. A push to bestow respect and dignity, absent an accompanying effort to provide practical individual assistance to open up new opportunity, leaves many women like Olivia abandoned and invisible. As one reviewer of Sennett's book has noted:

> But he is surely remiss not to emphasize more strongly that the greatest lack of respect at present is the equanimity with which the affluent majority in the richest and most wasteful country on earth accepts the misery of the poor minority, as though it was a fact of nature that had nothing to do with them and about which they need feel neither shame nor indignation.[79]

Certainly society's opprobrium toward women in prostitution has played a role in Olivia's lack of self-esteem, but she does not think that during her years on the streets she really cared about what other people thought. "I didn't really know the views of anybody other than the people I was around who were doing the same thing. It was like a subculture, everybody's doing the same thing and everybody reinforces the behavior."

The major problem for Olivia was not the opinions of others, but the experience of the sexual violence itself, the verbal abuse from customers, the drug addiction, and, most fundamentally, the self-hatred that developed from this humiliation and the knowledge that she was allowing all this to happen to her. Olivia's comments finally forced this author, very much against her will, to recognize that the problem of altering perceptions of others in society was the author's issue but not

Olivia's, and was simply missing the point: what Olivia needed was not to be abused, humiliated, and degraded by customers, managers, and pimps.

This is the recognition that Olivia needed. The recognition advocated by those who argue that prostitution is legitimate "sex work" might have left Olivia on the street and dead today. And where is Katrinka today? Is she dead or alive? Olivia needed all of us to see her, but not as a simplistic stereotype—not as a dope fiend or a slut, or as a naive victim needing our protection, or even as a person freely electing prostitution whose choice should be recognized.

Olivia has told her story so that we can understand her personhood in all its complexities and contradictions. We do her and others like her no real favors if we do not validate her experience by moving beyond the stereotypes of women in the sex trade presented by all sides in the great prostitution debate.

Epilogue

And that I should feel this transcendent joy simply because
I have been helped to go on living suggests that I know
something I have not yet told my mind, that within me, I
hold some assurance regarding the value of life, which
makes my fate different from what it appears, different, not
lamentable, grandiose.

— REBECCA WEST, *The Strange Necessity*

As Olivia was driving home after work from a Saturday health fair a
few years ago, she saw Strych on the street. Much to her own surprise,
she pulled the car up and honked the horn. Strych ambled over, and
they had a short conversation.

*There was blood and snot on his sleeve, his arm was in a sling.
He was limping, and still addicted, very much so. He was a
burnt-out case, and obviously living a rough life. I think I was
shocked. I wanted to make sure that was him, because I really
thought he was dead by now after all these years.*

During the conversation Olivia gave him information about entering
drug treatment at the center at which she worked. She could tell Strych
was ashamed. Tears ran down Olivia's cheeks as she drove away. She
knew she had introduced Strych to heroin, and she wondered if things
would have been different for him if he hadn't started shooting dope

with her. This question haunts Olivia still. At the same time, her feelings about all the abuse and violence quickly came to the surface.

> The anger. God, what I'd like to repay him with. But I
> wouldn't like to see him die on the streets like that, especially
> because I know now that there is another way. It was dangerous
> to pull up and stop. I wouldn't want to have a conversation with
> him or come face-to-face with him again, but I think I needed
> that one time. That closed something for me.

Since 1992 Olivia has worked in a variety of responsible positions in the field of social services. In 2002 she finished a three-year stint as coordinator of professional services at a major Chicago drug treatment center, where she was responsible for marketing, community relations, and monitoring of the programs from the standpoint of client satisfaction. Olivia opened up a new chapter in her working life when she assumed a position as director of addiction services at a community counseling center in the western suburbs in April 2002.

Olivia's main personal goal to return to school to complete college was recently realized in 2002, when she finally completed her bachelor's degree. Eventually she wants to possess a graduate degree as well.

> I want a master's degree. I've done very well with what I have,
> but there are a lot of positions that I know that I can do. I have
> trained people who knew less than me for jobs that I wanted and
> couldn't compete for because I didn't have the credential. I am
> going to find a way to do this. It is a dream.

Olivia's work is extremely important to her.

> It is my calling. I feel that I have a responsibility in many
> ways. I am afforded a life that I didn't do anything to deserve,
> and I believe it is because I have a story to tell. It is because I
> can bring some hope to women who are struggling. Because of
> things that have happened and how they have happened, I'm
> beginning to get a clearer picture of my mission. It is to be a
> good example. No matter how far down you go, that there is

> hope. That no matter what situations that come before you, you
> can overcome them. There is a way out.
>
> I had become so comfortable with the idea that this is how
> I was going to die, that I just wanted it to happen and get it
> over with, because it was so painful. How much brighter it
> could have been had there been someone there to take my hand
> and walk me through. I know that is what I'm here for.

Just at the point when Olivia gets tired and thinks it would be so much easier to get a nine-to-five job, the telephone rings or some new offer or situation arises that reminds her of her mission and its central importance in her life.

> I'll never make the money I thought I wanted to make. I really
> have gotten comfortable enough. The richness of my life far
> exceeds anything I could expect as compensation. I know I have
> to do this. I have to pay back what I have been given. That is
> why I am still here.

Olivia also serves as president of Exodus, a program designed and run by women who have escaped prostitution. Exodus aims to provide a support network for prostitution survivors to prevent recidivism and to help the women succeed in their new lives. The women need help with rent, clothing, and getting a job, but they also need ongoing personal and psychological support. Even years later, flashbacks can be triggered through new intimate relationships or other occurrences that can interfere with prostitution recovery.

The Exodus women have developed some creative approaches for support. For example, they believe, as Olivia explains, that spiritual retreats are absolutely essential for them.

> Once or twice a year it is so important to come home, connect
> with your sisters who have been there, and rejuvenate so you
> can come back and continue to do what you need to do in
> society. Talking, dancing, sharing, looking back on your life,
> setting goals, playing. Last year we found a water park, we went
> on a yacht for lunch. We have learned that we deserved a vaca-
> tion, but as we can't afford it, through the graciousness of our

funder, Sophie's Circle, we have been able to continue it over
the years. We're hoping to raise funds so that women never have
to stop enjoying these. It is such a major piece of healing,
especially since you are out of crisis. This is freedom. You talk
about the exodus, out of the bondage into the freedom to be you.
Exodus wants to provide that.

Edwina Gateley comments today about Olivia's role in Exodus:

> Look at women like Olivia, like Louise, look at these
> women, look at the dignity, the inherent pride, the self-
> respect. This is recovery. These women have not just quit
> prostitution and drugs, they have changed who they are.
> They have become proud of themselves. They have become
> women to be reckoned with. These women are in leader-
> ship. They are not just plodding on and surviving, they are
> leadership.[1]

A good percentage of Olivia's time is still devoted to her own personal
recovery. She still makes evening meetings three or four times a week,
and on Saturday she attends a women's group that has a spiritual component, after which the group goes out to eat. She also sponsors many
women in the twelve-step program.

Does Olivia still need to go to all these twelve-step meetings? She
thinks so.

> I'm not seriously worried about lapsing into drinking, drugging,
> or prostituting, but I'm concerned about other behaviors. Part
> of the disease of addiction involves honesty. I have to be totally
> honest with myself and keep a balance in my life. One of the
> things the twelve-step groups do for me now is help me maintain
> balance. You have to realize that everything that happens in life
> is almost brand new for me—whether it's coping with a death
> or opening a bank account at age forty.

Group members help and support one another. The need for balance,
however, cannot be overestimated. As a former drug addict, Olivia has
had to learn to cope with the vicissitudes of life without medicating to

relieve depression, to create peace of mind and even euphoria without drugs. Another important task she focuses on is learning to trust her own instincts: "I know I've always had some good instincts about people. I didn't always follow them. I never learned to listen to those voices inside, but growing spiritually, I've learned to listen to them."

Olivia is a morning person who is usually up by 5:30 A.M. She started rising early when the kids were in the house, because she needed some minutes for herself before the children got up for school. She still keeps that time for herself, a few minutes of meditation and reading, mostly self-help books and novels.

Olivia currently suffers from a long list of health problems. She has a weekly or a twice-weekly headache that she has only recently connected with the many times customers slammed her head against steering wheels, walls, or car windows. Her gallbladder has been removed, and she has ulcers, which she attributes to the effects of years of stress. Olivia says she also suffers from muscle aches, joint pain, painful menstruation, and hepatitis C, as well as memory, vision, and hearing problems. Miraculously, she is not HIV-positive.

> I am not impacted by HIV, escaped by nothing that I ever
> protected or did, [it] just wasn't meant to be. I did everything
> to put myself at risk, everything, with no consciousness of it.
> Even after I heard of AIDS, guys would pay you more not to use
> protection. Another sickness. And so I didn't. I did nothing to
> protect myself. It has been a gift. Because I realize the risks to
> women like myself, I have served on the city and state HIV
> planning groups, and now work as a consultant to a women's
> project providing HIV education throughout the state.

Olivia has also experienced irregular heartbeats. In February 2002 she was hospitalized for chest pains, which traveled down her arm. Tests revealed neither a heart attack nor any artery blockages. A heart valve was found not to be completely functioning, but the condition was not serious enough to cause the symptoms. The episode caused Olivia to substantially cut back on her cigarette smoking, but not to altogether eliminate it.

Olivia's three boys, now in their early twenties, are getting on well with their lives. Her oldest is married and the loving stepfather of a seven-year-old boy, and her middle son recently married his high school sweetheart.

Olivia says repeatedly that she can only be responsible for the choices she makes now; what is past is past. As author Andrew Solomon has written about his depression, "The medicine will not reinvent you. We can never escape from choice itself. One's self lies in the choosing, every choice everyday."[2]

Olivia agrees.

> I do have the power of the choices I make on a daily basis,
> sometimes on an hourly basis. The thoughts may come that I
> choose not to entertain, or I can choose what thoughts I do
> entertain. I have some tools in recovery so that I know what to
> do when I get those kinds of thoughts or urges. It is a real
> freedom of choice, not a false sense of choice.

Solomon has written movingly of the many harrowing depressive episodes he has experienced. He does not regret his depression, because that would be expressing sorrow over the most fundamental part of himself:

> On the happy day when we lose depression, we will lose a
> great deal with it. If the earth could feed itself and us with-
> out rain, and if we conquered the weather and declared
> permanent sun, would we not miss grey days and summer
> storms? As the sun seems brighter and more clear when it
> comes on a rare day of English summer after ten months of
> dismal skies than it can ever seem in the tropics, so recent
> happiness feels enormous and embracing and beyond any-
> thing I have ever imagined. Curiously enough, I love my
> depression. I do not love experiencing my depression, but
> I love the depression itself. I love who I am in the wake
> of it.[3]

Similarly Olivia does not regret having been involved in prostitution for nineteen years.

> When I think about the richness of the experiences that I bring
> to the women I work with today, I realize that I needed, my

God needed me to go through those things. I needed to turn every
single trick. I needed to be sick and stomped on, so that I would
really have a depth of understanding that makes me really good
at what I know and what I can tell women will happen before
it happens. I did everything not to be here. I really know that
whatever I do today, this is what I am supposed to be doing.
God has some work for me to do.

Toward the end of her book about her experiences with women on the
streets of Chicago, Edwina Gateley reproduces a letter she received
from a woman named Mezzie, written from the Cook County Jail,
where she had landed when the police picked her up on some old
warrants. An orphan, Mezzie had been physically abused in two foster
homes at age nine and ran away at age fourteen. After twenty years on
the streets in prostitution and heroin addiction, she joined Gateley's
program. Mezzie's letter from jail means the world to Olivia. It covers
everything that Olivia thinks needs to be said about girls and women
in prostitution. Here is part of that letter:

> Dear Edwina,
>
> Here I am, sitting in familiar surroundings . . .
>
> I can't afford to feel comfortable, Edwina. For me that's
> accepting my dope mentality. I need to look at my life and
> see where I'm all screwed up. But I also need to let the
> positive things I've done soak in and become me. If I do
> this I won't keep thinking of myself as worthless and nega-
> tive. I'll see me as you do.
>
> You believed in me and I tried. Someday, I'll believe in
> me too. I'd hate to die here in jail or die face down in some
> cooker of dope. But if I do, remember that I knew you
> loved me.[4]

Seven years later, in 1992, Mezzie died of AIDS. At the end, Mezzie, in the words of Gateley, too battered to make it and too bruised to
survive, was still in prostitution and using drugs. Olivia attended her
funeral.

Notes

Prologue

1. Olivia is her real name. To protect the privacy of her family members, however, Olivia has chosen not to use her last name in this work.

2. In 1996 U.S. profits in stripclubs, private dancing, and escort services were calculated at $4.25 billion a year. This figure does not include adult entertainment on the Internet, adult videos, pay-per-view TV, and the like. Anthony Flint, "Ads Generate Dollars, Allies," *Boston Globe*, 2 December 1996.

3. Jody Raphael, *Saving Bernice: Battered Women, Welfare, and Poverty* (Boston: Northeastern University Press, 2000).

Chapter One

1. Alta, interview by author, 28 September 2001.

2. Ibid.

3. Ibid.

4. Surprisingly, many prostitution researchers neglect to ask about family dysfunction, dwelling instead on the behaviors of women in prostitution as if they had occurred in a vacuum.

5. Jody Raphael and Deborah Shapiro, "Sisters Speak Out: The Lives and Needs of Prostituted Women in Chicago: A Research Study" (Chicago: Center for Impact Research, 2001), 16.

6. In a group of thirty-five adolescents involved in prostitution, 20 percent had a parent involved in drug or alcohol abuse; see Magnus J. Seng, "Child Sexual Abuse and Adolescent Prostitution: A Comparative Analysis," *Adolescence* 24, no. 95 (1989): 669. Fifty-eight percent of the fifty women incarcerated for prostitution in 1998 and 1999 in a northeastern city's jail had one or both parents addicted to alcohol, and 40 percent had at least one parent addicted to illegal drugs; see Maureen A. Norton-Hawk, "The Life-course of Prostitution," *Women, Girls & Criminal Justice* 3, no. 1 (2002): 7. Fifty-eight percent of 200 women involved in street prostitution in San Francisco

reported that their parents were involved in excessive drinking, and 28 percent had parents who used drugs excessively; see Mimi H. Silbert and Ayala M. Pines, "Entrance into Prostitution," Youth & Society 13, no. 4 (1982): 484. In research with forty-five adolescent females involved in prostitution, compared with thirty-seven adolescents in the same locations who were not, 83 percent of the girls in prostitution had excessive drinking in their parents' homes, compared with a figure of 77 percent for the girls not involved in prostitution; see Susan M. Nadon, Catherine Koverola, and Eduard H. Schludermann, "Antecedents to Prostitution: Childhood Victimization," Journal of Interpersonal Violence 13, no. 2 (1998): 215. Of twenty women involved in exotic dancing in stripclubs in more than ten U.S. cities, 75 percent stated that one or both of their parents abused alcohol, and 50 percent had at least one parent who abused drugs; see Nova Sweet and Richard Tewksbury, "'What's a Nice Girl Like You Doing in a Place Like This?' Pathways to a Career in Stripping," Sociological Spectrum 20 (2000): 334. Sixty-two percent of women in prostitution interviewed in the Los Angeles County Jail said their parents abused substances. Sixty percent of a larger sample of 159 women in prostitution, not in the jail, indicated substance abuse by one of both parents; see the Mary Magdalene Project, "Research Report on Street Prostitution" (report, Los Angeles, 2001), 169.

7. James A. Inciardi et al., "Prostitution, IV Drug Use, and Sex-For-Crack Exchanges among Serious Delinquents: Risks for HIV Infection," Criminology 29, no. 2 (1991): 226.

8. Nadon, Koverola, and Schludermann, "Antecedents to Prostitution," 215.

9. Joseph B. Kuhns III, Kathleen M. Heide, and Ira Silverman, "Substance Use/Misuse among Female Prostitutes and Female Arrestees," International Journal of the Addictions 27, no. 11 (1992): 1289. Fifty-one percent of the women in prostitution in the Los Angeles County jail began using drugs at the age of fifteen and under, most between the ages of fourteen and fifteen. Mary Magdalene Project, "Research Report," 192.

10. Mary Magdalene Project, "Research Report," 169, 179.

11. Raphael and Shapiro, "Sisters Speak Out," 15.

12. Sixty percent of a jail sample of women in prostitution witnessed their parents separating or divorcing, and 56 percent experienced the death of a family member or close relative; see Norton-Hawk, "Lifecourse of Prostitution," 7. Twenty-four percent of a Los Angeles sample had a father deceased; see Mary Magdalene Project, "Research Report," 169. In a San Francisco sample, 39 percent were raised by mothers only, and in 67 percent of the cases one of the parents was periodically absent from home; see Silbert and Pines, "Entrance into Prostitution," 475. Sixty-five percent of a sample of 43 women in prostitution in a Midwestern city suffered abandonment through death

or desertion; see Rochelle L. Dalla, "Exposing the 'Pretty Woman' Myth: A Qualitative Examination of the Lives of Female Streetwalking Prostitutes," *Journal of Sex Research* 37, no. 4 (2000): 349.

13. Cecilia Benoit and Alison Millar, "Dispelling Myths and Understanding Realities: Working Conditions, Health Status, and Exiting Experiences of Sex Workers" (report, Victoria, B.C.: 2001), 28–29. Although the majority of the respondents in the sample were living with both biological parents at the time of birth, by age five, less than half were still living with both parents, and by the age of ten, the figure had dropped to 34.4 percent. The number of respondents going into foster care steadily increased with age. Aboriginal respondents were three times more likely to have been in state institutions than others in the sample. Sixty-four percent of the women in a western Canadian sample had been involved in the welfare system as children, and of these, 78 percent had been taken into care and resided in foster care or group homes; see Nixon et al., "The Everyday Occurrence: Violence in the Lives of Girls Exploited through Prostitution," *Violence against Women* 8, no. 9 (2002): 1023.

14. Silbert and Pines, "Entrance into Prostitution," 476–77.

15. Mary Magdalene Project, "Research Report," 179.

16. Silbert and Pines, "Entrance into Prostitution," 478. The most recent national study found that 25.5 percent of all women will be subject to violence from an intimate partner during their lifetime. Patricia Tjaden and Nancy Thoennes, "Extent, Nature, and Consequences of Intimate Partner Violence: Findings from the National Violence against Women Survey 2000" (report, Washington, D.C., 2000), 9.

17. Chicago Coalition for the Homeless, "Unlocking Options for Women: A Survey of Women in Cook County Jail" (report, Chicago, 2001), 14.

18. Raphael and Shapiro, "Sisters Speak Out," 15.

19. Ibid., 16. Forty-nine percent of a large sample of women in prostitution in San Francisco reported that as children they had been hit or beaten by a caregiver until they were injured or bruised; see Melissa Farley et al., "Prostitution in Five Countries: Violence and Post-Traumatic Stress Disorder," *Feminism & Psychology* 8, no. 4 (1998), posted at www.prostitutionresearch. com. Fifty percent of a Canadian sample suffered physical abuse from their mother or father, using a hand, wooden spoon, rope, metal-end belt, chair, willow switch, or razor strap; see Benoit and Millar, "Dispelling Myths," 32. Thirty-nine percent of a sample of one hundred women in street prostitution in Washington, D.C., said they were beaten as children until bruised; see Roberto J. Valera et al., "Perceived Health Needs of Inner-City Street Prostitutes: A Preliminary Study," *American Journal of Health Behavior* 25, no. 1 (2001): 53. Forty-six percent of a jail sample of women in prostitution reported physical abuse at the hands of an immediate family member; see Norton-Hawk,

238   "Lifecourse of Prostitution," 7. Almost 77 percent of women in street prostitution in Florida had been victims of physical abuse in childhood; see Elizabeth Mayfield Arnold, J. Chris Stewart, and C. Aaron McNeece, "Perpetrators as Victims: Understanding Violence by Female Street-Walking Prostitutes in Florida," *Violence and Victims* 16, no. 2 (2001): 150. Fifty-one percent of the women in prostitution in the Cook County Jail sample in Chicago reported physical abuse in their households while growing up; see Chicago Coalition, "Unlocking Options," 15. A slightly smaller number, 41 percent, reported physical abuse in the Los Angeles Jail research; see Mary Magdalene Project, "Research Report," 181. In another San Francisco sample, 62 percent of the subjects were beaten while they were growing up. Forty-five percent were physically abused regularly (once a month or more often), and 12 percent several times a month. In over three-quarters of the cases, the beater was a male in some position of authority over the girl. See Silbert and Pines, "Entrance into Prostitution," 479. A third of the females sampled in the Canadian National Juvenile Prostitution Survey indicated they were victims of physical abuse while growing up; see Deborah R. Brock, *Making Work, Making Trouble: Prostitution as a Social Problem* (Toronto: University of Toronto Press, 1998), 111.

20. For an extended discussion of the relationship of running away and prostitution, see chapter 2, beginning at endnote 19.

21. Claudine O'Leary, interview with author, 19 January 2001.

22. Ibid.

23. D. Kelly Weisberg, *Children of the Night: A Study of Adolescent Prostitution* (Lexington, Mass.: Lexington Books, 1985), 90.

24. Silbert and Pines, "Entrance into Prostitution," 477, 484.

25. Weisberg, *Children of the Night*, 90.

26. Raphael and Shapiro, "Sisters Speak Out," 17. There could be more than one person in a household involved in prostitution activities.

27. Ibid.

28. O'Leary, interview.

29. These comments were noted in a review of the Center for Impact Research's completed survey forms.

30. Ibid.

31. In a sample from Victoria, B.C., researchers found that 55.3 percent of the females had been victims of sexual abuse, mostly at the hands of their fathers or male guardians; see Benoit and Millar, "Dispelling Myths," 33. Sixty-eight and two-thirds percent of a sample of women in prostitution on the streets in Florida said they had been sexually abused as children; see Arnold, Stewart, and McNeece, "Perpetrators as Victims," 150. In a San Francisco sample, 60 percent were victims of sexual abuse, 67 percent by father figures; see Silbert and Pines, "Entrance into Prostitution," 126. Thirty-nine percent of a sample of women in the Los Angeles jail were sexually abused as

children, and of these, 69 percent were abused at age ten or younger. See Mary Magdalene Project, "Research Report," 181. Fifty-three percent of the women in the Chicago jail sample had experienced sexual abuse as children; see Chicago Coalition, "Unlocking Options," 15. In a larger Los Angeles sample, 87 percent were sexually assaulted, and of these assaults 62 percent involved incest, with the father or father figure being the primary abuser; see Mary Magdalene Project, "Research Report," 164. Forty-four percent of a sample of 100 women in street prostitution in Washington, D.C., reported unwanted sexual contact as children; see Valera et al., "Perceived Health Needs," 53. Forty-five percent of the exotic dancers in a recent sample were raped or molested as children; see Jennifer K. Wesley, "Growing Up Sexualized: Issues of Power and Violence in the Lives of Female Exotic Dancers," *Violence against Women* 8, no. 10 (2002): 1193. Sexual abuse or molestation as a child was reported by a third of a group of strippers in another sample; see Sweet and Tewksbury, "'What's a Nice Girl Like You?'" 338. Sixty-eight percent of another study's adolescents involved in prostitution were sexually abused in childhood; see Nadon, Koverola, and Schludermann, "Antecedents to Prostitution," 214. In intensive interviews with women on the street in a Midwestern city, researchers found that 84 percent had been sexually abused as children; see Rochelle L. Dalla, "'Et Tu Brute?' A Qualitative Analysis of Streetwalking Prostitutes' Interpersonal Support Networks," *Journal of Family Issues* 22, no. 8 (2001): 1075. Sixty-five percent of women in another U.S. sample reported childhood sexual assault; see Janice Raymond and Donna M. Hughes, "Sex Trafficking of Women in the United States: International and Domestic Trends" (report, Kingston, R.I., 2001), 46. To compute the national prevalence of childhood sexual assault, the author used the figure from the well-regarded 1998 research of the Tjaden & Thoennes "National Violence against Women Study," commissioned by the U.S. Department of Justice and posted on its Web site at www.csom.org on 29 May 2003.

32. Melissa Farley and Howard Barkan, "Prostitution, Violence against Women, and Posttraumatic Stress Disorder," *Women & Health* 27, no. 3 (1998): 40. In another San Francisco sample, researchers found an average of two perpetrators per respondent; see Silbert and Pines, "Entrance into Prostitution," 126. Just under a quarter of another sample in Victoria, B.C., said they had multiple abusers; see Benoit and Millar, "Dispelling Myths," 33.

33. Norton-Hawk, "Lifecourse of Prostitution," 7. The early age of this sexual abuse is confirmed in other studies. For example, the sexual abuse reported in a sample of exotic dancers took place between the ages of seven and ten, although for some it began as early as age four or as late as age thirteen; see Sweet and Tewksbury, "'What's a Nice Girl?'" 338.

34. Dalla, "Exposing the 'Pretty Woman' Myth," 349.

35. Nixon et al., "The Everyday Occurrence," 1039.

36. Chicago Coalition, "Unlocking Options," 15.

37. Susan F. McClanahan et al., "Pathways into Prostitution among Female Jail Detainees and Their Implications for Mental Health Services," *Psychiatric Services* 50, no. 12 (1999): 1611.

38. Jody M. Greene, Susan T. Ennett, and Christopher L. Ringwalt, "Prevalence and Correlates of Survival Sex among Runaway and Homeless Youth," *American Journal of Public Health* 89, no. 9 (1999): 1408.

39. Diana E. H. Russell, "The Making of a Whore," in *Issues in Intimate Violence*, ed. R. Bergen (Thousand Oaks, Calif.: Sage, 1998), 67.

40. Ibid., 74.

41. Ibid., 70–71.

42. Ibid., 76.

43. Ibid., 70.

44. Larissa Branin, "Back on the Streets," *Hope*, no. 12 (January/February 1998): 54.

45. David Finkelhor, "The Trauma of Child Sexual Abuse: Two Models," in *Lasting Effects of Child Abuse*, eds. G. Powell and G. Wyatt (Newbury Park, Calif.: Sage, 1988), 69. A more psychological approach focuses on the disassociation that is always involved in incest. Sex that is not mutually interactive will eventually involve women in disengagement, dissociation, and disembodiment. Children who are abused develop enhanced capacities to disassociate. According to incest expert Judith Lewis Herman, "Studies have documented the connection between the severity of childhood abuse and the degree of familiarity with dissociative states." See Judith Lewis Herman, *Trauma and Recovery* (New York: Basic Books, 1992), 102. Eventually disassociation becomes not merely a defensive adaptation but "the fundamental principle of personality organization" (ibid., 102). Herman believes that the fragmentation in consciousness that occurs prevents the ordinary integration of knowledge, memory, emotional states, and bodily experience, which, in terms of childhood development, can be disastrous. Incest victims seek freedom from coercion and control but in early adulthood experience major impairments relating to self-care, cognition, and identity that often cause the trauma to be reencountered or reenacted, with deficiencies in self-protection common (ibid., 111). Herman also believes that children who are victims of child abuse develop a sense of themselves as bad, taking upon themselves the shame and guilt of their abusers. "The profound sense of inner badness becomes the core around which the abused child's identity is formed, and it persists into adult life" (ibid., 105).

46. Leon E. Pettiway, *Workin' It: Women Living through Drugs and Crime* (Philadelphia: Temple University Press, 1997), xxx.

47. Michele Harway and Marsha Liss, "Dating Violence and Teen Prostitution: Adolescent Girls in the Justice System," in *Beyond Appearance: A New Look at*

Adolescent Girls, eds. J. Worell, M. Roberts, and N. Johnson (Washington, D.C.: American Psychological Association, 1999), 292–93.

48. Ruth Rosen, *The Lost Sisterhood: Prostitution in America, 1900–1918* (Baltimore: Johns Hopkins University Press, 1982), 143.

49. Ibid.

50. Ibid., 159.

51. Ibid., 144.

52. Ibid., 162.

53. Ibid., 161.

54. Ibid., 162.

55. Ibid., 167. The memoirs of Madeleine (first published in 1919), describing her experiences in brothels in St. Louis and Chicago in the 1890s, demonstrate the validity of Rosen's point. Madeleine's alcoholic father was absent, and her mother struggled to care for a large family. Madeleine describes how the combination of poverty, lack of guidance, weakened family bonds, lack of friends, and the attractions of sex worked to influence her entry into prostitution at age seventeen:

> One would have to live through it to realize the agony a high-spirited sensitive girl may endure when she is the town drunkard's daughter, especially when that town drunkard had once been one of the leading citizens.
>
> I was never permitted to forget that this was my position. I had no girl companions—my sisters were too small. Instead of girl friends, I made clandestine visits to ignorant, corrupt women who wore a scanty garb of respectability, and whose influence was far more pernicious than a public prostitute's would have been. I had no boy friends. Our home was far too squalid to invite them to, even if there had been any boys who would have gone with me openly. I was fair game for any predacious male who might be attracted by my youthful face or my well-developed figure. . . .
>
> I had not only lost my father's support in material matters; I had lost his protection as well. My mother was tied hand and foot by ill health, poverty, a sickly baby, and the care of a large family. I needed both my parents; I had neither. The mating instinct was developing strongly and I had no legitimate outlet of study, amusement, companionship, or recreation.

Madeleine, *Madeleine: An Autobiography* (New York: Persea Books, 1986), 12–13.

56. Rosen, *The Lost Sisterhood*, 175.

57. Ibid.

CHAPTER TWO

1. Alta, interview by author, 20 January 2003.

2. In determining the mean age of entry into prostitution, it is essential

242   to separate samples of teens in prostitution from those encompassing both teens and adults; obviously the average age of entry in teen-only samples will be lower. For example, in a sample of forty-five juveniles ranging in age from thirteen to eighteen years, interviewed in the mid-1990s, the average age of initial involvement was fourteen years; 89 percent of the girls were sixteen or younger when they began; see Nadon, Koverola, and Schludermann, "Antecedents to Prostitution," 213. When researchers questioned women, all of whom had begun in prostitution before age eighteen, they found that almost two-thirds began their involvement when they were fifteen years old or less. Over a third were between the ages of eleven and thirteen, and another third were between fourteen and fifteen; see Nixon et al., "The Everyday Occurrence," 1022. In a San Francisco sample, the mean age for juvenile entry into prostitution was thirteen years; see Silbert and Pines, "Entrance into Prostitution," 483.

3. Chicago Coalition, "Unlocking Options," 14.

4. Raphael and Shapiro, "Sisters Speak Out," 13.

5. In a San Francisco sample, the average age of starting prostitution was sixteen. Of the respondents, 62 percent were under sixteen when they began; see Silbert and Pines, "Entrance into Prostitution," 483. Researchers in Victoria, B.C., found that the female respondents' median age of entry was eighteen years, with that of Aboriginal women still younger at the median age of seventeen; see Beloit and Millar, "Dispelling Myths," 35. African-American women in one Cook County (Chicago) Jail sample began prostitution earlier than the other women in the sample; see McClanahan et al., "Pathways into Prostitution," 1609. In a jail sample in a northeastern U.S. city, the median age of the first paid sexual intercourse was eighteen years; see Norton-Hawk, "Lifecourse of Prostitution," 7. In a research sample in the Los Angeles Jail, the average age of beginning in prostitution was fourteen, as was the average number of years the women had been involved in prostitution; see Mary Magdalene Project, "Research Report," 142. The mean entry age for a sample in Washington, D.C., was 17.85 years; see Valera et al., "Perceived Health Needs," 53. The mean entry age in a sample in a Midwestern city was 19.4 years; see Dalla, "Exposing the 'Pretty Woman' Myth," 349. The mean age of entry in a sample from Minneapolis of women in both indoor and outdoor prostitution was eighteen; see Ruth Parriott, "Health Experiences of Twin Cities Women Used in Prostitution: Survey Findings and Recommendations" (report, Minneapolis, 1994), 10. In a sample of almost two thousand women in Vancouver, the average age of entry into the sex trade was 16.98; see Leonard Cler-Cunningham, "Violence against Women in Vancouver's Street Level Sex Trade and the Police Response" (report, Vancouver, 2001), 5. Fifty percent of a small sample of U.S. women interviewed who were trafficked for prostitution began between the ages of thirteen and eighteen; see H. Patricia

Hynes, "The United States Interview Findings and Data Analysis: A Survey of Trafficked Women and Women in Prostitution," in "A Comparative Study of Women Trafficked in the Migration Process: Patterns, Profiles, and Health Consequences of Sexual Exploitation in Five Countries" (report, Kingston, R.I., 2002).

6. Raphael and Shapiro, "Sisters Speak Out," 13–14.

7. Maureen A. Norton-Hawk, "Prostitution Is Not about Sex: The Vicious Circle of Street Violence," unpublished manuscript.

8. Pariott, "Health Experiences," 10.

9. Priscilla Pyett and Deborah Warr, "Women at Risk in Sex Work: Strategies for Survival," *Journal of Sociology* 35, no. 2 (1999): 186, 194.

10. Stephanie Church et al., "Violence by Clients towards Female Prostitutes in Different Work Settings: Questionnaire Survey," *British Medical Journal* 322, no. 7285 (2001): 524.

11. S. T. Green et al., "Female Streetworker-Prostitutes in Glasgow: A Descriptive Study of Their Lifestyle," *AIDS Care* 5, no. 3 (1993): 323.

12. Eleanor Maticka-Tyndale et al., "Exotic Dancing and Health," *Women & Health* 31, no. 1 (2000): 93.

13. Kelly Holsopple, "Stripclubs according to Strippers," in *Making the Harm Visible: Global Sexual Exploitation of Women and Girls* (Kingston, R.I.: Coalition against Trafficking in Women, 1999), 255.

14. Wesley, "Growing Up," 1192.

15. Sweet, "'What's a Nice Girl like You?'" 335.

16. Marcia Hood-Brown, "Trading for a Place: Poor Women and Prostitution," *Journal of Poverty* 2, no. 3 (1989): 19.

17. Prostitution Unit Officers, interview by author, 8 November 2000.

18. Adrienne Sanders, "A Hack's View of Hookers," *Examiner*, 9 May 2002.

19. Richard J. Estes and Neil Alan Weiner, "The Commercial Sexual Exploitation of Children in the U.S., Canada, and Mexico" (report, Philadelphia, 2001), 27.

20. Over two-thirds of the women in the sample were runaways, but almost all the juveniles (96 percent) had run away from home. Silbert and Pines, "Entrance into Prostitution," 485.

21. Almost three-quarters of the Vancouver women had left their parents' or guardian's home permanently at age sixteen or younger. Cler-Cunningham, "Violence against Women," 5.

22. The National Juvenile Prostitution Survey in Canada found that three-quarters of the respondents had run away from home on at least one occasion, and almost three-fifths described their action as a means of escaping family problems. Brock, *Making Work*, 110.

23. Almost 75 percent of this sample ran away from home as children,

with 29 percent running away more than ten times. The median age of first running away was thirteen years, and 25 percent first ran away between the ages of seven to ten. Norton-Hawk, "Lifecourse of Prostitution," 7.

24. In this jail sample, 62 percent left home under the age of eighteen years. Mary Magadelene Project, "Research Report," 178.

25. Almost 56 percent of these women stated they had run away from home at least once, with a mean age of the first running away episode at 13.4 years. About a third of the women said they ran away two to four times, 21 percent five to ten times, and 30 percent more than ten times. Raphael and Shapiro, "Sisters Speak Out," 16.

26. Forty percent of this sample ran away from home during early adolescence. Dalla, "Exposing the 'Pretty Woman' Myth," 349.

27. Norton-Hawk, "Lifecourse of Prostitution," 7.

28. Benoit and Millar, "Dispelling Myths," 28.

29. McClanahan et al., "Pathways into Prostitution," 1611.

30. Seng, "Child Sexual Abuse," 672–73.

31. Ronald L. Simons and Les B. Whitbeck, "Sexual Abuse as a Precursor to Prostitution and Victimization among Adolescent and Adult Homeless Women," *Journal of Family Issues* 12, no. 3 (1991): 375.

32. Nadon, Koverola, and Schludermann, "Antecedents to Prostitution," 219.

33. Andrea Dworkin, *Life and Death*, (New York: Free Press, 1997), 143.

34. Maggie O'Neill, *Prostitution and Feminism: Towards a Politics of Feeling* (Malden, Mass.: Blackwell Publishers, 2001), 112.

35. Norma Hotaling, "Increased Demand Resulting in the Flourishing Recruitment and Trafficking in Women and Girls" (paper presented at the Annual Conference on Criminal Justice Research and Evaluation, Washington, D.C., July 2001), 2. See also Diane Cardwell, "Fears That City's Flesh Trade May Be Getting Younger," *New York Times*, 7 December 2002, quoting New York City law enforcement officials that some girls in prostitution in that city are as young as eleven.

36. Hotaling, "Increased Demand," 4.

37. *Chicago after Dark: An Upscale Adult Leisure-Time Guide*, April 2002, 12.

38. Adrienne Sanders, "Pimp in Tiffany's Series Charged," *Examiner*, 18 December 2002.

39. A half-page ad featuring a young woman in such a schoolgirl pose appeared in *Chicago after Dark*, April 2002, 36.

40. Maureen Norton-Hawk, "Social Class, Drugs, Gender and the Limitations of the Law: Contrasting the Elite Prostitute with the Street Prostitute," *Studies in Law, Politics, and Society* 29 (2003): 123.

41. Sarah Lyall, "Britain's Hunt for Child Pornography Users Nets Hundreds besides Pete Townshend," *New York Times*, 15 January 2003. Certainly

the writings of some male customers on the Internet describing their sex-oriented tours abroad reveal a stunning disregard for issues of child abuse. Many, well aware of the ages of the girls, convince themselves that in developing countries sex with minors is both legal as well as culturally acceptable, which frees them to act upon what might have remained fantasies back home:

> I was among a couple of girls and they came very close and I could feel they wanted me. I called a taxi and we got to my hotel, my friend and me in the back of the car and her sister in front and when we took off I put my arm around her and gently kissed her and found her breasts to be naked under her shirt and she could not wait until we got to my room and she sat on my lap and my hands discovered that she was wet and I found it very difficult to get my dick out of my trouser and I couldn't help making love to her while the taxi got stuck in the Jakarta traffic on the way back to the hotel.
>
> When we got to my room her sister said that she was tired and got into my bed while I first jumped in the shower and my friend followed me and we washed each other and I never forget her small breasts and her hard nibbles and she was shaved completely and I sat in front of her and licked her under the running water. We got back completely naked and her sister slept on one side of the large bed while I got into the other side and took my friend in the middle. She was a schoolgirl and had her homework with her and I told her about places I have seen or lived in but she had to learn about in geography. She was very close and completely naked and under the cool air from the air con I felt her body heat. I placed my head on her lap while she sat in the middle of the bed with her schoolbooks and I could smell her and I kissed her lower body. . . .
>
> Only when we were finished and she rested on my chest and I gently kissed her face and touched her nice black hair I discovered that her sister wasn't asleep at all but had watched us all of the time.

Another English-speaking man has written:

> The hotel girls are usually younger than most other "available" girls in Bangkok, 14–15 year olds being rather common. They are in effect "owned" by the hotel, which means that you can treat them more or less any way you want—and many men do. Hotels like this should be like paradise for those of us who are into S & M [sadomasochism].

Both these descriptions were found on the Internet World Sex Guide under Indonesia at www.porncave.com/content/worldsex on 2 April 2001.

42. Amy O'Neill Richard, "International Trafficking in Women to the United States: A Contemporary Manifestation of Slavery and Organized Crime" (report, Washington, D.C., 1999), 3, 5.

43. Audrey Gillan and Peter Moszynski, "Aid Workers in Africa 'Bought Child Sex with Food,'" *Guardian Weekly*, 7–13 March 2002.

44. Jay Reeves, "Charges of Sex Acts Shake Girls' Lockup," *Chicago Tribune*, 18 June 2001.

45. "Classified ads," *Chicago after Dark*, April 2002, 52.

46. Louise Eek, "Prostitution as Male Violence against Women" (speech delivered at the Swedish Embassy, Paris, France, 11 March 2003).

47. Raoul V. Mowatt, "Where There's Smoking . . . There's B96 with a Message," *Chicago Tribune*, 24 May 2002, Section 5.

48. Others who regularly listen to the radio station have supplied this information to the author. *Chicago Reporter* journalist Rupa Shenoy also heard one of these ads and followed up with a story. She found that the same advertisement had run on WKSC-FM, known as KISS-FM. John Gehron, regional vice president and marketing manager for Clear Channel Radio, owner of KISS-FM, told Shenoy, "I don't think that this commercial is unethical, it's a legitimate business and they are looking for people to work. I think it's an individual's choice to decide whether they want to work in that business or not. . . . I think it could create an opportunity for the right woman." B-96 confirmed that the station had played the ad, which, according to Shenoy, nets it $500 a day in revenue, for the last four years. The *Chicago Reporter* received no response to its story from the stations, the club, or the general public. Rupa Shenoy, "Clubs Promise Path from Poverty," *Chicago Reporter*, February 2003; Rupa Shenoy, interview by author, 11 March 2003.

49. This description was found at www.stripclublist.com on 17 April 2002 under the Chicago listings.

50. O'Leary, interview by author, 19 January 2001.

51. Ann Goetting, *Getting Out: Life Stories of Women Who Left Abusive Men* (New York: Columbia University Press, 1999), 6.

52. Alexa Albert, *Brothel: Mustang Ranch and Its Women* (New York: Random House, 2001), 77–79.

53. Maya Angelou, *Gather Together in My Name* (New York: Bantam Books, 1997), 161–63, 191.

54. Mike Goens, "Girl's Mom: Daughter Forced into Prostitution," *Florence (AL) Times Daily*, 11 February 2000.

55. Many of these girls were said to be homeless runaways who were treated with lavish generosity, alternated with harsh physical and sexual violence, to get them to cooperate in the prostitution scheme; see Shia Kapos, "Alleged Sex Ring Detailed," *Chicago Tribune*, 16 January 2003, Metro Section. In Quebec City, authorities said that the Wolf Pack gang lured girls into prostitution, showering them with expensive gifts, money, and drugs until they fell in love with their recruiters. When the girls turned eighteen they were often required to work as strippers or lap dancers in clubs operated by a biker gang;

see Rheal Saguin, "Web Site Lured Girls, Officials Say," *Toronto Globe and Mail*, 20 December 2002. The New England–based Paul and Lisa Program has been providing services to runaways and girls in the sex trade since 1980. Pimps, it tells the girls, masquerade as talent scouts, professional businessmen, sports persons, teachers, and photographers, and often remind someone of the man next door—in other words, well cultured, well informed, and very manipulative and convincing. The program advises that the recruiting tactics and skills of both pimps and madams should never be underestimated, and lists several examples of recruitment strategies of which girls should be aware. They include:

> A photographer approaches you in a shopping mall.
>
> You are approached by a person with a business card or other business credentials, promoting modeling or business careers.
>
> Being asked to leave familiar surroundings and/or go to an out of the ordinary or questionable location for a job interview, photo session, meeting with others, hotel, warehouse, parking lot or out of town location.
>
> The "Pretty Woman" Syndrome—being offered travel, parties, new friends, excitement, with no strings or responsibilities attached.

This material was taken from the Paul and Lisa Web site at www.pauland lisa.org/escapemyth.html on 16 April 2002.

56. O'Leary, interview.

57. Barnardo's, "Stolen Childhood," (report, Ilford, U.K., 2002), 8.

58. Angus Stickler, "Child Prostitution Crisis," BBC News, 29 July 2001.

59. Cardwell, "Fears That City's Flesh Trade."

60. These excerpts from the Tom Leykis Show of 27 December 1999 were found at www.mediawatch.com/leykis.html on 27 November 2001.

61. O'Neill, *Prostitution and Feminism*, 79.

62. Cherry Kingsley and Melanie Mark, "Sacred Lives: Canadian Aboriginal Children & Youth Speak Out about Sexual Exploitation" (report, Vancouver, B.C., 2001), 31.

63. O'Leary, interview.

64. Jannit Rabinovitch and Megan Lewis, "'Impossible, eh?' The Story of PEERS" (report, Vancouver, B.C., 2001), 8. One Fulton County (Atlanta) Juvenile Court judge reports that he sees twelve-year olds in love with twenty-two- and twenty-three-year-old men: "They'll do anything for them, including prostitution"; see Jane O. Hansen, "Selling Atlanta's Children: Prostitutes Getting Younger as Sex Trade Grows, Judges Say," *Atlanta Journal-Constitution*, 7 January 2001. Another judge remarked, "They come in on charges that are relationship-based. But how do you replace an exploitative relationship?" see

248

Jane O. Hansen, "Selling Atlanta's Children: The Girls—Promise of Easy Life Pulls the Young to Streets," *Atlanta Journal-Constitution*, 7 January 2001.

65. In 70 percent of the cases, the pimps were much older than the women, with age differences from eleven to thirty-five years. Hynes, "The United States Interview Findings," 195.

66. Brock, *Making Work*, 110. In a small sample in New Zealand, the majority of whom were involved in indoor prostitution activities, 10 percent reported that their boyfriends had arranged their first prostitution encounter; see Sarah E. Romans et al., "The Mental and Physical Health of Female Sex Workers: A Comparative Study," *Australian and New Zealand Journal of Psychiatry* 35, no. 1 (2001): 78.

67. Rabinovitch and Lewis, "'Impossible, eh?'" 57.

68. Raphael and Shapiro, "Sisters Speak Out," 17.

69. Nixon et al., "The Everyday Occurrence," 1025; Benoit and Millar, "Dispelling Myths," 36.

70. Valera et al, "Perceived Health Needs," 55.

71. Silbert and Pines, "Entrance into Prostitution," 484.

72. Claire E. Sterk, *Tricking and Tripping: Prostitution in the Era of AIDS* (Putnam Valley, N.Y.: Social Change Press, 2000), 32.

73. Raphael and Shapiro, "Sisters Speak Out," 17.

74. Mary Magdalene Project, "Research Report," 155.

75. "Monica," interview by author, 21 September 2001.

76. Estes and Weiner, "Commercial Sexual Exploitation," 10. These and other prevalence rates were computed by estimating the number of homeless youth and applying a figure of 60 to 70 percent of that number who are said to be involved in prostitution. Both figures used in this calculation are merely estimates. For example, the Chicago Coalition for the Homeless recently estimated that over the course of a year approximately 26,000 youth in Illinois experience homelessness. Of these, 12,000 experience chronic homelessness. That would mean that about 8,400 youth in the state are involved in prostitution. See Chicago Coalition for the Homeless, "Youth on the Streets and on Their Own: Youth Homelessness in Illinois" (report, Chicago, 2001), 1.

77. Willy Pedersen and Kristinn Hegna, "Children and Adolescents Who Sell Sex: A Community Study," *Social Science & Medicine* 56 (2003): 140.

78. Ibid.

79. Ibid., 143.

80. Curtis Lawrence, "Ex-Teen Hooker Tells of Stag Party Sex," *Chicago Sun-Times*, 12 September 2002.

81. This figure comes from information on the Barnardo's Web site www.barnardos.org.uk on 25 November 2002.

82. Judith Levine, *Harmful to Minors: The Perils of Protecting Children from Sex* (Minneapolis, Minn.: University of Minnesota Press, 2002), 225. Levine deals

with coerced sex and dating violence only in passing, blithely quoting experts' opinions that most girls can differentiate between abuse, coercion, and consent (see p. 87). Her general prescription for more information and frank discussion about sex for teens may, in the end, help girls avoid these pitfalls, but her failure to squarely confront the susceptibility of needy young girls to this kind of grooming and coercion weakens her text. Dealing with this issue would have strengthened, not weakened, her argument.

83. Sterk, *Tricking and Tripping*, 41.

84. Katherine Joslin, "Introduction," in Jane Addams, *A New Conscience and an Ancient Evil* (Urbana: University of Illinois Press, 2002), x, xiii.

85. Addams, *A New Conscience*, 56.

86. Ibid., 17.

87. Ibid., 69.

88. Ibid., 85.

89. Ibid., 65.

90. Ibid., 64. Novelist Ignazio Silone also has written movingly of how an ancient cruelty produces indifference:

> For twenty years I knew the monotony of the earth, the rain, the wind, the snow, the saints' days, the worries, the troubles and the poverty—the everlasting poverty handed down by fathers who inherited it from grandfathers, and in the face of which honest toil had never been of any use. The hardest injustices were of such long standing that they had acquired the naturalness of the rain, the wind and the snow. The life of men, of the beast of the field, and of the earth itself seemed enclosed in an immovable ring, held in the viselike grip of the mountains and the changes of the season, welded into an unchanging natural cycle as in a kind of never-ending imprisonment.

From Ignazio Silone, *Fontamara*, in *The Abruzzo Trilogy* (South Royalton, Vt.: Steerforth Press, 2000), 6–7.

CHAPTER THREE

1. Alta, interview.

2. Laure Adler, *Marguerite Duras: A Life* (Chicago: University of Chicago Press, 1998), 65.

3. Ibid., 60–61.

4. Ibid., 62.

5. Ibid., 52, 66.

6. Ibid., 348.

7. Ibid., 61.

8. Marguerite Duras, *The Lover* (New York: HarperPerennial, 1992), 35.

9. Ibid., 42.

250

10. Vivian Gornick, *The Situation and the Story: The Art of Personal Narrative* (New York: Farrar, Straus and Giroux, 2001), 145.

11. Rosemary Sullivan, *Labyrinth of Desire: Women, Passion, and Romantic Obsession* (Washington, D.C.: Counterpoint, 2001), 55.

12. David Sherman, "Sexually Oriented Businesses: An Insider's View," Testimony before the Michigan House Committee on Ethics and Constitutional Law, 12 May 2000, 2.

13. Ibid.

14. Ibid.

15. Ibid., 3.

16. Ibid. Women interviewed by Raymond and Hughes about their stripping experiences corroborate Sherman's scenario. The women said they were hired to serve drinks and then were pressured to dance and eventually to undertake prostitution to make more money. One social service provider explained that it takes about six months on average for the women to get drawn into prostitution from stripping. See Raymond and Hughes, "Sex Trafficking," 58.

17. O'Neill, *Prostitution and Feminism*, 84.

18. Jody Miller and Dheeshana Jayasundara, "Prostitution, the Sex Industry, and Sex Tourism," in *Sourcebook on Violence against Women*, eds. C. Renzetti, J. Edleson, and R. Bergen (Thousand Oaks, Calif.: Sage, 2001), 465.

19. Laurie Shrage, *Moral Dilemmas of Feminism: Prostitution, Adultery, and Abortion* (New York: Routledge, 1994), 155. Shrage provides an extended discussion of the reasons for the racially determined nature of this demand.

20. Siobhan Brooks, "Working the Streets: Gloria Lockett's Story," www .spectator.net.

21. Claudine O'Leary and Olivia Howard, "The Prostitution of Women and Girls in Metropolitan Chicago: A Preliminary Prevalence Report" (report, Chicago, 2001), 24–26.

22. Raymond and Hughes, "Sex Trafficking," 35.

23. Ibid., 32.

24. Lily Burana, *Strip City: A Stripper's Farewell Journey across America* (New York: Talk Miramax Books, 2001), 44. With an average daily audience at each of 200, this estimate amounts to more than 500,000 viewers a night, or 3.5 million each week. The *Boston Globe* has reported an estimate of 2,200 stripclubs in the United States and puts the total stripclub annual revenue at $3 billion in 1996; see Flint, "Ads Generate Dollars." Another journalist has quoted *Stripper Magazine*'s estimate of as many as 3,000 stripclubs in North America; see David A. Scott, *Behind the G-String: An Exploration of the Stripper's Image, Her Person and Her Meaning* (Jefferson, N.C.: McFarland, 1996), 5.

25. Jeff Horwich, "Exotic Dancing: Is It Art?" Minnesota Public Radio, 4 March 2002.

26. Melissa Farley made these remarks at a training session on prostitution sponsored by the Prostitution Alternatives Roundtable in Chicago on 23 May 2001.

27. Lily Burana, a former stripper who returned to the business, has written: "Things have changed drastically since I left San Francisco. . . . Finding clubs that don't allow customer contact has been difficult. And establishments that were once familiar to me have transformed dramatically—or vanished." Burana, *Strip City*, 246. See also Elisabeth Eaves, *Bare: On Women, Dancing, Sex, and Power* (New York: Alfred A. Knopf, 2002).

28. Kelly Holsopple, presentation at Moorhead State University, Moorhead, Minn., 25 October 1996.

29. See chapter 9 of this work for an extended discussion of this issue.

30. Although Burana explains that she wanted to return to stripping to "bring closure" and to come to terms with that part of her life, this explanation seems contrived.

31. Lily Burana, interview by Jeni McDonald, 11 January 2002, www .BookReview.com.

32. Ibid.

33. Burana, *Strip City*, 68–69.

34. Ibid., 162.

35. Ibid., 105.

36. Ibid., 300.

37. Lily Burana, interview by Suzy Hansen, 9 October 2001, www .salon.com.

38. Burana, *Strip City*, 318.

39. Ibid., 221.

40. Ibid., 327–28.

41. Eaves, *Bare*, 21, 78.

42. Ibid., 47.

43. Ibid., 154.

44. Ibid., 287.

45. Ibid., 100.

46. Ibid., 79.

47. Ibid., 97.

48. Ibid., 103.

49. Ibid, 139.

50. Ibid., 223.

51. Ibid., 225.

52. Ibid.

53. Ibid., 288.

54. Ibid.

55. This description of activities available at the Little Red Mill in Gary, Indiana, was found at www.worldsexguide.org on 27 September 2001.

56. This description of the prostitution on offer at the Pure Gold and Doll Lounge in Cicero was found at the World Sex Guide, www.worldsexguide.org on 14 December 1999, Chicago section.

57. These comments were all found at www.stripclublist.com on 17 October 2002.

58. Dan Geringer, "Wheelchair-bound Man Sues Fla. Strip Club," *Philadelphia Daily News*, 23 September 2002.

59. Claudine O'Leary provided the author with this description of her visit to a Chicago club on 25 January 2001.

CHAPTER FOUR

1. Farley et al., "Prostitution in Five Countries."

2. Wendy McElroy, "Prostitutes, Anti-Pro Feminists, and the Economic Associates of Whores," in *Prostitution: On Whores, Hustlers, and Johns*, eds. James E. Elias et al. (Amherst, N.Y.: Prometheus Books, 1998), 336.

3. Holsopple, "Stripclubs According to Strippers," 261.

4. Ibid.

5. Ibid., 263.

6. Ibid., 266.

7. Ibid., 265.

8. Ibid., 271.

9. Ibid., 268.

10. Raphael and Shapiro, "Sisters Speak Out," 18.

11. Ibid.

12. Ibid., 19.

13. Jody Raphael and Deborah L. Shapiro, "Violence in Indoor and Outdoor Prostitution Venues," *Violence against Women*, forthcoming.

14. Stephanie Church et al., "Violence by Clients towards Female Prostitutes in Different Work Settings: Questionnaire Survey," *British Medical Journal* 322, no. 7285 (2001): 524–25.

15. Pyett and Warr, "Women at Risk," 190–91.

16. Sheila Jeffreys, "Trafficking in Women versus Prostitution: A False Distinction" (keynote address, Townsville International Women's Conference, James Cook University, 3–7 July 2002), 5.

17. Maticka-Tyndale et al., "Exotic Dancing and Health," 95.

18. Ibid., 101. A 1990 study in Winnipeg, Manitoba, that interviewed twenty exotic dancers, twenty patients diagnosed with multiple personality disorder, and twenty women in street prostitution found that seven of the exotic dancers and one of the women in prostitution met the criteria for multiple personality disorder on the Dissociative Disorders Interview Schedule. Substance abuse was equally common in the three groups: eleven multiple personality disorder subjects, sixteen women in prostitution, and eight danc-

ers reported problems with drugs and alcohol. See Colin A. Ross et al., "Dissociation and Abuse among Multiple-Personality Patients, Prostitutes, and Exotic
Dancers," *Hospital and Community Psychiatry*, 41, no. 3 (1990): 330.

19. Wesley, "Growing Up Sexualized," 1207.

20. Ibid., 1201.

21. Ibid., 1202.

22. Ibid., 1206.

23. Ibid., 1207.

24. Ibid., 1209. Elizabeth Anne Wood, who spent 110 hours as a customer in two New England stripclubs between 1996 and 1998 observing the
action and formally interviewing twelve of the dancers, corroborates Wesley's
findings. When they had first started stripping, the women told her, the positive attention they had received from the customers along with the money
was positively addictive. Wood found that the power dynamics were complex:
the women were cooperating in portraying one-dimensional, paper-doll fantasy figures for the customer, which cost them a significant amount of physical and emotional labor, and they also had to "manage the negativity that
customers sometimes direct at dancers, which must be balanced with the financial rewards and affirmation from customers." Elizabeth Anne Wood,
"Working in the Fantasy Factory: The Attention Hypothesis and the Enacting
of Masculine Power in Strip Clubs," *Journal of Contemporary Ethnography* 29, no. 1
(2000): 28.

25. Carol Rambo Ronai and Carolyn Ellis, "Turn-Ons for Money: Interactional Strategies of the Table Dancer," *Journal of Contemporary Ethnography* 18, no.
3 (1989): 275–76.

26. Ibid., 292.

27. Ibid.

28. Ibid., 296.

29. Raphael and Shapiro, "Sisters Speak Out," 23–24.

30. Ibid., 23.

31. Ibid., 23.

32. These quotations are taken from the questionnaires completed during
the Center for Impact Research study between July and October 2001.

33. Maticka-Tyndale et al., "Exotic Dancing and Health," 101–2.

34. Holsopple, "Stripclubs according to Strippers," 261.

35. Janet Lever and Deanne Dolnick, "Clients and Call Girls: Seeking Sex
and Intimacy," in *Sex for Sale: Prostitution, Pornography, and the Sex Industry*, ed. R.
Weitzer (New York: Routledge, 2000), 94.

36. Pyett and Warr, "Women at Risk," 189.

37. R. De Graaf et al., "Alcohol and Drug Use in Heterosexual and Homosexual Prostitution, and Its Relation to Protection Behavior," *AIDS Care* 7, no.
1 (1995): 39. Pariott's sample of sixty-eight included women involved in a

wide variety of prostitution activities in the mid-1990s in the Minnesota Twin Cities area. She reported that half of her subjects stated they were high "all the time" while involved in prostitution, and another 34 percent described themselves as high at least half the time; see Parriott, "Health Experiences," 15. Raymond and Hughes found that 50 percent of the U.S-born women in their sample, which consisted of women in both indoor and outdoor prostitution, began alcohol and drug use after they entered prostitution, stating that without the drugs or alcohol they would not have been able to survive in the sex industry; see Raymond and Hughes, "Sex Trafficking," 86. Alexa Albert found that all the women in a legal brothel in Nevada were addicted to drugs: "Quite a few, sadly, embarked on their drug and alcohol habits while at Mustang." See Albert, *Brothel*, 160.

38. Scott, *Behind the G-String*, 74.

39. This entry was submitted on 17 February 1998 by "Traveling Man" at www.worldsexbank.com/usa/illinois.htm on 3 May 2002. Other entries talk about women "hopped up on speed" and ladies in strip clubs who are "obviously drug-addicted."

40. Norton-Hawk, "Social Class," 122.

41. Benoit and Millar, "Dispelling Myths," 79.

42. Melissa Farley and Vanessa Kelly, "Prostitution: A Critical Review of the Medical and Social Sciences Literature," *Women & Criminal Justice* 11, no. 4 (2000): 48.

43. Benoit and Millar, "Dispelling Myths," 46, 53.

44. Scott, *Behind the G-String*, 42.

45. Ibid., 53.

46. Ibid., 228.

47. Lillian Faderman, *Naked in the Promised Land* (New York: Houghton Mifflin, 2003).

48. Lillian Faderman, interview by author, 14 March 2003.

49. Faderman, *Naked*, 128, 267.

CHAPTER FIVE

1. Alta, interview, 28 September 2001.

2. Ibid.

3. Ibid.

4. In a large sample in Victoria, B.C., 67 percent of respondents said that at some time they had received treatment for physical injury, and 36 percent reported being hospitalized because of injuries incurred in the sex trade. Aboriginal respondents had been hospitalized at slightly higher rates than non-Aboriginals (40 percent compared with 35.7 percent); see Benoit and Millar, "Dispelling Myths," 68. Researchers found that in a sample of 113 women on the streets in Harlem and the Bronx, 32 percent had been victims of physi-

cal or sexual assault from customers. Those who had been incarcerated during the past year were more likely to have been physically abused by commercial partners than those who had not, and being homeless significantly increased the risk of customer abuse. If the sex trade was the major source of income, the more often the woman exchanged sex for money or drugs the more likely she was to be physically and sexually abused by customers; see Nabila El-Bassel et al., "Correlates of Partner Violence among Female Street-based Sex Workers: Substance Abuse, History of Childhood Abuse, and HIV Risks, "*AIDS Patient Care and STDs* 15, no. 1 (2002): 46. Sixty-one percent of a sample of women on the streets in Washington, D.C., reported being physically assaulted, nearly 80 percent reported being threatened with a weapon, and 44 percent had been raped in prostitution, with 60 percent of these rapes by customers; see Valera, "Perceived Health Needs," 54. In a sample in a Midwestern city, 72 percent reported incidents of severe abuse suffered in prostitution, including rapes at knifepoint; see Dalla, "Exposing the 'Pretty Woman' Myth," 350. In another sample in a large northeastern city, 36 percent had been hit, 30 percent robbed, 30 percent had a weapon used on them, 32 percent had a customer attempt to rape them, and 26 had been raped by customers; see Norton-Hawk, "Lifecourse of Prostitution," 9. Researchers found that 75 percent of a sample of women incarcerated in a Midwestern jail for prostitution-related charges had been raped by one or more customers, and almost 63 percent had been raped on the streets by others. Almost 98 percent had been victims of physical assaults, which ranged from being punched or kicked (31 percent) to being beaten (61 percent), stabbed or slashed (31percent), or hit with an object like a baseball bat or a brick (25 percent). One respondent had been tortured by electric shock. See Jody Miller and Martin D. Schwartz, "Rape Myths and Violence against Street Prostitutes," *Deviant Behavior: An Interdisciplinary Journal* 16, no. 1 (1995): 8. In a survey of women in the Cook County (Chicago) Jail, 74 percent said they had been sexually assaulted as adults by someone other than a partner (compared with 29 percent among those who were not regularly involved in prostitution) and 69 percent reported they had been attacked with a weapon by someone other than a partner (compared with 33 percent of those not regularly involved in prostitution); see Chicago Coalition, "Unlocking Options," 15. Ninety-five percent of 800 participants in Oregon's Council for Prostitution Alternatives recovery program who entered the program in 1991 had been assaulted by customers, and 71 percent had been raped, 78 percent by the customer; see Nanette J. Davis, "From Victims to Survivors: Working with Recovering Street Prostitutes," in *Sex for Sale: Prostitution, Pornography, and the Sex Industry*, ed. R. Weizer (New York: Routledge, 2000), 143. In a large street sample in Victoria, B.C., 44.5 percent had been threatened with a weapon, 51 percent had been physically assaulted, 30 percent assaulted with a weapon, 45.8 percent forced to have sex against their will, and almost 41 percent raped with a weapon involved; see Cler-Cunningham, "Violence against Women," 7. The customer beatings reported in San Francisco (65 percent of the respondents had been physically abused) were seen as arbitrary. Seventy percent had been victimized by customer rape an average of 31.3 times; see Mimi H. Silbert and Ayala M. Pines, "Victimization of Prostitutes," *Victimology: An International Journal* 7, no. 1–4 (1983): 127.

5. Farley and Barkan, "Prostitution," 40–41.

6. Ibid., 42. The symptoms were placed in three groups: intrusive re-experiencing (called B symptoms), numbing and avoidance (C symptoms), and hyperarousal (D symptoms). Eight-eight percent reported one or more B symptoms, 79 percent three or more C symptoms, and 74 percent two or more D symptoms.

7. Ibid.

8. Ibid., 45.

9. "Getting Real Facts about Prostitution: An Interview with Melissa Farley," 1998, www.mergemag.org/1998/farley.html.

10. Valera, "Perceived Health Needs," 57. The prevalence of PTSD in the general population is 7.8 percent.

11. Elizabeth Arnold et al., "Perpetrators as Victims: Understanding Violence by Female Street-Walking Prostitutes," *Violence and Victims* 16, no. 2 (2001): 147.

12. Nabila El-Bassel et al., "Sex Trading and Psychological Distress among Women Recruited from the Streets of Harlem," *American Journal of Public Health* 97, no. 1 (1997): 69. A study in Los Angeles with adolescent homeless youth not involved in prostitution, compared to a sample in prostitution, found that the teens in prostitution were twice as likely to have a serious mental health problem (such as personality or thought disorder) and almost twice as likely to be actively suicidal or to have previously attempted suicide. See Gary L. Yates and Julia Pennbridge, "A Risk Profile Comparison of Homeless Youth Involved in Prostitution and Homeless Youth Not Involved," *Journal of Adolescent Health* 12 (1991): 547.

13. Raymond and Hughes, "Sex Trafficking," 83.

14. Hood-Brown, "Trading for a Place," 24. Ten percent of the respondents in a Victoria, B.C., sample had attempted suicides; see Benoit and Millar, "Dispelling Myths," 69.

15. Valera, "Perceived Health Needs," 58.

16. Pariott, "Health Experiences," 19.

17. Raphael and Shapiro, "Sisters Speak Out," 18. Large percentages of the women involved in street-level prostitution in this sample stated that they had no home while trading sex for money in this way, 22. These data corroborate research finding that 84 percent of the women surveyed on the streets

of San Francisco reported current or past homelessness, thought to contribute to vulnerability and susceptibility to violence on the street; see Farley and Barkan, "Prostitution," 41.

18. Maureen Norton-Hawk, "The Counterproductivity of Incarcerating Female Street Prostitutes," *Deviant Behavior: An Interdisciplinary Journal* 22 (2001): 411.

19. Miller and Schwartz, "Rape Myths," 12.

20. Sterk, *Tricking and Tripping*, 123, 134.

21. Lisa Maher, *Sexed Work: Gender, Race, and Resistance in a Brooklyn Drug Market* (New York: Oxford University Press, 1997), 157.

22. Neil McKeganey and Marina Barnard, *Sex Work on the Streets: Prostitutes and Their Clients* (Philadelphia: Open University Press, 1996), 72.

23. Phillipe Bourgois and Eloise Dunlap, "Exorcising Sex-for-Crack: An Ethnographic Perspective from Harlem," in *Crack as Pimp*, ed. M. Ratner (Lanham, Md.: Lexington Books, 1992), 114–15.

24. Ibid., 115.

25. Raymond and Hughes, "Sex Trafficking," 77.

26. If the jokes in the "humor column" of *Chicago after Dark*, a free monthly guide to upscale prostitution venues in the metropolitan area, are any guide, power and control are much on the minds of the customers:

> Q: If your wife keeps coming out of the kitchen to nag at you, what have you done wrong?
> A. Made her chain too long.
>
> Q. Why do women fake orgasms?
> A. Because they think men care.
>
> Q. What is the definition of "making love"?
> A. Something a woman does while a guy is screwing her.
>
> Q. What is the difference between a battery and a woman?
> A. A battery has a positive side.

Chicago after Dark, April 2002, 48.

27. This comment was posted on 19 November 1997 at www.porn cave.com/content/worldsex/United-States.html on 7 May 2002.

28. This review of a Chicago escort service was posted on 31 December 1999 at www.worldsexguide.com/guide/North_America/United_States/Illinois/Chicago on 9 April 2002.

29. Chester's guide was found at www.porncave.com/content/world sex/United-States.html on 18 September 2000.

30. Donna M. Hughes, "'Welcome to the Rape Camp': Sexual Exploitation and the Internet in Cambodia" (report, Kingston, R.I., 2001), 2.

31. Martin A. Monto, "Why Men Seek Out Prostitutes," in *Sex for Sale:*

258   *Prostitution, Pornography, and the Sex Industry,* ed. R. Weizer (New York: Routledge, 2000), 68.

32. Ibid.

33. The Nokomis Foundation, "We Can Do Better: Helping Prostituted Women and Girls in Grand Rapids Make Healthy Choices" (report, Grand Rapids, Mich., 2002), 36.

34. Ibid., 35–36.

35. Michigan Family Impact Seminars, "Prostituted Teens: More Than a Runaway Problem" (Briefing Report no. 2002–2, East Lansing, Mich., 2002), 7.

36. Martin Monto, "A Comparison of the Male Clients of Female Street Prostitutes with National Samples of Men," unpublished manuscript.

37. Ibid.

38. Ibid.

39. Martin Monto, "Conceiving of Sex as a Commodity: A Study of Arrested Clients of Female Street Prostitutes," unpublished manuscript.

40. Noel Bridget Busch et al., "Male Customers of Prostituted Women: Exploring Perceptions of Entitlement to Power and Control and Implications for Violent Behavior toward Women," *Violence against Women* 8, no. 9 (2002): 1107.

41. Jody Miller, e-mail exchange with author, 16 April 2003.

42. Dennis Altman, *Global Sex* (Chicago: University of Chicago Press, 2001), 159. Altman also usefully remarks that those who publicly flout the gender/sexual order seem particularly vulnerable to violence; see *Global Sex,* 7.

43. Martin Monto, "Female Prostitution, Customers, and Violence," unpublished manuscript.

44. For a lucid discussion of the routine activities theory, see Martin D. Schwartz et al., "Male Peer Support and a Feminist Routine Activities Theory: Understanding Sexual Assault on the College Campus," *Justice Quarterly* 18, no. 3 (2001): 625–27.

45. Ibid., 645–46.

46. Helen Rumbelow, "Fallen Men: At 'John School,' Students Review a Lesson Picked Up on the Street," *Washington Post,* 28 August 2002, Section C.

CHAPTER SIX

1. Alta, interview, 28 September 2001.

2. Ibid.

3. Ibid.

4. Ibid.

5. Ibid.

6. In a Chicago study with 222 women in prostitution, 100 percent of the women used drugs and alcohol while in the streets; see Raphael and Sha-

piro, "Sisters Speak Out," 23. Ninety-five percent of women in a smaller Midwestern sample reported routine drug use; see Dalla, "Exposing the 'Pretty Woman' Myth," 349. Ninety-four percent of the women in a Los Angeles jail sample used drugs while in prostitution; see Mary Magdalene Project, "Research Report," 191. Almost 100 percent of the women in the prostitution sample in a northeastern city used at least one drug; see Norton-Hawk, "Lifecourse of Prostitution," 8. Fifty-one percent of a sample of 998 women in street prostitution in Los Angeles used drugs before interaction with a customer, and 39 percent used alcohol; see Lever and Dolnick, "Clients and Call Girls," 94. Seventy-five percent of the women in a San Francisco street sample reported a drug abuse problem, and 27 percent reported an alcohol problem; see Farley and Barkan, "Prostitution," 41. Fifty-seven percent of a sample of women in the streets in Washington, D.C., used drugs, and 64 percent used alcohol; see Valera, "Perceived Health Needs," 54. Fifty percent of a sample on the East Harlem streets reported current drug use; see El-Bassel et. al., "Correlates of Partner Violence," 47. Seventy-four percent of the women disclosing prostitution in the Cook County (Chicago) Jail used drugs, as compared with 43 percent of those women in the jail sample who were not in prostitution; see Chicago Coalition, "Unlocking Options," 15. The same pattern held true among arrestees detained at a Florida work release center. Ninety-two percent of the women in prostitution (compared with 38 percent of the women not in prostitution) had used crack, and 87 percent of the women in prostitution (compared with 45 percent of those not in prostitution) had used cocaine. Over a third of the women in the sex trade had used heroin, compared with less than 10 percent of the other women. See Kuhns et al., "Substance Use/Misuse," 1286. Prostitution was associated with greater current drug use levels among seriously delinquent Miami youth; see Inciardi et al., "Prostitution," 226. Among homeless youth in Los Angeles, 74.5 percent of those involved in prostitution used drugs, compared with 36 percent of the youth not active in prostitution; see Yates and Pennbridge, "A Risk Profile," 546.

7. Nanette Graham and Eric D. Wish, "Drug Use among Female Arrestees: Onset, Patterns, and Relationships to Prostitution," *Journal of Drug Issues* 24 (1994): 325.

8. McClanahan et al., "Pathways into Prostitution," 1611.

9. Sterk, *Tricking and Tripping*, 4.

10. Jody Miller, "Gender and Power on the Streets: Street Prostitution in the Era of Crack Cocaine," *Journal of Contemporary Ethnography* 23, no. 4 (1995): 435.

11. Pariott, "Health Experiences," 15.

12. Dalla, "Exposing the 'Pretty Woman' Myth," 349.

13. Maureen Norton-Hawk, "Drugs and Prostitution: A Complex Equation," unpublished manuscript.

14. Amy M. Young et al., "Prostitution, Drug Use, and Coping with Psychological Distress," *Journal of Drug Issues* 30, no. 4 (2000): 795–96.

15. Norton-Hawk, "Drugs and Prostitution."

16. Raphael and Shapiro, "Sisters Speak Out," 23–24.

17. R. De Graaf et al., "Alcohol and Drug Use," 42–3. Twenty-nine percent of a sample of girls in prostitution aged sixteen to eighteen in northern England also said they were coerced into selling sex to support a boyfriend's drug habit; see Joseph Rowntree Foundation, "Findings from the Choice and Opportunity Project: Young Women and Sexual Exploitation" (report, York, U.K., 2003).

18. S. T. Green et al., "Female Streetworker-Prostitutes," 330.

19. El-Bassel et al., "Correlates of Partner Violence," 48.

20. Claire Sterk, communication with author, 20 June 2001.

21. Raphael and Shapiro, "Sisters Speak Out," 11. Close to 29 percent of the respondents had participated in one activity, 26 percent in two, 23 percent in three, 10 percent in four, 6 percent in five, and 6 percent in six or more activities. Forty-one women reported simultaneous prostitution activities.

22. Ibid., 25–26. The researchers placed drug houses with outside prostitution because the clientele, duration of the encounters, and quality of the surroundings were similar.

23. Ibid., 24–25.

24. Mary Magdalene Project, "Research Project," 159, 184.

25. Rabinovitch and Lewis, "'Impossible, eh?'" 60.

26. Benoit and Millar, "Dispelling Myths," 39.

27. See Maher, *Sexed Work*, for an example of this kind of analysis.

28. For a history of the recent crack epidemic, see Maria Szalavitz, "Cracked Up," Salon.com, 1999. However, the U.S. government states that women continue to be introduced to crack cocaine and that the proportion of women with long-term use of smoked cocaine has grown; see Drug and Alcohol Services Information System, "The DASIS Report," 13 July 2001.

29. Estes and Weiner, "Commercial Sexual Exploitation," 7.

30. The young men are called "Metrocard pimps" because they are too young to afford cars. For a detailed description of what is known about young girls and their pimps in New York City, see Alexis J. Loinaz, "From the Cradle to the Street," *Village Voice*, 17–23 July 2002. See also Cardwell, "Fears That City's Flesh Trade May Be Getting Younger."

31. Sterk, *Tricking and Tripping*, 74, 78.

32. Norton-Hawk, "Lifecourse of Prostitution," 7–8. Forty percent of the women in a Midwestern city sample were also controlled by pimps; see Dalla, "Exposing the 'Pretty Woman' Myth," 350.

33. Norton-Hawk, "Prostitution Is Not about Sex."

34. Mary Magdalene Project, "Research Report," 187.

35. Miller, "Gender and Power," 440.

36. Raymond and Hughes, "Sex Trafficking," 48.

37. Raphael and Shapiro, "Sisters Speak Out," 20–21.

38. Ibid., 21.

39. Ibid.

40. Davis, "From Victims to Survivors," 143.

41. Raymond and Hughes, "Sex Trafficking," 62–63. Violence was used for sexual gratification of the pimps, as a form of punishment, to threaten and intimidate women, and to punish them for alleged violations.

42. Celia Williamson, "Pimp Controlled Prostitution: Still an Integral Part of Street Life," *Violence against Women* 8, no. 9 (2002): 1090.

43. Ibid., 1081.

44. Ibid., 1085.

45. Adrienne Sanders, "Heartland Daughters for Sale," *Examiner*, 9 May 2002.

46. *Pimps Up, Ho's Down*, directed by Brent Owens, was released on 12 December 2000 by Mti Home Video 2.

47. Williamson, "Pimp Controlled Prostitution," 1088.

48. Albert, *Brothel*, 75–76.

49. Ibid., 79–80.

50. Joseph Parker, "How Prostitution Works," report from the Lola Greene Baldwin Foundation, at www.prostitutionrecovery.org on 29 February 2003.

CHAPTER SEVEN

1. Melissa Farley, speech, Conference on Prostitution and Homelessness, Chicago, 23 May 2001.

2. Norton-Hawk, "Counterproductivity of Incarcerating Female Street Prostitutes," 405.

3. Ibid., 414.

4. Raphael and Shapiro, "Sisters Speak Out," 28.

5. Chicago Coalition, "Unlocking Options," 14.

6. Mary Magdalene Project, "Research Report," 185.

7. Kuhns, Heide, and Silverman, "Substance Use/Misuse," 1284. In another Florida study of 102 women in a community-based case management program, all but one had histories of felony charges, with the mean number at 6.5; see Arnold, Stewart, and McNeece, "Perpetrators as Victims," 147. The average length of incarceration in a Midwestern sample was 1.2 years; see Dalla, "Exposing the 'Pretty Woman' Myth," 351.

8. Terrie McDermott, interview by author, 7 August 2001.

9. Julie Pearl, "The Highest Paying Customers: America's Cities and the Costs of Prostitution Control," *Hastings Law Journal* 38 (1987): 772, 781.

10. San Francisco Task Force on Prostitution, "Final Report 1996," 4.

11. Mary Magadelene Project, "Research Report," 158.

12. Norton-Hawk, "Counterproductivity of Incarcerating Female Street Prostitutes," 412.

13. Raphael and Shapiro, "Sisters Speak Out," 19–20.

14. Ibid., 20.

15. Brock, Making Work, 114.

16. Sterk, Tricking and Tripping, 142.

17. Liz Armstrong, "No Apologies: A New-Model Porn Queen Revels in Her Own Raunch," The Reader, 9 March 2002, 12.

18. Jody Miller, "'Your Life Is on the Line Every Night You're on the Streets': Victimization and the Resistance among Street Prostitutes," Humanity & Society 17, no. 4 (1993): 440–41.

19. Linda A. Fairstein, Sexual Violence: Our War against Rape, (New York: William Morrow, 1993), 172.

20. Ibid., 173.

21. Jannit Rabinovitch and Susan Strega, "The PEERS Story: Effective Services Side-Step the Controversies," Violence against Women, forthcoming.

22. Sterk, Tricking and Tripping, 42.

23. Pettiway, Workin' It, 95.

24. Brenda Myers, interview by author, 30 May 2003. Another survivor has said, "If you're white and educated, you might see stripping as an option, but if you're poor, a woman of color, drug-addicted, or were turned out into the trade when you were 12, it's not an option. Your choice has been taken." See Katia Dunn, "Prostitution: Pro or Con?" Portland (Ore.) Mercury, 9 May 2002.

25. Rabinovitch and Strega, "The PEERS Story."

26. Primo Levi, Survival in Auschwitz (New York: Collier Books, 1961), 155.

27. Ibid., 138–39.

28. Barbara Ehrenreich, Nickel and Dimed: On (Not) Getting By in America (New York: Henry Holt, 2001), 211.

29. Rhonda Hammer, Antifeminism and Family Terrorism: A Critical Feminist Perspective (Lanham, Md.: Rowman & Littlefield, 2002), 175.

30. Hughes, "'Welcome to the Rape Camp,'" 18. Some researchers believe this response involves the Stockholm Syndrome: the terror created in the woman by the pimp causes a sense of helplessness and dependence, which leads to the captive's acceptance of the world of the captor and hypervigilance with respect to his needs, to the exclusion of her own. See Farley and Kelly, "Prostitution: A Critical Review," 45.

31. K. Sue Jewell, From Mammy to Miss America and Beyond: Cultural Images and the Shaping of U.S. Social Policy (New York: Routledge, 1993), 37.

32. Ibid., 46.

33. Shrage, Moral Dilemmas, 155.

34. These advertisements were viewed in the January 2001 edition of Chicago after Dark and at www.eros-Chicago.com/sections/escort.htm on 8 January 2003.

35. Tameka A. Gillum, "Exploring the Link Between Stereotypic Images and Intimate Partner Violence in the African-American Community," *Violence against Women* 8, no. 1 (2002): 74–75, 83.

36. Vednita Carter and Evelina Giobbe, "Duet: Prostitution, Racism and Feminist Discourse," *Hastings Women's Law Journal* 10 (1999): 40.

37. Patricia Hill Collins, *Black Feminist Thought: Knowledge, Consciousness, and the Politics of Empowerment* (New York: Routledge, 2000), 145.

38. Vednita Nelson, "Prostitution: Where Racism and Sexism Intersect," *Michigan Journal of Gender & Law* 1 (1993), at www.prostitutionresearch.com.

39. Ibid.

40. Federal Bureau of Investigation, "Crime in the United States, 2000," Table 33, www.fbi.gov/ucr/00cius.htm on 9 April 2002.

41. Ibid., Table 49.

42. O'Leary and Howard, "Prostitution of Women and Girls," 10.

43. Nelson, "Prostitution."

44. Ibid.

45. Mary Magdalene Project, "Research Report," 115.

46. Kingsley and Mark, "Sacred Lives," 8.

47. Nixon et al., "The Everyday Occurrence," 1022.

48. Benoit and Millar, "Dispelling Myths," 35.

49. McClanahan et al., "Pathways into Prostitution," 1609.

50. Carter and Giobbe, "Duet," 12.

51. Dunn, "Prostitution: Pro or Con?"

52. Shrage, *Moral Dilemmas*, 144.

53. Ibid., 145, 149.

54. Rosen, *Lost Sisterhood*, 139.

55. Shrage, *Moral Dilemmas*, 156.

56. Primo Levi, *The Drowned and the Saved* (New York: Vintage International, 1989), 125–26.

Chapter Eight

1. Niki Surico, interview by author, 26 January 2001.

2. Edwina Gateley, interview by author, 29 March 2001.

3. Kim, interview by author, 22 June 2001.

4. Surico, interview.

5. Ibid.

6. Ibid.

7. Ibid.

8. Kim, interview.

9. Ibid.

10. Gateley, interview.

11. Kim, interview.

12. Gateley, interview by author, 19 March 2001.

13. Ibid.

14. Gateley, interview by author, 12 April 2002.

15. Louise, interview by author, 29 March 2001.

16. Surico, interview by author, 16 January 2001.

17. Ibid.

18. Herman, *Trauma and Recovery*, 53–54, 105.

19. Primo Levi, quoted in Frederic D. Homer, *Primo Levi and the Politics of Survival*, (Columbia: University of Missouri Press, 2001), 209.

20. Levi, *The Drowned and the Saved*, 73.

21. Ibid., 75–76.

22. Ibid., 199.

23. Jenny Horsman, interview by author, 27 October 2001.

24. Farley, speech, Prostitution Alternatives Roundtable, Chicago, 23 May 2001.

25. Anne Heche, *Call Me Crazy* (New York: Scribner, 2001), 139.

26. Horsman, interview.

27. Scott, *Behind the G-String*, 221.

28. Andrew Solomon, *The Noonday Demon: An Atlas of Depression* (New York: Scribner, 2001), 34–37.

29. Joseph Parker, "Between the Hammer and the Anvil: Working with Complex Post-Traumatic Stress Disorder in a Hostile Environment," www .prostitutionrecovery.org on 29 January 2003.

30. Ibid. This is common theme in survivor testimonies; see Pettiway, *Workin' It*. Women's perceptions of the difficulty of shedding the stigma are not misplaced. The Kentucky Bar Association's Character and Fitness Committee denied admission to the Kentucky Bar to Taylor Strasser, who as a juvenile had run away from home and been involved in an escort service, in which capacity she had been arrested. The committee stated that her "abusive childhood and prior lifestyle" left her lacking the "mental and emotional fitness to be admitted to the Kentucky Bar." Following a lawsuit, the Kentucky Supreme Court ruled in her favor, lauding her for having "taken appropriate steps to deal with the residue of her early life." See Charles Wolfe, "Court: Prostitution Doesn't Disqualify Prospective Lawyer," *Cincinnati Enquirer*, 21 March 2003.

31. Horsman, interview.

32. Parker, "Between the Hammer and the Anvil."

33. Edwina Gateley, *I Hear a Seed Growing: God of the Forest, God of the Streets* (Trabuco Canyon, Calif.: Source Books, 1998), 115, 148.

34. Ibid., 168.

35. Jean Bethke Elshtain, *Jane Addams and the Dream of American Democracy: A Life* (New York: Basic Books, 2002), 92.

36. Ibid., 125.

37. Ibid., 93.

38. Ibid., 122.

39. Horsman, interview.

40. Ibid.

41. Brenda Myers, testimony, Illinois House Prison Management Reform Committee Hearing, Chicago, 8 August 2001.

42. Gateley, interview, 29 March 2001.

43. Gateley, I Hear a Seed, 195–96.

44. Solomon, The Noonday Demon, 432.

45. Rita Nakashima Brock and Susan Thistlethwaite, Casting Stones: Prostitution and Liberation in Asia and the United States (Minneapolis: Fortress Press, 1996), 295.

46. Alta, interview, 28 September 2001.

47. Ibid.

CHAPTER NINE

1. Lyndall Maccowan, "Organizing in the Massage Parlor: An Interview with Denise Turner," in Whores and Other Feminists, ed. J. Nagle (New York: Routledge, 1997), 237.

2. Barbara and Carole, "Interview with Barbara," in Sex Work: Writings by Women in the Sex Industry, eds. F. Delacoste and P. Alexander (Pittsburgh: Cleis Press, 1987), 174.

3. Cosi Fabian, "The Holy Whore: A Woman's Gateway to Power," in Whores and Other Feminists, 44.

4. Ann Renee, "A Sex Protector/Pervert Speaks Out," in Whores and Other Feminists, 56.

5. Liz Highleyman, aka Mistress Vronika Frost, "'Professional Dominance: Power, Money, and Identity," in Whores and Other Feminists, 152.

6. Nicole Grasse, "Dancing Lessons," www.salon.com.

7. Ann D'Lorenzo, "A San Francisco Whore in a Nevada Brothel," www .headlightjournal.com/issue05/whore/whore.html on 4 April 2002. Indeed, research with strippers estimates that 50 to 75 percent of the women tend toward lesbian contacts in their private lives. However, it is not known whether strippers begin with this orientation, or turn to other women because of their disillusioning experiences with men in the stripclubs. See Charles H. McCaghy and James K. Skipper Jr., "Lesbian Behavior As an Adaptation to the Occupation of Stripping," in Bisexuality in the United States: A Social Science Reader, eds. L. Faderman and L. Gross (New York: Columbia University Press, 2000), 271. One analyst notes that minority women in prostitution have little or no chance of being considered rebels against conventional sexuality, but are considered instead to be criminals; see Regina Austin, "The Black Community, Its Lawbreakers and a Politics of Identification," in Criminology at the Crossroads:

Feminist Readings in Criminal Justice, eds. K. Daly and L. Maher (New York: Oxford University Press, 1998), 271.

8. D'Lorenzo, "A San Francisco Whore."

9. Ibid. For a full explication of this point of view, see Nickie Roberts, *Whores in History* (London: Grafton, 1993).

10. Julia O'Connell Davidson, *Prostitution, Power and Freedom* (Ann Arbor: University of Michigan Press, 1998), 103.

11. Ibid., 103–4.

12. Drucilla Cornell, *At the Heart of Freedom: Feminism, Sex, and Equality* (Princeton: Princeton University Press, 1998), 55.

13. Ibid., 56.

14. Davidson, *Prostitution, Power and Freedom*, 114.

15. Carter and Giobbe, "Duet," 39.

16. Ibid., 38–39.

17. Martin Vander Weyer, "Diary," *Spectator*, 30 March 2002, 8.

18. Judith Lynne Hanna, "Wrapping Nudity in a Cloak of Law," *New York Times*, 29 July 2001, Arts and Leisure Section.

19. Katherine Liepe-Levinson, *Strip Show: Performances of Gender and Desire* (New York: Routledge, 2002), 7.

20. Ibid., 55, 89.

21. Ibid., 60, 126.

22. Ibid., 144–45.

23. Ibid., 146.

24. Brian McNair, *Striptease Culture: Sex, Media and the Democratization of Desire* (New York: Routledge, 2002).

25. Ibid., 12, 108, 205.

26. Ibid., 91.

27. Ibid, 54.

28. This report was heard on National Public Radio's "Morning Edition" on 27 September 2002.

29. Ruth La Ferla, "Those Naughty Victorians Find New Takers," *New York Times*, 6 October 2002, Sunday Styles. See also Georgia Sauer, "Fashion Shows Put the S-E-X in the City of Paris," *Chicago Tribune*, 11 October 2002.

30. Toni Bentley, *Sisters of Salome* (New Haven, Conn.: Yale University Press, 2002), 11.

31. Ibid., 13.

32. Leo Carey, "The Dream Master: The Stories of Arthur Schnitzler, the Amoral Voice of Fin-de-Siècle Vienna," *New Yorker*, 9 September 2002, 154.

33. Alex Kuczynski, "The Sex-Worker Literati," *New York Times*, 4 November 2001.

34. Clearly Albert's purpose is to convey to her readers her surprised finding that the women at the Mustang Ranch were human: "In a business

built largely on desire and fantasy, it's easy to be deceived by our assumptions and, in doing so, overlook the humanity that's at the core of this complex and timeless profession." See Albert, *Brothel*, 260. One prostitution survivor, who faults the book for its glossing over of issues of pimping and drug addiction, which she finds "maddening," is, however, grateful for the work's compassion toward its subjects; see Victoria Martinelli, "Let Them Meat Cake: My sabbatical from internecine warfare amongst feminists," *Feminista!* 4, no. 7, www.feminista.com.

35. John D. Thomas, "Author Reveals the Stripper's View," *Chicago Tribune*, 5 November 2002, Tempo Section.

36. Heidi Mattson, *Ivy League Stripper* (New York: Arcade Publishing, 1995), 116, 183.

37. Ibid., 155.

38. Ibid., 253.

39. Ibid., 223, 243.

40. This review, posted by Georgina Pacoa on 28 December 2000 and accessed on 24 October 2002, can be found at www.amazon.com on the Mattson book's Web page. Pacoa's concerns are corroborated by a reader from Dallas who posted this comment at the site on 27 July 2002: "I read this book when I was 23 and thought, 'Wow! Even I could be a stripper!' Heidi makes this profession seem easy, fun, and extremely profitable. I worked part-time as a stripper for three years after that and it was nothing like her book. She shows the fantasy side of stripping but doesn't touch on the realistic side. Now that I have survived through that experience, I realize how misleading the book was."

41. Norton-Hawk, "Social Class," 128–29.

42. Bernadette Barton, "Dancing on the Mobius Strip: Challenging the Sex War Paradigm," *Gender & Society* 16, no. 5 (2002): 590–91.

43. Ibid., 595.

44. Ibid., 599.

45. Sarah Lyall, "A Writer's Tale Is Victorian; His Past, Gothic," *New York Times*, 28 October 2002.

46. Emma Donoghue, interview by Linda Richards, *January Magazine*, November 2000, at www.januarymagazine.com/profiles/donoghue.html.

47. Valerie Jenness, *Making It Work: The Prostitutes' Rights Movement in Perspective* (New York: Aldine de Gruyter, 1993), 79.

48. These explanations of COYOTE's mission and principles were found at its Web site: www.bayswan.org/coyote.html on 5 May 2003.

49. Priscilla Alexander, "The International Sex Worker's Rights Movement," in *Sex Work*, eds. Delacoste and Alexander, 16.

50. Jenness, *Making It Work*, 48.

51. This story was told to the author by a prostitution survivor who needs to remain anonymous to protect the identity of the victim.

52. Rabinovitch and Lewis, "'Impossible, eh?'" 9.

53. The author received this issue alert from the National Organization for Women on 25 January 2002. More information about Grand Theft Auto III can be found at http://gamespot.com/gamespot/stories/reviews/0m10867,2820025,00.html on 21 March 2002.

54. Brenda Myers, interview by author, 30 May 2003.

55. Ronald Weitzer, "Prostitutes' Rights in the United States: The Failure of a Movement," *Sociological Quarterly* 32, no. 1 (1991): 34.

56. Siobhan Brooks, "Working the Streets: Gloria Lockett's Story," spectator.net interviews, www.spectator.net.

57. For a detailed description of sexual liberalism and its history, see Linda R. Hirshman and Jane E. Larson, *Hard Bargains: The Politics of Sex* (New York: Oxford University Press, 1998).

58. Altman, *Global Sex*, 162.

59. Cornell, *At the Heart of Freedom*, 59.

60. Helen Lefkowitz Horowitz, *Rereading Sex: Battles over Sexual Knowledge and Suppression in Nineteenth-Century America* (New York: Knopf, 2002), 149.

61. Ibid., 147.

62. Roberts, *Whores in History*, 354. Some feminists remain troubled by prostitution recovery groups today for this reason. Although she admires the work of the Portland, Oregon–based CPA group, one researcher concludes: "At its best, radical feminist advocacy serves as a reclamation process for some prostitutes, empowering the disempowered. At its worst, it reinforces stereotypes about prostitutes as unfit and degraded persons. It also encourages alliances with other antiprostitution groups (police, local community groups, moralists), some of which may be less interested in rescuing street women than in eradicating public displays of prostitution. Prostitution historically has been subjected to moral crusades that have scapegoated poor women prostitutes. The link between these earlier events and contemporary gender politics is often lost. The insistence that prostitutes are incapable of making sound decisions, except to leave prostitution, is a subtext among intervention specialists." Nanette J. Davis, "From Victims to Survivors: Working with Recovering Street Prostitutes," in *Sex for Sale: Prostitution, Pornography, and the Sex Industry*, ed. R. Weizer (New York: Routledge, 2000), 154–55. Davis's comments well characterize the conflicted stance of many sexual liberals on the issue of prostitution.

63. Martha C. Nussbaum, *Sex & Social Justice* (New York: Oxford University Press, 1999), 292.

64. Ibid., 289. Although some writers may be ignorant of the real facts of prostitution, others willfully disregard them. Consider this statement of Camille Paglia: "Feminists like to quote these absolutely specious statistics, a typical trick of the feminist movement of the last twenty years. For example,

they'll say the majority of prostitutes have been sexually abused as children. But there's no evidence for this! . . . The ones who get into the surveys have drug problems or psychological problems. They're the ones who were sexually abused. Feminists are using amateurs to condemn a whole profession. This is appalling!" See Tracy Quan, "The Prostitute, The Comedian—and Me," www.desires.com/1.2/sex/docs/paglia2.html on 9 April 2002. One proponent of pornography has found it necessary to disbelieve Linda Marchiano, now deceased, who wrote that she was physically coerced into performing oral sex in the film *Deep Throat*. "As someone who's seen *Deep Throat* several times, I can report that it certainly doesn't *seem* as though Marchiano—or Linda Lovelace, to use her *nom de porn*—is doing anything against her will. . . . In the vast majority of cases, the only thing actresses harm by appearing in adult films is their chances of doing something more mainstream." See Toby Young, "Confessions of a Porn Addict," *Spectator* (10 November 2001), 32.

65. Leah Platt, "Regulating the Global Brothel: As Feminization of Migration Continues, Prostitution Becomes the Protypical Industry. How Do We 'Protect' Its Workers?" *American Prospect*, Summer 2001, 11. The approach in the Platt article is not atypical. One academic has written, "Women sex workers and the lives they lead are far more mundane than is implied in the excesses of attention and stereotype"; see Graham Scambler, "Conspicuous and Inconspicuous Sex Work: The Neglect of the Ordinary and the Mundane," in *Rethinking Prostitution: Purchasing Sex in the 1990s*, eds. G. Scambler and A. Scambler (New York: Routledge, 1997), 112. Yet another feminist wonders why it is that we want "to believe so badly that women are choosing this life, profiting from it?" She continues: "In other forms of exploitation, such as minimum wage jobs, no one is standing next to the worker masturbating because the thought of paying them poorly excites them sexually. Nobody is sexualizing and then selling their exploitation. No one is claiming that they wanted it, they really enjoyed getting paid $5 an hour, and even though they said they wanted more, they really wanted less." These comments were found at www.angelfire.com/wa/onestorm1/101.html on 16 March 2001.

66. Kemala Kempadoo, "The Exotic Dancers Alliance: An Interview with Dawn Passar and Johanna Breyer," in *Global Sex Workers: Rights, Resistance, and Redefinition*, eds. K. Kempadoo and J. Doezema (New York: Routledge, 1998), 185.

67. Hughes, "'Welcome to the Rape Camp,'" 17.

68. Janice Raymond, "Sex: From Intimacy to 'Sexual Labor' Or Is It a Human Right to Prostitute?" (Coalition against Trafficking in Women, Kingston, R.I.), 1998.

69. Herman, *Trauma and Recovery*, 107. See also Jenny Horsman, *Too Scared to Learn: Women, Violence, and Education* (Mahwah, N.J.: Lawrence Erlbaum Associates, 2000), 180.

70. Herman, *Trauma and Recovery*, 108.

71. Horsman, *Too Scared to Learn*, 54.

72. Harry Kreisler, "The Case of Trauma and Recovery: Conversation with Judith Herman, M.D., Psychiatrist and Author," 21 September 2000, http://globetrotter.berkeley.edu/people/Herman/herman-con0.html on 13 May 2003. For this reason, some call the use of sexual violence against women a form of terrorism: "Sexual terrorism is the system by which males frighten, and by frightening, dominate and control females. It is manifested through actual and implied violence. All females are potential victims—at any age, any time, or any place, and through a variety of means: rape, battery, incest, sexual abuse of children, sexual harassment, prostitution, and sexual slavery. The subordination of women in all spheres of the society rests on the power of men to intimidate and to punish women sexually." See Carole J. Sheffield, "Sexual Terrorism: The Social Control of Women," in *Feminist Jurisprudence: Taking Women Seriously*, eds. M. Becker, C. G. Bowman, and M. Torrey (St. Paul: West Group, 2001), 269.

73. "That is, there is nothing in the nature of the work itself, insofar as we can separate it from its working conditions, that would prevent it from being performed by men for men, by women for women, or most significantly by men for women." Christine Overall, "What's Wrong with Prostitution? Evaluating Sex Work," *Signs: Journal of Women in Culture and Society* 17, no. 4 (1992): 718.

74. Sheila Jeffreys, interview by author, 1 April 2001.

75. Lisa D. Brush, *Gender & Governance* (Lanham, Md.: AltaMira Press, 2003), 125.

76. Diana E. H. Russell, "Husbands Who Rape Their Wives," in *Feminist Jurisprudence*, eds. Becker, Bowman, and Torrey, 317.

77. Ann Snitow, Christine Stansell, and Sharon Thompson, "Introduction" in *Powers of Desire: The Politics of Sexuality*, eds. A. Snitow, C. Stansell, and S. Thompson (New York: Monthly Review Press, 1983), 42.

78. Maher, *Sexed Work*, 7.

79. Ibid., 166.

80. Ibid.

81. O'Neill, *Prostitution and Feminism*, 27.

82. Dunn, "Prostitution: Pro or Con?"

83. Ibid.

84. McElroy, "Anti-Pro Feminists," 335–36.

85. Ronald Weitzer, "Why We Need More Research on Sex Work," in *Sex for Sale: Prostitution, Pornography, and the Sex Industry*, ed. R. Weitzer (New York: Routledge, 2000), 3. Wendy Chapkis also cautions that there is "no true story," and that prostitution involves both "victimization and agency, exploitation and engaged complicity; in short both the violence and wild defiance

of sex." See Wendy Chapkis, *Live Sex Acts: Women Performing Erotic Labor* (New York: Routledge, 1997), 212.

86. Weitzer, "Why We Need More Research," 4.

87. Ibid., 5.

88. Ibid., 6.

89. Ibid., 6. Given that traffickers most often place women in indoor prostitution venues (see chapter 10 of this work for a full discussion), Weitzer's call for more in-depth research on the indoor sex trade is not misplaced.

90. Elshtain, *Jane Addams*, 61. Another iteration of this philosophy comes from Albert Camus, who took a stand against all ideological dogma: "We are all in the plague. . . . All I know is that one must do one's best not to be a plague victim. . . . And this is why I have decided to reject everything that, directly or indirectly, makes people die or justifies others in making them die." See Tony Judt, "On the Plague," *New York Review of Books*, 29 November 2001, 8.

91. Elshtain, *Jane Addams*, 60.

92. Ann Russo, *Taking Back Our Lives: A Call to Action for the Feminist Movement* (New York: Routledge, 2001), 45.

93. Jane E. Larson, "Imagine Her Satisfaction: The Transformative Task of Feminist Tort Work," *Washburn Law Journal* 33 (1993): 73.

94. I am indebted to Melissa Farley for this observation.

Chapter Ten

1. Mary Lucille Sullivan and Sheila Jeffreys, "Legalization: The Australian Experience," *Violence against Women* 8, no. 9 (2002): 1142. Many brothel owners still prefer to operate illegally, since they can thereby avoid paying taxes and can more easily employ children and women and children trafficked illegally.

2. Janice G. Raymond, "10 Reasons for Not Legalizing Prostitution," Coalition against Trafficking in Women, www.catwinternational.org on 7 April 2003.

3. Ibid.

4. Ibid. The Coalition against Trafficking in Women maintains a "Fact Book on Global Exploitation," containing reports on specific countries, at its Web site. There readers can obtain information about the number of trafficked women and their pimps who have been detained by governments. See www.catwinternatinal.org/fb.

5. Raymond, "10 Reasons."

6. Migration Information Programme, "Trafficking in Women to Austria for Sexual Exploitation" (Brussels, 1996), 5.

7. Sullivan and Jeffreys, "Legalization: The Australian Experience," 1145–46.

8. Raymond, "10 Reasons."

272

9. Sullivan and Jeffreys, "Legalization," 1146.

10. Raymond, "10 Reasons."

11. Rabinovitch and Strega, "The PEERS Story."

12. Carter and Giobbe, "Duet," 53.

13. Nussbaum, *Sex & Social Justice*, 298.

14. Francine du Plessix Gray, *Simone Weil* (New York: Viking, 2001), 197.

15. Martha C. Nussbaum, *Women and Human Development: The Capabilities Approach* (New York: Cambridge University Press, 2000), 73.

16. Ibid., 78–80, 113.

17. Ibid., 87.

18. Among the basic needs are health and bodily integrity, capacity for sexual pleasure, and having the power to participate in the planning and managing of one's own life. Larson, "Imagine Her Satisfaction," 65.

19. Ibid., 71.

20. John Fountain, "Study Finds Teenagers Smoking Less; Campaign Is Cited," *New York Times*, 20 December 2001.

21. Elizabeth Olson, "W.H.O. Treaty Would Ban Cigarette Ads Worldwide," *New York Times*, 22 July 2002.

22. Mowatt, "Where There's Smoking."

23. Claudine O'Leary's comments are taken from a presentation she made at the Donors Forum of Chicago on 22 March 2002.

24. Jannit Rabinovitch, "Creating an Atmosphere of Hope for All Children and Youth: Teen Prostitutes Speak Up & Speak Out" (Victoria, B.C., 1998), 6.

25. Ibid.

26. This ad for Club "O" was found on page 35 of the April 2002 *Chicago after Dark*, picked up in a kiosk in the Chicago Water Tower area.

27. Alex Kuczynski, "Racy Magazine Ads Expose Inconsistency in Publishers' Stance," *New York Times*, 12 March 2001, Section C.

28. Ibid.

29. Ibid. The *Boston Phoenix* publisher has admitted that adult ads account for about 10 percent of the paper's advertising revenue. The ads run in an adult entertainment advertising supplement, which industry analysts say brings in about $100,000 in revenue each week; see Flint, "Ads Generate Dollars."

30. Kuczynski, "Racy Magazine Ads."

31. Sylvia Law, "Commercial Sex: Beyond Decriminalization," *Southern California Law Review* 73 (2000): 539. Eric Schlosser's new book documents America's thriving underground economy—the buying and selling of illegal items. "The current demand for marijuana and pornography is deeply revealing. Here are two commodities that Americans publicly abhor, privately adore, and buy in astonishing amounts." See Eric Schlosser, *Reefer Madness: Sex, Drugs, and Cheap Labor in the American Black Market* (New York: Houghton Mifflin, 2003), 8.

32. Rabinovitch and Strega, "The PEERS Story." For a more in-depth description of peer-led services, see Rabinovitch and Lewis, " 'Impossible, eh?' "

33. Raphael and Shapiro, "Sisters Speak Out," 28.

34. Norton-Hawk, "Lifecourse of Prostitution," 9.

35. Mary Magdalene Project, "Research Report," 188, 161.

36. Benoit and Millar, "Dispelling Myths," 60.

37. Dalla, "Exposing the 'Pretty Woman' Myth," 351. As one social services provider explains, "Leaving the streets is a process, not an event." Experienced programs know how to manage the process. See May Otto, "In Baltimore, New Ambitions on the Street," *Baltimore Sun* 3 June 2003.

38. Information about government benefits available to trafficked persons can be found at www.ojp.gov/ovc/help/tip.htm on 15 May 2003.

39. A listing of the few programs in the U.S. can be found at www.prosti tutionresearch.com on 20 May 2003.

40. See fact sheets posted at the SAGE Web site at www.sageprojectinc.org on 31 May 2003.

41. O'Leary and Howard, "The Prostitution of Women and Girls," 30.

42. Adrienne Sanders, "Tiffany's Legacy," *Examiner*, 27 May 2002.

43. Brenda Myers, interview by author, 23 January 2003.

44. Joyce made this statement at a presentation on 12 March 2003 at a community forum on prostitution in the Chicago Wicker Park community.

45. Brenda Myers, interview by author, 22 January 2003.

46. Ibid.

47. Ibid. Brenda's statement about not knowing any other way to live echoes observations by French philosopher Simone de Beauvoir, who wrote that the lot of the most severely oppressed appears to them so natural, so immovable, that no other choice of how to live their situation appears possible: "The less economic and social circumstances allow an individual to act upon the world, the more this world appears to him as given." See Sonia Kruks, "Beauvoir: The Weight of Situation," in *Simone de Beauvoir: A Critical Reader*, ed. E. Fallaize (New York: Routledge, 1998), 56–57.

48. For information on the Prostitution Alternatives Roundtable, see www.chicagohomeless.org on 31 May 2003. Information on the Grand Rapids initiative can be found at www.nokomisfoundation.org on 31 May 2003.

49. For information on Angela's Fund and other initiatives against child prostitution in Atlanta, see http//cwf.techbridge.org/initiatives/initiatives_ childprost.asp on 15 May 2003.

50. Author interviews with the staff of the Chicago Police Department's Prostitution Unit, 1 and 8 November, 2000.

51. This scheme is not without its critics, because the girls are not free to leave the police station during the intervention. See Neil Herland, "Operation

274   Help: Saskatoon Police Try a New Approach to Get Hookers off the Street,"
CBC Television Saskatchewan, 18 May 2002 at http://sask.cbc.ca/archives/
operationhelp on 18 October 2002.

52. These statistics were supplied to the author by the Chicago Police
Department.

53. A. N. Wilson, The Victorians (New York: W.W. Norton, 2003), 473.
The discrepancies result because the police do not take legal action against the
buyers. However, many states also have established lesser penalties for the
male customers than for those selling sex. This practice reflects the approach
of the Model Penal Code, which enshrines the differential treatment, classify-
ing the patronization of women as an infraction that carries no jail time. One
commentator writes that the American Law Institute believes that because
women earn the money, their involvement is greater and the law should punish them more harshly. See Julie Lefler, "Shining the Spotlight on Johns: Moving toward Equal Treatment of Male Customers and Female Prostitutes," Hastings Women's Law Journal 11 (1999): 17.

54. This information is taken from the 1999 fact sheet, "Violence against
Women," at the Swedish Government Offices Web site: www.naring.reger
ingen.se/pressinfo/fatablad/PDF/n2001_038e.pdf on 17 January 2003.

55. Gunilla Ekberg, special adviser to Sweden's Division for Gender
Equality, interview by author, 16 January 2003.

56. Robert R. Weidner, "I Won't Do Manhattan": Causes and Consequences of a
Decline in Street Prostitution (New York: LFB Scholarly Publishing, 2001), 151–63.

57. Ekberg, interview.

58. Ibid. The only study measuring the number of women in prostitution
in the general U.S. population occurred in St. Louis, Missouri. There researchers found a lifetime prevalence of prostitution to be 2 percent in females. See
Linda B. Cottler, John E. Helzer, and Jayson E. Tripp, "Lifetime Patterns of
Substance Use among General Population Subjects Engaging in High Risk Sexual Behaviors: Implications for HIV Risk," American Journal of Drug and Alcohol Abuse
16, nos. 3 & 4 (1990): 214.

59. This information comes from fact sheets posted at the SAGE Web site
at www.sageprojectinc.org on 31 May 2003.

60. Monto, "Female Prostitution, Customers, and Violence."

61. "2 Women Found Strangled on West Side," Chicago Tribune, Metropolitan Digest, 9 September 2002.

62. Adrienne Sanders, "S. F.: A Haven for Pedophiles," Examiner, 8 January
2003.

63. Youth Advocate Program, "Children for Sale: Youth Involved in Prostitution, Pornography, and Sex Trafficking," (Washington, D.C., 1998), at
www.yapi.org/publications/resourcepapers.htm on 12 May 2003.

64. Adrienne Sanders, "The City Killed Tiffany Mason," Examiner, 20 May
2002.

65. "Prosecutors: Sex Ring Resembled Cult," 17 January 2003, at www .cbsnews.com on 18 May 2003.

66. "Focus: Teenage Prostitution in Britain," *Sunday Telegraph*, 14 March 1999. Focus Section.

67. "Blunkett in Radical Shake-up of Sex Laws," *London Times Online*, 19 November 2002. For complete details on the new legislation, see the Home Office's Web site, www.homeoffice.gov.uk. The U.K. Home Office found that there were only 204 prosecutions for unlawful sex with girls under fifteen in 1996, compared with 1,000 in 1960; see "Child Prostitutes 'Victims Not Criminals,'" BBC News, 21 May 2000 at http://news.bbc.co.uk/2/hi/ uk_news/757145.stm on 25 November 2002.

68. Jamie Smyth, "Enjo Kosai: Teen Prostitution, a Reflection of Society's Ills," *Tokyo Weekender*, 4 September 1998.

69. Susanna Capelouto, "Combatting [sic] Child Prostitution in Atlanta," National Public Radio Morning Edition, 9 May 2001.

70. Adrienne Sanders, "Tiffany's Legacy," *Examiner*, 27 May 2002.

71. Rhonda Copelon, "Recognizing the Egregious in the Everyday: Domestic Violence as Torture," *Columbia Human Rights Law Review* 25 (1994): 309, 341.

72. These costumes were viewed at www.buycostumes.com on 1 October 2002.

73. Robert E. Pierre, "In Chicago Stories of Prostitution Are Part of Plea for Help: Activists Urge Social Services over Arrests," *Washington Post*, 13 May 2003, Section A. See also Richard Roeper, "Solving Prostitution Takes More Than Just Outrage," *Chicago Sun-Times*, 10 March 2003.

74. Raymond, "10 Reasons," 11.

75. "It's Their Business," *Economist*, 6 January 2001.

76. Nancy Fraser, *Justice Interruptus: Critical Reflections on the 'Postsocialist' Condition* (New York: Routledge, 1997), 14.

77. Richard Sennett, *Respect in a World of Inequality* (New York: W. W. Norton, 2003), 263.

78. Ibid., 262.

79. Alan Ryan, "Call Me Mister," *New York Review of Books*, 27 February 2003, 34.

Epilogue

1. Gateley, interview, 29 March 2001.

2. Solomon, *The Noonday Demon*, 432.

3. Ibid., 442–43.

4. Gateley, *I Hear a Seed*, 285.

Bibliography

Addams, Jane. *A New Conscience and an Ancient Evil*. Urbana: University of Illinois Press, 2002.

Adler, Laure. *Marguerite Duras: A Life*. Chicago: University of Chicago Press, 1998.

Albert, Alexa. *Brothel: Mustang Ranch and Its Women*. New York: Random House, 2001.

Alexander, Priscilla. "The International Sex Worker's Rights Movement." In *Sex Work: Writings by Women in the Sex Industry*, eds. F. Delacoste and P. Alexander, 14–19. Pittsburgh: Cleis Press, 1987.

Altman, Dennis. *Global Sex*. Chicago: University of Chicago Press, 2001.

Anderson, Laura. "Working in Nevada." At www.bayswan.org/Laura.html on 9 August 2002.

Angelou, Maya. *Gather Together in My Name*. New York: Bantam Books, 1997.

Angier, Carole. *The Double Bond: Primo Levi, A Biography*. New York: Farrar, Straus and Giroux, 2002.

Armstrong, Liz. "No Apologies: A New-Model Porn Queen Revels in Her Own Raunch." *The Reader*, 8 March 2002.

Arnold, Elizabeth Mayfield, J. Chris Stewart, and C. Aaron McNeece. "Perpetrators as Victims: Understanding Violence by Female Street-Walking Prostitutes." *Violence and Victims* 16, no. 2 (2001): 145–59.

Austin, Regina. "The Black Community, Its Lawbreakers, and a Politics of Identification." In *Criminology at the Crossroads: Feminist Readings in Criminal Justice*, eds. K. Daly and L. Maher, 262–90. New York: Oxford University Press, 1998.

Balos, Beverly. *Teaching Prostitution Seriously*. Buffalo Criminal Law Review 4 (2001): 709–53.

Barbara and Carole. "Interview with Barbara." In *Sex Work: Writings by Women in the Sex Industry*, eds. F. Delacoste and P. Alexander, 166–74. Pittsburgh: Cleis Press, 1987.

Barnardo's. "Stolen Childhood: Barnardo's Work with Children Abused through Prostitution." Report, Ilford, U.K., 2002. At www.barnardos.org.uk on 25 November 2002.

Barry, Kathleen. *The Prostitution of Sexuality*. New York: New York University Press, 1995.

Bartlett, Katharine T. *Gender and Law: Theory, Doctrine, Commentary*. Boston: Little, Brown, 1993.

Barton, Bernadette. "Dancing on the Mobius Strip: Challenging the Sex War Paradigm." *Gender & Society* 16, no. 5 (2002): 585–602.

Benoit, Cecilia, and Alison Millar. "Dispelling Myths and Understanding Realities: Working Conditions, Health Status, and Exiting Experiences of Sex Workers." Report, Victoria, B.C., 2001. At www.peers.bc.ca on 25 February 2003.

Bentley, Toni. *Sisters of Salome*. New Haven: Yale University Press, 2002.

"Blunkett in Radical Shake-Up of Sex Laws." *Times of London*, 19 November 2002.

Boghossian, Paul. "The Gospel of Relaxation." *The New Republic*, 10 September 2001, 35–39.

Bourgois, Philippe, and Eloise Dunlap. "Exorcising Sex-for-Crack: An Ethnographic Perspective from Harlem." In *Crack as Pimp*, ed. M. Ratner, 97–132. Lanham, Md.: Lexington Books, 1992.

Branin, Larissa. "Back on the Streets." *Hope*, no. 12, January/February 1998, 52–57.

Brannigan, Augustine, and Erin G. Van Brunschot. "Youthful Prostitution and Child Sexual Trauma." *International Journal of Law and Psychiatry* 20, no. 3 (1997): 337–54.

Brock, Deborah R. *Making Work, Making Trouble: Prostitution as a Social Problem*. Toronto: University of Toronto Press, 1998.

Brock, Rita Nakashima, and Susan Thistlethwaite. *Casting Stones: Prostitution and Liberation in Asia and the United States*. Minneapolis: Fortress Press, 1996.

Brooks, Siobhan. "Working the Streets: Gloria Lockett's Story." At www.spectator.net.

Brush, Lisa D. *Gender & Governance*. Lanham, Md.: AltaMira Press, 2003.

Burana, Lily. *Strip City: A Stripper's Farewell Journey across America*. New York: Talk Miramax Books, 2001.

Busch, Noel Bridget, et al. "Male Customers of Prostituted Women: Exploring Perceptions of Entitlement to Power and Control and Implications for Violent Behavior toward Women." *Violence against Women* 8, no. 9 (2002): 1093–1112.

Capelouto, Susanna. "Combatting [sic] Child Prostitution in Atlanta." National Public Radio, Morning Edition, 9 May 2001.

Cardwell, Diane. "Fears That City's Flesh Trade May Be Getting Younger." *New York Times*, 7 December 2002.

Carey, Leo. "The Dream Master: The Stories of Arthur Schnitzler, the Amoral Voice of Fin-de-Siècle Vienna." *New Yorker*, 9 September 2002, 154–60.

Carter, Vednita, and Evelina Giobbe. "Duet: Prostitution, Racism, and Feminist Discourse." *Hastings Women's Law Journal* 10 (1999): 37–56.

Chapkis, Wendy. *Live Sex Acts: Women Performing Erotic Labor*. New York: Routledge, 1997.

Chicago Coalition for the Homeless: "Unlocking Options for Women: A Survey of Women in Cook County Jail." Report, Chicago, 2002.

———. "Youth on the Streets and on Their Own: Youth Homelessness in Illinois." Report, Chicago, 2001.

"Child Prostitutes 'Victims Not Criminals.'" BBC News, 21 May 2001.

Church, Stephanie, et al. "Violence by Clients towards Female Prostitutes in Different Work Settings: Questionnaire Survey." *British Medical Journal* 322 , no. 7285 (2001): 524–25.

"Class and Respect," The Talk Show, 6 January 2003, at www.bbc.co.uk/bbcfour.

Cler-Cunningham, Leonard. "Violence against Women in Vancouver's Street Level Sex Trade and the Police Response." Report, Vancouver, B.C., 2001. At www.vcn.bc.ca/pacekids/report on 18 January 2002.

Coalition against Trafficking in Women. "Factbook." At www.catwinternational.org/fb on 2 December 2002.

———. "Sex from Intimacy to 'Sexual Labor' or Is It a Human Right to Prostitute?" Report, Kingston, R.I., at www.catwinternational.org on 4 April 2002.

Collins, Patricia Hill. *Black Feminist Thought: Knowledge, Consciousness, and the Politics of Empowerment*. New York: Routledge, 2000.

Cook, Rhonda. "'Selling Dreams' Helps Lure Girls, Defendant Says." *Atlanta Journal-Constitution*, 23 January 2002.

Copelon, Rhonda. "Recognizing the Egregious in the Everyday: Domestic Violence as Torture." *Columbia Human Rights Review* 25 (1994): 291–367.

Cornell, Drucilla. *At the Heart of Freedom*. Princeton: Princeton University Press, 1998.

Cottler, Linda B., John E. Helzer, and Jayson E. Tipp. "Lifetime Patterns of Substance Abuse among General Population Subjects Engaging in High Risk Sexual Behaviours: Implications for HIV Risk." *American Journal of Drug and Alcohol Abuse* 16, nos. 3 & 4 (1990): 207–22.

"Counting the Money: Living the Pimp Life in Atlanta," at www.abcnews.com.

Dalla, Rochelle L. "'Et Tu Brute?' A Qualitative Analysis of Streetwalking Prostitutes' Interpersonal Support Networks." *Journal of Family Issues* 22, no. 8 (2001): 1066–85.

————. "Exposing the 'Pretty Woman' Myth: A Qualitative Examination of the Lives of Female Streetwalking Prostitutes." *Journal of Sex Research* 37, no. 4 (2000): 344–53.

Davidson, Julia O'Connell. *Prostitution, Power and Freedom.* Ann Arbor: University of Michigan Press, 1998.

Davis, Nanette J. "From Victims to Survivors: Working with Recovering Street Prostitutes." In *Sex for Sale: Prostitution, Pornography, and the Sex Industry,* ed. R. Weitzer, 139–55. New York: Routledge, 2000.

de Beauvoir, Simone. *The Second Sex.* New York: Bantam Books, 1970.

De Graaf, R., et al. "Alcohol and Drug Use in Heterosexual and Homosexual Prostitution, and Its Relation to Protection Behaviour." *AIDS Care* 7, no. 1 (1995): 35–47.

DeKeseredy, Walter S. *Women, Crime, and the Canadian Criminal Justice System.* Cincinnati: Anderson Publishing, 2000.

Dines, Gail, Robert Jensen, and Ann Russo. *Pornography: The Production and Consumption of Inequality.* New York: Routledge, 1998.

D'Lorenzo, Ann. "A San Francisco Whore in a Nevada Brothel." At www .headlightjournal.com on 4 April 2002.

Donoghue, Emma. *Slammerkin.* New York: Harcourt, 2000.

Drug and Alcohol Services Information System. "The DASIS Report." Report, Washington, DC, 2001. At www.samhsa.gov/oas/2k1/femCrack/ femCrack.htm on 24 May 2003.

Dunn, Katia. "Prostitution Pro or Con?" *Portland (Ore.) Mercury,* 9 May 2002.

Duras, Marguerite. *The Lover.* New York: HarperPerennial, 1985.

Dworkin, Andrea. *Heartbreak: The Political Memoir of a Feminist Militant.* New York: Basic Books, 2002.

————. *Life and Death.* New York: Free Press, 1997.

Eaves, Elisabeth. *Bare: On Women, Dancing, Sex, and Power.* New York: Knopf, 2002.

Eek, Louise. "Prostitution as Male Violence against Women." Speech, Swedish Embassy, Paris, 11 March 2003. At www.sos-sexisme.org/news on 28 May 2003.

Ehrenreich, Barbara. *Nickel and Dimed: On (Not) Getting By in America.* New York: Henry Holt, 2001.

Ehrenreich, Barbara, and Arlie Russell Hochschild. *Global Woman: Nannies, Maids, and Sex Workers in the New Economy.* New York: Metropolitan Books, 2002.

El-Bassel, Nabila, et al. "Correlates of Partner Violence among Female Street-based Sex Workers: Substance Abuse, History of Childhood Abuse, and HIV Risks." *AIDS Patient Care and STDs* 15, no. 1 (2001): 41–51.

————. "Sex Trading and Psychological Distress among Women Recruited from the Streets of Harlem." *American Journal of Public Health* 87, no. 1 (1997): 66–70.

————. "Social Support among Women in Methadone Treatment Who Experience Partner Violence: Isolation and Male Controlling Behavior." *Violence against Women* 7, no. 3 (2001): 246–74.

Elshtain, Jean Bethke. *Jane Addams and the Dream of American Democracy: A Life.* New York: Basic Books, 2002.

Erickson, Patricia G., et al. "Crack and Prostitution: Gender, Myths, and Experiences." *Journal of Drug Issues* 30, no. 4 (2000): 767–88.

Estes, Richard J., and Neil Alan Weiner. "The Commercial Sexual Exploitation of Children in the U.S., Canada, and Mexico: Executive Summary." Report, Philadelphia, 2001.

Faber, Michel. *The Crimson Petal and the White.* New York: Harcourt, 2002.

Fabian, Cosi. "The Holy Whore: A Woman's Gateway to Power." In *Whores and Other Feminists*, ed. J. Nagle, 44–54. New York: Routledge, 1977.

Faderman, Lillian. *Naked in the Promised Land.* New York: Houghton Mifflin, 2003.

Fairstein, Linda A. *Sexual Violence: Our War against Rape.* New York: William Morrow, 1993.

Farley, Melissa, et al. "Prostitution in Five Countries: Violence and Post-Traumatic Stress Disorder." *Feminism & Psychology* 8, no. 4 (1998): 405–26.

Farley, Melissa, and Howard Barkan. "Prostitution, Violence against Women, and Posttraumatic Stress Disorder." *Women & Health* 27, no. 3 (1998): 37–49.

Farley, Melissa, and Vanessa Kelly. "Prostitution: A Critical Review of the Medical and Social Sciences Literature." *Women & Criminal Justice* 11, no. 4 (2000): 29–63.

Federal Bureau of Investigation. "Crime in the United States, 2000," Tables 33 and 49. At www.fbi.gov/ucr/00cius.htm on 9 April 2002.

Finkelhor, David. "The Trauma of Child Sexual Abuse." In *Lasting Effects of Child Sexual Abuse*, eds. G. Powell and G. Wyatt, 61–82. Newbury Park, Calif.: Sage, 1988.

Flint, Anthony. "Ads Generate Dollars, Allies." *Boston Globe*, 2 December 1996.

Flowers, R. Barri. *The Prostitution of Women and Girls.* Jefferson, N.C.: McFarland, 1998.

"Focus: Teenage Prostitution in Britain." *Sunday Telegraph*, 14 March 1999, Focus Section.

Fountain, John W. "Study Finds Teenagers Smoking Less; Campaign Is Cited." *New York Times*, 20 December 2001.

Franki. "Good Practice Guide for Agencies Working with Women Who Work in Prostitution." Report, Bolton, U.K., 2001. At www.franki-wsp.org .uk on 1 March 2001.

Fraser, Nancy. *Justice Interruptus: Critical Reflections on the "Postsocialist" Condition.* New York: Routledge, 1997.

Gateley, Edwina. *I Hear a Seed Growing: God of the Forest, God of the Streets*. Trabuco Canyon, Calif.: Source Books, 1998.

Geringer, Dan. "Wheelchair-bound Man Sues Fla. Strip Club." *Philadelphia Daily News*, 23 September 2002.

"Getting Real Facts about Prostitution: An Interview with Melissa Farley." At www.mergemag.org/1998/farley.html.

Gibson-Ainyette, Ivan, et al. "Adolescent Female Prostitutes." *Archives of Sexual Behavior* 17, no. 5 (1998): 431–38.

Gillan, Audrey, and Peter Moszynski. "Aid Workers in Africa 'Bought Child Sex with Food.'" *Guardian Weekly*, 7–13 March 2002.

Gillum, Tameka L. "Exploring the Link between Stereotypic Images and Intimate Partner Violence in the African-American Community." *Violence against Women* 8, no. 1 (2002): 64–86.

Giobbe, Evelina. "An Analysis of Individual, Institutional, and Cultural Pimping." *Michigan Journal of Gender Law* 1 (1993): 33–57.

Goens, Mike. "Girl's Mom: Daughter Forced into Prostitution." *Florence (AL) Times Daily*, 11 February 2000.

Goetting, Ann. *Getting Out: Life Stories of Women Who Left Abusive Men*. New York: Columbia University Press, 1999.

Gornick, Vivian. *The Situation and the Story: The Art of Personal Narrative*. New York: Farrar, Straus and Giroux, 2001.

Gossop, M., et al. "Female Prostitutes in South London: Use of Heroin, Cocaine, and Alcohol, and Their Relationship to Health Risk Behaviors. *AIDS Care* 7, no. 3 (1995): 253–60.

Graham, Nanette, and Eric D. Wish. "Drug Use among Female Arrestees: Onset, Patterns, and Relationships to Prostitution." *Journal of Drug Issues* 24, no. 2 (1994): 315–29.

"Grand Theft Auto III" Review. At gamespot.com/gamespot/stories/reviews/0,10867,2820025,00.html on 21 March 2002.

Grasse, Nicole. "Dancing Lessons." At www.salon.com.

Gray, Francine du Plessix. *Simone Weil*. New York: Viking, 2001.

Green, S.T., et al. "Female Streetworker–Prostitutes in Glasgow: A Descriptive Study of Their Lifestyle." *AIDS Care* 5, no. 3 (1993): 321–35.

Greene, Elizabeth. "Shining the Light on a Hidden Tragedy: Charities Take On a Problem Few Care to Acknowledge—Commercial Sex Involving Youngsters." *Chronicle of Philanthropy*, 1 November 2001, 9–14.

Greene, Jody M., Susan T. Ennett, and Christopher L. Ringwalt. "Prevalence and Correlates of Survival Sex among Runaway and Homeless Youth." *American Journal of Public Health* 89, no. 9 (1999): 1406–9.

Greer, Germaine. *The Whole Woman*. New York: Knopf, 1999.

Hammer, Rhonda. *Antifeminism and Family Terrorism: A Critical Feminist Perspective*. Lanham, Md.: Rowman & Littlefield, 2002.

Hanna, Judith Lynne. "Wrapping Nudity in a Cloak of Law." *New York Times,* 29 July 2001, Arts Section.

Hansen, Jane O. "Selling Atlanta's Children: Feds, Police Elsewhere Finding Solutions." *Atlanta Journal-Constitution,* 7 January 2001.

———. "Selling Atlanta's Children: The Girls: Promise of Easy Life Pulls the Young to Streets." *Atlanta Journal-Constitution,* 7 January 2001.

———. "Selling Atlanta's Children: Prostitutes Getting Younger As Sex Trade Grows, Judges Say." *Atlanta Journal-Constitution,* 7 January 2001.

———. "Selling Atlanta's Children: Runaway Girls Lured into the Sex Trade Are Being Jailed for Crimes While Their Adult Pimps Go Free." *Atlanta Journal-Constitution,* 7 January 2001.

Hansen, Suzy. "Interview with Lily Burana." 9 October 2001. At www.salon.com.

Harway, Michele, and Marsha Liss. "Dating Violence and Teen Prostitution: Adolescent Girls in the Justice System." In *Beyond Appearance: A New Look at Adolescent Girls,* eds. J. Worell, M. Roberts, and N. Johnson, 277–300. Washington, D.C.: American Psychological Association, 1999.

Heche, Anne. *Call Me Crazy.* New York: Scribner, 2001.

Herland, Neil. "Operation Help: Saskatoon Police Try a New Approach to Get Hookers off the Street." CBC Radio, 18 May 2002. At sask.cbc.ca/archives/operationhelp on 2 June 2002.

Herman, Judith Lewis. *Trauma and Recovery.* New York: Basic Books, 1992.

Highleyman, Liz, aka Mistress Vronika Frost. "Professional Dominance: Power, Money, and Identity." In *Whores and Other Feminists,* ed. J. Nagle, 145–55. New York: Routledge, 1997.

Hirshman, Linda R., and Jane E. Larson. *Hard Bargains: The Politics of Sex.* New York: Oxford University Press, 1998.

Hobson, Barbara Meil. *Uneasy Virtue: The Politics of Prostitution and the American Reform Tradition.* New York: Basic Books, 1987.

Hofstede Committee. "Juvenile Prostitution in Minnesota." Report, St. Paul, 1999.

Hoigard, Cecilie, and Liv Finstad. *Backstreets: Prostitution, Money, and Love.* University Park: Pennsylvania State University Press, 1992.

Holsopple, Kelly. Remarks at Moorhead State University, Moorhead, Minn., 25 October 1996. At rrnet.com/~wnrrv/msu.htm on 7 February 2001.

———. "Stripclubs According to Strippers." In *Making the Harm Visible: Global Sexual Exploitation of Women and Girls: Speaking Out and Providing Services,* 252–76. Kingston, R.I.: Coalition against Trafficking in Women, 1999.

Holzman, Harold R., and Sharon Pines. "Buying Sex: The Phenomenology of Being a John." *Deviant Behavior* 4 (1982): 89–116.

Homer, Frederic D. *Primo Levi and the Politics of Survival.* Columbia: University of Missouri Press, 2001.

284

Hood-Brown, Marcia. "Trading for a Place: Poor Women and Prostitution." *Journal of Poverty* 2, no. 3 (1998): 13–33.

Horowitz, Helen Lefkowitz. *Reading Sex: Battles over Sexual Knowledge and Suppression in Nineteenth-Century America.* New York: Knopf, 2002.

Horsman, Jenny. *Too Scared to Learn: Women, Violence, and Education.* Mahwah, N.J.: Lawrence Erlbaum Associates, 2000.

Horwich, Jeff. "Exotic Dancing—Is It Art?" Minnesota Public Radio, 4 March 2002. At news.mpr.org/features on 15 March 2002.

Hotaling, Norma, and L. Levitas. "Increased Demand Resulting in the Flourishing Recruitment and Trafficking in Women and Girls." Speech, Annual Conference on Criminal Justice Research and Evaluation, Washington, D.C., 25 July 2001.

Hughes, Donna M. "Pimps and Predators on the Internet." Report, Kingston, R.I., 1999.

———. "'Welcome to the Rape Camp': Sexual Exploitation and the Internet in Cambodia." Report, Kingston, R.I., 2001.

Hynes, H. Patricia. "The United States: Interview Findings and Data Analysis," in "A Comparative Study of Women Trafficked in the Migration Process: Patterns, Profiles, and Health Consequences of Sexual Exploitation in Five Countries." At www.catwinternational.org on 9 August 2002.

Inciardi, James A., et al. "Prostitution, IV Drug Use, and Sex-For-Crack Exchanges among Serious Delinquents: Risks for IV Infection." *Criminology* 29, no. 2 (1991): 221–35.

"It's Their Business." *The Economist,* 6 January 2001.

Jacobs, Michelle S. "Symposium: Prostitutes, Drug Users, and Thieves: The Invisible Women in the Campaign to End Violence against Women." *Temple Political & Civil Rights Law Review* 8 (1999): 459–76.

Jeffreys, Sheila. *The Idea of Prostitution.* North Melbourne: Spinifex, 1997.

———. "Trafficking in Women versus Prostitution: A False Distinction." Address, Townsville International Women's Conference, James Cook University, 3–7 July 2002. At www.austdvclearinghouse.unsw.edu/au on 5 December 2002.

Jenness, Valerie. *Making It Work: The Prostitutes' Rights Movement in Perspective.* New York: Aldine De Gruyter, 1993.

Jewell, K. Sue. *From Mammy to Miss America and Beyond: Cultural Images and the Shaping of U.S. Social Policy.* New York: Routledge, 1993.

Jordan, Winthrop D. *White over Black: American Attitudes toward the Negro, 1550–1812.* Baltimore: Penguin Books, 1969.

Joseph Rowntree Foundation. "Findings from the Choice and Opportunity Project: Young Women and Sexual Exploitation." Report, York, U.K., 2003. At www.jrf.org/uk/knowledge/findings/social policy/513.asp on 30 April 2003.

Judt, Tony. "On the Plague." *New York Review of Books*, 29 November 2001, 6–9.

Kapos, Shia. "Alleged Sex Ring Detailed." *Chicago Tribune*, 16 January 2003.

Kelly, Liz. *Surviving Sexual Violence*. Minneapolis: University of Minnesota Press, 1988.

Kempadoo, Kamala. "The Exotic Dancers Alliance: An Interview with Dawn Passar and Johanna Breyer." In *Global Sex Workers: Rights, Resistance, and Redefinition*, eds. K. Kempadoo and J. Dozema, 182–91. New York: Routledge, 1998.

Kidd, Sean A., and Michael J. Kral. "Suicide and Prostitution among Street Youth: A Qualitative Analysis." *Adolescence* 37, no. 146 (2002): 411–30.

Kilvington, Judith, Sophie Day, and Helen Ward. "European Prostitution Policy: A Time of Change?" At www.med.ic.ac.uk on 22 November 2002.

Kingsley, Cherry, and Melanie Mark. "Sacred Lives: Canadian Aboriginal Children and Youth Speak Out about Sexual Exploitation." Report, Vancouver, B.C., 2001. At www.savethechildren.ca/en/whatwedo/pdf/sacredlives.pdf on 4 September 2002.

Kipke, Michele D., et al. "Street Youth in Los Angeles: Profile of a Group at High Risk for Human Immunodeficiency Virus Infection." *Archives of Pediatric and Adolescent Medicine* 149, no. 5 (1995): 513–19.

Kreisler, Harry. "The Case of Trauma and Recovery: Conversation with Judith Herman, M.D., Psychiatrist and Author," 21 September 2000. At glob trotter.berkeley.edu/people/Herman/herman-con0.html on 24 May 2003.

Kristeva, Julia. *Hannah Arendt*. New York: Columbia University Press, 2001.

Kruks, Sonia. "The Weight of Situation." In *Simone de Beauvoir: A Critical Reader*, ed. E. Fallaize, 43–71. New York: Routledge, 1998.

Kuczynski, Alex. "Racy Magazine Ads Expose Inconsistency in Publishers' Stance." *New York Times*, 12 March 2001, Section C.

———. "The Sex-Worker Literati." *New York Times*, 4 November 2001.

Kuhns, Joseph B., III, Kathleen M. Heide, and Ira Silverman. "Substance Use/Misuse among Female Prostitutes and Female Arrestees." *International Journal of the Addictions* 27, no. 11 (1992): 1283–92.

La Ferla, Ruth. "Those Naughty Victorians Find New Takers." *New York Times*, 6 October 2002.

Larson, Jane E. "Imagine Her Satisfaction: The Transformative Task of Feminist Tort Work." *Washburn Law Journal* 33 (1993): 56–75.

Law, Sylvia A. "Commercial Sex: Beyond Decriminalization. *Southern California Law Review* 73 (2000): 523–610.

Lawrence, Curtis. "Ex-Teen Hooker Tells of Stag Party Sex." *Chicago Sun Times*, 12 September 2002.

Lefler, Julie. "Shining the Spotlight on Johns: Moving toward Equal Treatment of Male Customers and Female Prostitutes." *Hastings Women's Law Journal* 11 (1999): 11–35.

Leidholdt, Dorchen, and Janice G. Raymond. *The Sexual Liberals and the Attack on Feminism*. Elmsford, N.Y.: Pergamon Press, 1990.

Lerner, Gerda. *The Creation of Patriarchy*. New York: Oxford University Press, 1986.

Lever, Janet, and Deanne Dolnick. "Clients and Call Girls: Seeking Sex and Intimacy." In *Sex for Sale: Prostitution, Pornography, and the Sex Industry*, ed. R. Weitzer, 85–100. New York: Routledge, 2000.

Levi, Primo. *The Drowned and the Saved*. New York: Vintage International, 1989.

———. *Survival in Auschwitz: The Nazi Assault on Humanity*. New York: Collier Books, 1961.

Levine, Judith. *Harmful to Minors: The Perils of Protecting Children from Sex*. Minneapolis: University of Minnesota Press, 2002.

Liepe-Levinson, Katherine. *Strip Show: Performances of Gender and Desire*. New York: Routledge, 2002.

Liptak, Adam. "Disabled Man Sues Club over Privacy of Lap Dance." *New York Times*, 18 July 2002.

Loinaz, Alexis. "From the Cradle to the Street." *Village Voice*, 17–23 July 2002. At www.villagevoice.com/issues/0229/loinaz.php on 25 July 2002.

Lyall, Sarah. "Britain's Hunt for Child Pornography Users Nets Hundreds besides Pete Townshend." *New York Times*, 15 January 2003.

———. "Easing of Marijuana Laws Angers Many Britons." *New York Times* 12 August 2002.

———. "A Writer's Tale Is Victorian; His Past, Gothic." *New York Times*, 28 October 2002.

Maccowan, Lyndall. "Organizing in the Massage Parlor: An Interview with Denise Turner." In *Whores and Other Feminists*, ed. J. Nagle, 232–41. New York: Routledge, 1997.

MacKinnon, Catherine A., and Andrea Dworkin. *In Harm's Way: The Pornography Civil Rights Hearings*. Cambridge, Mass.: Harvard University Press, 1997.

Madeleine. *Madeleine: A Biography*. New York: Persea Books, 1986.

Maher, Lisa. *Sexed Work: Gender, Race, and Resistance in a Brooklyn Drug Market*. New York: Oxford University Press, 1997.

Main, Frank. "Chicago Fights Growing Female 'Slave' Trade." *Chicago Sun-Times*, 25 February 2002.

Martinelli, Victoria. "Let Them Meat Cake: My sabbatical from internecine warfare amongst feminists." *Feminista!* 4, no. 7, at www.feminista.com.

Mary Magdalene Project. "Research Report on Street Prostitution." Report, Los Angeles, 2001.

Maticka-Tyndale, Eleanor, et al. "Exotic Dancing and Health." *Women & Health* 31, no. 1 (2000): 87–108.

Mattson, Heidi. *Ivy League Stripper*. New York: Arcade Publishing, 1995.

Maxwell, Sheila R., and Christopher D. Maxwell, "Examining the 'Criminal Careers' of Prostitutes within the Nexus of Drug Use, Drug Selling, and Other Illicit Activities." *Criminology* 38, no. 3 (2000): 787–809.

McCaghy, Charles H., and James K. Skipper. "Lesbian Behavior as an Adaptation to the Occupation of Stripping." In *Bisexuality in the United States: A Social Science Reader*, eds. L. Faderman and L. Gross, 267–75. New York: Columbia University Press, 2000.

McCain, John, and Mark Salter. *Faith of My Fathers: A Family Memoir*. New York: Random House, 1999.

McClanahan, Susan F., et al. "Pathways into Prostitution among Female Jail Detainees." *Psychiatric Services* 50, no. 12 (1999): 1606–13.

McDonald, Jeni. Interview with Lily Burana. At www.bookreview.com.

McElroy, Wendy. "Prostitutes, Anti-Pro Feminists, and the Economic Associates of Whores." In *Prostitution: On Whores, Hustlers, and Johns*, eds. J. Elias, V. Bullough, V. Elias, and G. Brewer, 333–44. Amherst, N.Y.: Prometheus Books, 1998.

McKeganey, Neil, and Marina Barnard. *Sex Work on the Streets: Prostitutes and Their Clients*. Buckingham, U.K.: Open University Press, 1996.

McNair, Brian. *Striptease Culture: Sex, Media and the Democratization of Desire*. New York: Routledge, 2002.

Mead, Rebecca. "American Pimp: How to Make an Honest Living from the Oldest Profession." *New Yorker*, April 23 and 30, 2001, 74–86.

Media Watch, "Pseudo-Rebel Radio Jock Stoops to New Low." At www.mediawatch.com/leykis.html on 27 November 2001.

Metropolitan Digest. "2 Women Found Strangled on West Side." *Chicago Tribune*, 9 September, 2002.

Michigan Family Impact Seminars. "Prostituted Teens: More Than a Runaway Problem." Report, East Lansing, Mich., 2002. At www.icyf.msu.edu/publi-cats/briefs.html on 22 December 2002.

Migration Information Programme. "Trafficking in Women to Austria for Sexual Exploitation." Report, Brussels, 1996. At www.iom.int.iom/publications on 15 February 2001.

Miller, Jody. "Gender and Power on the Streets: Street Prostitution in the Era of Crack Cocaine." *Journal of Contemporary Ethnography* 23, no. 4 (1995): 427–52.

———. "Violence and Coercion in Sri Lanka's Commercial Sex Industry: Intersections of Gender, Sexuality, Culture and the Law." *Violence against Women* 8, no. 9 (2002): 1044–73.

———. "'Your Life Is on the Line Every Night You're on the Streets': Victimization and the Resistance among Street Prostitutes." *Humanity & Society* 17, no. 4 (1993): 422–46.

Miller, Jody, and Dheeshana Jayasundara. "Prostitution, the Sex Industry, and Sex Tourism." In *Sourcebook on Violence against Women*, eds. C. Renzetti, J. Edleson, and R. Bergen, 459–80. Thousand Oaks, Calif.: Sage, 2001.

Miller, Jody, and Martin D. Schwartz "Rape Myths and Violence against Street Prostitutes." *Deviant Behavior* 16 (1995): 1–23.

Monto, Martin A. "A Comparison of the Male Clients of Female Street Prostitutes with National Samples of Men." Unpublished manuscript.

———. "Conceiving of Sex as a Commodity: A Study of Arrested Clients of Female Street Prostitutes." Unpublished manuscript.

———. "Female Prostitution, Customers, and Violence." *Violence against Women*, forthcoming.

———. "Why Men Seek Out Prostitutes." In *Sex for Sale: Prostitution, Pornography, and the Sex Industry*, ed. R. Weitzer, 67–83. New York: Routledge, 2000.

Monto, Martin A., and Norma Hotaling. "Predictors of Rape Myth Acceptance among Male Clients of Female Street Prostitutes." *Violence against Women* 7 no. 3 (2001): 275–93.

Mowatt, Raoul. "Where There's Smoking . . . There's B96 with a Message." "At Random Column," *Chicago Tribune*, 24 May 2002.

Nadon, Susan M., Catherine Koverola, and Eduard H. Schludermann. "Antecedents to Prostitution." *Journal of Interpersonal Violence* 13, no. 2 (1998): 206–21.

Nagel, Thomas, "Sheltered Lives and Public Postures." *Times Literary Supplement*, 25 January 2002, 8.

National Center for Missing and Exploited Children. "Female Juvenile Prostitution: Problem and Response." Report, Washington, D.C., 1992.

Nelson, Vednita. "Prostitution: Where Racism and Sexism Intersect." *Michigan Journal of Gender & Law* 1 (1993): 81–89.

Nixon, Kendra, et al. "The Everyday Occurrence: Violence in the Lives of Girls Exploited through Prostitution." *Violence against Women* 8, no. 9 (2002): 1016–43.

Nokomis Foundation. "We Can Do Better: Helping Prostituted Women and Girls in Grand Rapids Make Healthy Choices: A Prostitution Round Table Report to the Community." Report, Grand Rapids, Mich., 2002.

Norton-Hawk, Maureen A. "The Counter-Productivity of Incarcerating Female Street Prostitutes." *Deviant Behavior: An Interdisciplinary Journal* 22, no 5 (2001): 403–17.

———. "Drugs and Prostitution: A Complex Equation." Unpublished paper.

———. "The Lifecourse of Prostitution." *Women, Girls & Criminal Justice* 3, no. 1 (2002): 1, 7, 8–9.

———. "Prostitution Is Not about Sex." Unpublished paper.

———. "Social Class, Drugs, Gender and the Limitations of the Law: Contrasting the Elite Prostitute with the Street Prostitute." *Studies in Law, Politics, and Society* 29 (2003): 115–31.

Nussbaum, Martha C. *Sex & Social Justice*. New York: Oxford University Press, 1999.

————. *Women and Human Development: The Capabilities Approach*. New York: Cambridge University Press, 2000.

O'Leary, Claudine, and Olivia Howard. "The Prostitution of Women and Girls in Metropolitan Chicago: A Preliminary Prevalence Report." Report, Chicago, 2001. At www.impactresearch.org on 29 May 2003.

Olson, Elizabeth. "W.H.O. Treaty Would Ban Cigarette Ads Worldwide." *New York Times*, 22 July 2002.

O'Neill, Maggie. *Prostitution and Feminism: Towards a Politics of Feeling*. Malden, Mass.: Blackwell Publishers, 2001.

Otto, Mary. "In Baltimore, New Ambitions on the Street." *Baltimore Sun*, 3 June 1003, Metro Section.

Overall, Christine. "What's Wrong with Prostitution? Evaluating Sex Work." *Signs: Journal of Women in Culture and Society* 17, no. 4 (1992): 705–25.

Parker, Joseph. "Between the Hammer and the Anvil: Working with Complex Post-Traumatic Stress Disorder in a Hostile Environment." At www.prostitutionrecovery.org on 29 January 2003.

————. "How Prostitution Works." At www.prostitutionrecovery.org on 29 January 2003.

Parriott, Ruth. "Health Experiences of Twin Cities Women Used in Prostitution: Survey Findings and Recommendations." Report, Minneapolis, 1994.

Pearl, Julie. "The Highest Paying Customers: America's Cities and the Costs of Prostitution Control." *Hastings Law Journal* 38 (1987): 769–90.

Pedersen, Willy, and Kristinn Hegna. "Children and Adolescents Who Sell Sex: A Community Study." *Social Science & Medicine* 56, no. 1 (2003): 135–47.

Pettiway, Leon E. *Workin' It: Women Living through Drugs and Crime*. Philadelphia: Temple University Press, 1997.

Pheterson, Gail. *The Prostitution Prism*. Amsterdam: Amsterdam University Press, 1996.

Pierre, Robert E. "In Chicago Stories of Prostitution Are Part of Plea for Help: Activists Urge Social Services over Arrests." *Washington Post*, 12 May 2003, Section A.

Platt, Leah. "Regulating the Global Brothel: As Feminization of Migration Continues, Prostitution Becomes the Prototypical Industry. How Do We 'Protect' Its Workers?" *American Prospect*, Summer 2001, 10–14.

————. "Stopping at a Red Light." *The Nation*, 9 July 2001, 40–42.

Porter, Judith, and Louis Bonilla. "Drug Use, HIV, and the Ecology of Street Prostitution." In *Sex for Sale: Prostitution, Pornography, and the Sex Industry*, ed. R. Weitzer, 103–21. New York: Routledge, 2000.

Potterat, John J., et al. "Pathways to Prostitution: The Chronology of Sexual and Drug Abuse Milestones." *Journal of Sex Research* 35, no. 4 (199): 333–40.

"Prosecutors: Sex Ring Resembled Cult," 17 January 2003. At www.cbsnews.com on 18 May 2003.

Prostitution Alternatives Counseling Education. "Violence against Women in Vancouver's Street Level Sex Trade." Report, Vancouver, 2001. At www.vcn.bc.ca/pacekids/report on 18 January 2002.

"Protecting the Public, Strengthening the Law on Sex Offenders and Sex Offences." UK Home Office Press Release. At www.homeoffice.gov.uk on 25 November 2002.

Pyett, Priscilla, and Deborah Warr. "Women at Risk in Sex Work: Strategies for Survival." Journal of Sociology 35, no. 2 (1999): 183–197.

Quan, Tracy. "The Prostitute, the Comedian—and Me." At www.desires.com/1.2/sex/docs/paglia2.html on 9 April 2002.

Rabinovitch, Jannit. "Creating an Atmosphere of Hope for All Children and Youth: Teen Prostitutes Speak Up & Speak Out." Report, Vancouver, 1996.

Rabinovitch, Jannit, and Megan Lewis. "Impossible, eh? The Story of PEERS." Report, Vancouver, B.C., 2001. At www.sayso.net/resources/pdf/pub_16pdf on 16 August 2002.

Rabinovitch, Jannit, and Susan Strega. "The PEERS Story: Delivering Services by Side-Stepping the Current Controversies." Violence against Women, Forthcoming.

Raphael, Jody. Saving Bernice: Battered Women, Welfare, and Poverty. Boston: Northeastern University Press, 2000.

Raphael Jody, and Deborah L. Shapiro. "Sisters Speak Out: The Lives and Needs of Prostituted Women in Chicago: A Research Study." Report, Chicago, 2002. At www.impactresearch.org on 29 May 2003.

Raymond, Janice. "10 Reasons for not Legalizing Prostitution." Report, Amherst, Mass., 2003. At www.catwinternational.org on 14 May 2003.

Raymond, Janice G., and Donna M. Hughes. "Sex Trafficking of Women in the United States: International and Domestic Trends." Report: Kingston, R.I., 2001. At www.catwinternational.org on 29 March 2003.

Reeves, Jay. "Charges of Sex Acts Shake Girls' Lockup: Abuse Alleged at Alabama Campus." Chicago Tribune, 18 June 2001.

Renee, Ann. "A Sex Protector/Pervert Speaks Out." In Whores and Other Feminists, ed. J. Nagle, 55–56. New York: Routledge, 1997.

Richard, Amy O'Neill. "International Trafficking in Women to the United States: A Contemporary Manifestation of Slavery and Organized Crime." Report, Washington, D.C., 1999.

Richards, Linda. "Interview: Emma Donoghue." January Magazine, November 2000. At www.janmag.com/profiles/donoghue.html.

Roberts, Nickie. Whores in History. London: HarperCollins, 1992.

Roeper, Richard. "Solving Prostitution Takes More Than Just Outrage." Chicago Sun-Times, 10 March 2003.

Roffman, Deborah M. "The 'De-Meaning' of Sex: Value-Free Thinking Has Replaced Old Morality." Washington Post Weekly Edition, 1–14 July 2002, 19, 36, and 37.

Roiphe, Katie. *The Morning After: Sex, Fear, and Feminism on Campus*. Boston: Little, Brown, 1993.

Romans, Sarah E., et al. "The Mental and Physical Health of Female Sex Workers: A Comparative Study." *Australian and New Zealand Journal of Psychiatry* 35, no. 1 (2001): 75–80.

Ronai, Carol Rambo, and Carolyn Ellis. "Turn-Ons for Money: Interactional Strategies of the Table Dancer." *Journal of Contemporary Ethnography* 18, no. 2 (1989): 271–98.

Rosen, Ruth. *The Lost Sisterhood: Prostitution in America, 1900–1918*. Baltimore: Johns Hopkins University Press, 1982.

————. *The World Split Open: How the Modern Women's Movement Changed America*. New York: Penguin Books, 2000.

Ross, Colin A., et al. "Dissociation and Abuse among Multiple-Personality Patients, Prostitutes, and Exotic Dancers." *Hospital and Community Psychiatry* 41, no. 3 (1990): 328–30.

Roy, E., et al. "Prevalence of HIV Infection and Risk Behaviours among Montreal Street Youth." *International Journal of STD & AIDS* 11 (2000): 241–47.

Rumbelow, Helen. "Fallen Men: At 'John School,' Students Review a Lesson Picked Up on the Street." *Washington Post*, 28 August 2002, Section C.

Russell, Diana E. H. "Husbands Who Rape Their Wives." In *Cases and Materials on Feminist Jurisprudence: Taking Women Seriously*, eds. M. Becker, C. G. Bowman, and M. Torrey, 314–20. St. Paul: West Group, 2001.

————. "The Making of a Whore." In *Issues in Intimate Violence*, ed. R. Bergen, 65–76. Thousand Oaks, Calif.: Sage, 1998.

Russo, Ann. *Taking Back Our Lives: A Call to Action for the Feminist Movement*. New York: Routledge, 2001.

Ryan, Alan. "Call Me Mister." *New York Review of Books*, 27 February 2003, 31–34.

Saguin, Rheal. "Hells Angels, Prominent Citizens—Sex Slave Ring, School Girls." *Toronto Globe and Mail*, 19 December 2002.

————. "Web Site Lured Girls, Officials Say." *Toronto Globe and Mail*, 20 December 2002.

Sanders, Adrienne. "The City Killed Tiffany Mason." *Examiner*, 20 May 2002.

————. "A Hack's View of Hookers." *Examiner*, 9 May 2002.

————. "Heartland Daughters for Sale." *Examiner*, 9 May 2002.

————. "Pimp in Tiffany's Series Charged." *Examiner*, 18 December 2002.

————. "S.F.: A Haven for Pedophiles." *Examiner*, 8 January 2003.

————. "Tiffany's Legacy." *Examiner*, 27 May 2002.

San Francisco Task Force on Prostitution. "Final Report 1996." Report, San Francisco, 1996. At www.bayswan.org/4laws.html on 29 November 2000.

Sauer, Georgia. "Fashion Shows Put the S-E-X in the City of Paris." *Chicago Tribune*, 11 October 2002.

Scambler, Graham. "Conspicuous and Inconspicuous Sex Work: The Neglect of the Ordinary and the Mundane." In *Rethinking Prostitution: Purchasing Sex in the 1990s*, eds. G. Scambler and A. Scambler, 105–20. New York: Routledge, 1997.

Schissel, Bernard, and Kari Fedec. "The Selling of Innocence: The Gestalt of Danger in the Lives of Youth Prostitutes." *Canadian Journal of Criminology* 4, no. 1 (1999): 33–56.

Schlosser, Eric. *Reefer Madness: Sex, Drugs, and Cheap Labor in the American Black Market*. New York: Houghton Mifflin, 2003.

Schneider, Elizabeth M. *Battered Women & Feminist Lawmaking*. New Haven, Conn.: Yale University Press, 2000.

Schwartz, John. "Studies Detail Solicitation of Children for Sex Online." *New York Times*, 20 June 2001.

Schwartz, Martin, et al. "Male Peer Support and a Feminist Routine Activities Theory: Understanding Sexual Assault on the College Campus." *Justice Quarterly* 18, no. 3 (2001): 623–49.

Scott, David A. *Behind the G-String: An Exploration of the Stripper's Image, Her Person and Her Meaning*. Jefferson, N.C.: McFarland, 1996.

Seng, Magus J. "Child Sexual Abuse and Adolescent Prostitution: A Comparative Analysis." *Adolescence* 24, no. 95 (1989): 665–75.

Sennett, Richard. *Respect in a World of Inequality*. New York: Random House, 2003.

Sheffield, Carole J. "Sexual Terrorism: The Social Control of Women." In *Feminist Jurisprudence: Taking Women Seriously*, eds. M. Becker, C. G. Bowman, and M. Torrey, 269–70. St. Paul: West Group, 2001.

Shenoy, Rupa. "Clubs Promise Path from Poverty." *Chicago Reporter*, February 2003.

Sherman, David. "Sexually Oriented Businesses: An Insider's View." Testimony before the Michigan House Committee on Ethics and Constitutional Law, 12 January 2000. At www.a-stop.org/Testimony%20of%20David%20 Sherman.html on 5 December 2000.

Shrage, Laurie. *Moral Dilemmas of Feminism: Prostitution, Adultery, and Abortion*. New York: Routledge, 1994.

Silbert, Mimi H., and Ayala M. Pines. "Entrance into Prostitution." *Youth & Society* 13, no. 4 (1982): 471–500.

———. "Occupational Hazards of Street Prostitutes." *Criminal Justice and Behavior* 8, no. 4 (1981): 395–99.

———. "Victimization of Street Prostitutes." *Victimology: An International Journal* 7 (1982): 122–33.

Silone, Ignazio. *Fontamara*. In *The Abruzzo Trilogy*. South Royalton, Vt.: Steerforth Press, 2000.

Simons, Ronald L., and Les B. Whitbeck. "Sexual Abuse as a Precursor to

Prostitution and Victimization among Adolescent and Adult Homeless Women." *Journal of Family Issues* 12, no. 3 (1991): 361–79.

Smyth, Jamie. "Enjo Kosai: Teen Prostitution, a Reflection of Society's Ills." *Tokyo Weekender*, 4 September 1998. At www.weekender.co.jp/latest Edition/980904/oped.html on 29 May 2003.

Snitow, Ann, Christine Stansell, and Sharon Thompson. "Introduction." In *Powers of Desire: The Politics of Sexuality*, eds. A. Snitow, C. Stansell, and S. Thompson, 9–47. New York: Monthly Review Press, 1983.

Solomon, Andrew. *The Noonday Demon: An Atlas of Depression*. New York: Scribner, 2001.

Solomonson, Sonia C. "We Can't Just Be Spectators." *The Lutheran*, May 2000. At www.thelutheran.org/0005/page18a.html on 28 January 2002.

Spangenberg, Mia. "Prostituted Youth in New York City: An Overview." Report, New York, 2001.

Stanley, Alexandra. "Forget the Sex and Violence; Shame Is the Ratings Leader." *New York Times*, 20 November 2002.

Sterk, Claire E. *Tricking and Tripping: Prostitution in the Era of AIDS*. Putnam Valley, N.Y.: Social Change Press, 2000.

Stickler, Angus. "Child Prostitution Crisis." BBC News, 29 July 2001.

Sullivan, Mary, and Sheila Jeffreys. "Legalization: The Australian Experience." *Violence against Women* 8, no. 9 (2002): 1140–48.

Sullivan, Rosemary. *Labyrinth of Desire: Women, Passion, and Romantic Obsession*. Washington, D.C.: Counterpoint, 2001.

Sweet, Nova, and Richard Tewksbury. "'What's a Nice Girl Like You Doing in a Place Like This?' Pathways to a Career in Stripping." *Sociological Spectrum* 20 (2000): 325–43.

Szalavitz, Maria. "Cracked Up." Salon.com. At www.salon.com/news/feature/1999/05/11crack_media.

Teets, Janet M. "The Incidence and Experience of Rape among Chemically Dependent Women." *Journal of Psychoactive Drugs* 29, no. 4 (1997): 331–44.

Thomas, John D. "Author Reveals the Stripper's View." *Chicago Tribune*, 5 November 2002.

Tjaden, Patricia, and Nancy Thoennes. "Extent, Nature, and Consequences of Intimate Partner Violence: Findings from the National Violence against Women Survey 2000." Report, Washington, D.C., 2000.

"Two Women Found Strangled on West Side." *Chicago Tribune*, 9 September 2002, Metropolitan Digest.

Valera, Roberto J., et al. "Perceived Health Needs of Inner-City Street Prostitutes: A Preliminary Study." *American Journal of Health Behavior* 25, no. 1 (2001): 50–59.

Vander Weyer, Martin. "Diary." *Spectator*, 30 March 2002, 8.

"Violence against Women." Fact sheet about the Swedish prostitution law.

294   At www.naring.regeringen.se/pressinfo/fak/tablad/PDF/n2001-038e.pdf on 24 May 2003.

Volkonsky, Anastasia. "Legalizing the 'Profession' Would Sanction the Abuse." In *Taking Sides: Clashing Views on Controversial Issues in Human Sexuality*, eds. R. Rancoeur and W. Taverner, 140–44. Guilford, Conn.: Dushkin/McGraw-Hill, 2000.

Walby, Sylvia. *Theorizing Patriarchy*. Oxford, U.K.: Blackwell Publishers, 1990.

Waller, James. "Perpetrators of Genocide: An Explanatory Model of Extraordinary Human Evil." *Journal of Hate Studies* 1, no. 1 (2002): 5–22.

Weidner, Robert R. *"I Won't Do Manhattan": Causes and Consequences of a Decline in Street Prostitution*. New York: LFB Scholarly Publishing, 2001.

Weisberg, D. Kelly. *Applications of Feminist Legal Theory to Women's Lives: Sex, Violence, Work, and Reproduction*. Philadelphia: Temple University Press, 1996.

———. *Children of the Night: A Study of Adolescent Prostitution*. Lexington, Mass.: Lexington Books, 1985.

Weitzer, Ronald. "Prostitutes' Rights in the United States: The Failure of a Movement." *Sociological Quarterly* 32, no. 1 (1991): 23–41.

———. "Why We Need More Research on Sex Work." In *Sex for Sale: Prostitution, Pornography, and the Sex Industry*, ed. R. Weitzer, 1–13. New York: Routledge, 2000.

Wesley, Jennifer K. "Growing Up Sexualized: Issues of Power and Violence in the Lives of Female Exotic Dancers." *Violence against Women* 8, no. 10 (2002): 1186–1211.

West, Rebecca. *A Celebration: Selected from Her Writings by Her Publishers with Her Help*. New York: Penguin Books, 1978.

———. *The Fountain Overflows*. London: Pan Books, 1970.

———. *This Real Night*. New York: Penguin Books, 1986.

———. *The Young Rebecca: Writings of Rebecca West, 1911–17*, ed. J. Marcus. New York: Viking, 1982.

Widom, Cathy Spatz, and Joseph B. Kuhns. "Childhood Victimization and Subsequent Risk for Promiscuity, Prostitution, and Teenage Pregnancy: A Prospective Study." *American Journal of Public Health* 86, no. 11 (1996): 1607–12.

Williams, Robert R. *Recognition: Fichte and Hegel on the Other*. Albany: State University of New York Press, 1992.

Williamson, Celia. "Pimp Controlled Prostitution: Still an Integral Part of Street Life." *Violence against Women* 8, no. 9 (2002): 1074–92.

Wilson, A. N. *The Victorians*. New York: W. W. Norton, 2003.

Winberg, Margareta. Various speeches archived at www.regeringen.se/winberg on 22 November 2002.

Winterbauer, Nancy L. "Chicago Syphilis Ethnography: Interim Progress Report." Report, Chicago, 2000.

Wolf, Naomi. *Fire with Fire: The New Female Power and How It Will Change the 21st Century.* New York: Random House, 1993.

Wolfe, Charles. "Prostitution Doesn't Disqualify Prospective Lawyer." *Cincinnati Enquirer*, 21 March 2003.

Wood, Elizabeth Anne. "Working in Fantasy Factory: The Attention Hypothesis and the Enacting of Masculine Power in Strip Clubs." *Journal of Contemporary Ethnography* 29, no. 1 (2000): 5–31.

World Sex Guide. "Indonesia Trip." At www.porncave.com/content/worldsex/indonesia_trip.txt.html on 2 April 2001.

———. "Prostitution in Chicago." At www.porncave.com/content/worldsex/United-States.html on 18 September 2000.

———. "Re: Pure Gold (and the Spot) in Chicago." At www.sexatlas.com/wsg/chicago_gold.txt.html on 14 December 1999.

Yahne, Carolina E., et al. "Magdalena Pilot Project: Motivational Outreach to Substance Abusing Women Street Sex Workers." *Journal of Substance Abuse Treatment* 23, no. 1 (2002): 49–53.

Yates, Gary L., et al. "A Risk Profile Comparison of Homeless Youth Involved in Prostitution and Homeless Youth Not Involved." *Journal of Adolescent Health* 12 (1991): 545–48.

Young, Amy M., et al. "Prostitution, Drug Use, and Coping with Psychological Distress." *Journal of Drug Issues* 30, no. 4 (2000): 789–800.

Young, Toby. "Confessions of a Porn Addict." *Spectator*, 10 November 2001, 32–33.

Youth Advocate Program. "Children for Sale: Youth Involved in Prostitution, Pornography and Sex Trafficking." Report, Washington, D.C., 1998.

Zielbauer, Paul. "Prostitute Guilty in Ex-Mayor's Sex Abuse Case." *New York Times*, 11 September 2002.

Acknowledgments

I extend grateful thanks to the following: Olivia and her sister Alta, who shared their lives with me with complete candor; Lisa Brush, Walter DeKeseredy, Jody Miller, Claudine O'Leary, and Jannit Rabinowitch for their generosity in sharing insights, materials, and information; Jeanne Walsh and Pauline Grippando, Reference Department, River Forest Public Library, for interlibrary loan arrangements far beyond the call of duty; Dorothy Gardner and Jennifer McDonough, Michael Reese Health Trust, and Alice Cottingham, Robin Dix, and Julie Walther, Girl's Best Friend Foundation, for generous funding; and Lise Strom and Sandi Kim for eagle-eyed copy editing, and Alan Raphael for scrupulous copy editing and everything else.

This book is dedicated to three very special women. Editor Claire Renzetti's early enthusiasm carried me over many a bad patch and moment of doubt. Northeastern University Press Acquiring Editor Sarah Rowley's broad knowledge of the literature and tough-minded editing made sure that no flaccid thought or lazy argument slipped through. Her dedication to this project was a great gift.

Sheila Wellstone's tragic death in an airplane crash on October 25, 2002 left a gaping hole in my life, but more important, silenced one of this country's most dedicated and effective advocates for battered women. I would like to think that Sheila would have approved of this book.

Index